American Sectionalism in the British Mind, 1832–1863

AMERICAN SECTIONALISM IN THE BRITISH MIND 1832–1863

PETER O'CONNOR

LOUISIANA STATE UNIVERSITY PRESS BATON ROUGE

Published by Louisiana State University Press

Manufactured in the United States of America
First printing

Designer: Barbara Neely Bourgoyne
Typeface: MillerText
Printer and binder: Sheridan Books

Library of Congress Cataloging-in-Publication Data
Names: O'Connor, Peter (Historian), author.
Title: American sectionalism in the British mind, 1832–1863 / Peter O'Connor.
Description: Baton Rouge : Louisiana State University Press, [2017] | Includes bibliographical references and index.
Identifiers: LCCN 2017019258| ISBN 978-0-8071-6815-8 (cloth : alk. paper) | ISBN 978-0-8071-6816-5 (pdf) | ISBN 978-0-8071-6817-2 (epub)
Subjects: LCSH: United States—Foreign public opinion, British—History—19th century. | Sectionalism (United States)—History. | Slavery—Southern States—History. | Racism—United States—History—19th century. | United States—History—Civil War, 1861-1865—Foreign public opinion, British. | United States—Politics and government—19th century. | Great Britain—Relations—United States. | United States—Relations—Great Britain. | Public opinion—Great Britain—History—19th century.
Classification: LCC E183.8.G7 O39 2017 | DDC 327.73041/09034—dc23
LC record available at https://lccn.loc.gov/2017019258

The paper in this book meets the guidelines for permanence and durability of the Committee on Production Guidelines for Book Longevity of the Council on Library Resources. ♾

For Carly

CONTENTS

ACKNOWLEDGMENTS

It would not have been possible to produce this book without the assistance and encouragement of many people, and I would like to thank them.

This book began during my time at Northumbria University in 2010. My supervisors David Gleeson and James McConnel enthusiastically supported my work, providing me with thoughtful and detailed comments that kept my research progressing in the right direction. They also showed remarkable patience reading draft upon draft. I would also like to thank Jay Sexton and Brian Ward, whose comments were vital to the shaping of the final book.

Beyond this group I owe a debt to a wide range of people within the academic community who supported me through the research and writing. I would like to thank the Northumbria University postgraduate community who provided an incredibly supportive and enjoyable atmosphere in which to conduct the bulk of the research. I would also like to thank my colleagues at both Northumbria University and the University of Manchester. I am also indebted to those who offered comments on papers given over the last few years and to the helpful archival staff at the Merseyside Maritime Museum, the National Maritime Museum, the University of Liverpool Library, the British Library, and the Sheffield Archives.

I would also like to offer my thanks to Rand Dotson of Louisiana State University Press. His work has helped to make the daunting process of publishing a first book as easy and smooth as possible. I would also like to thank the reader of the original manuscript, whose comments helped me improve the text immeasurably.

Finally, I wish to thank my family and friends. My parents Alma and Steven have helped to support me throughout my studies, and this work would not have been possible without them. I would also like to thank my grandparents, Jimmy and Alma, as well as my Uncles Peter and Raymond and my Auntie Christine for their help. I wish to give particular thanks to my partner Carly, whose love and support have been vital to me completing this project.

American Sectionalism in the British Mind, 1832–1863

INTRODUCTION

On 7 October 1862, William Ewart Gladstone, the chancellor of the exchequer under British prime minister Lord Palmerston, gave a speech in Newcastle-Upon-Tyne about the situation in the United States that sparked a political and diplomatic furor. Despite the action taken by the Union against slavery in the early autumn, and the northern victory at the Battle of Antietam three weeks before, Gladstone told the crowd that Confederate president Jefferson Davis had "made a nation." The chancellor's implication was clear. It was time for Her Majesty's government to recognize the Confederacy. Given the recent developments in the American conflict, it seems natural to ask why Gladstone, the doyen of mid-Victorian liberalism and an avowed opponent of slavery, would come out in favor of the slaveholding Confederacy being admitted into the family of nations. In short, why did he believe that southern secession was justified?[1]

In order to understand the views of Gladstone, and countless others like him, it is necessary to reconsider the way the British engaged with America during the Civil War. In particular, it is vital that we understand that British observers did not isolate the conflict from its broader historical context. Instead, they examined the war with reference to their own set of ideas about antebellum America. Furthermore, it is important to reject any assumption that Britons automatically associated the northern states with the abolition of slavery. Simply put, for Gladstone and his counterparts the American conflict was not abolitionist crusade. While most Britons recognized the obvious division between the free Union and the slaveholding Confederacy, few believed that the existence of slavery was the only point of contention between the North and South. During the antebellum period, many Britons had developed a sophisticated understanding of sectionalism (meaning in this work the division between North and South), which led them to explicitly reject such a simplified formulation of the war. If, therefore, we are to account for British responses to the conflict, it is imperative that we reconstitute the existing framework in which they placed the war. Doing this requires us to go back to the 1830s and trace the ways in which the literate population of Britain engaged with the United States. Many prominent intellectuals traveled across the Atlantic and produced travel narratives about, set novels in, and published philosophical musings on the United States during the 1830s, 1840s, and 1850s. Crucially, these figures discussed divisions within the United States and thereby familiarized the British population with the notion of sectionalism. When the Civil War broke out, Britons understood it in terms of their preconceived ideas about the differences between North and South. The purpose of this book, therefore, is twofold. First, it expands the chronological boundaries of the study of British reactions to the Civil War. Second, it demonstrates the role of cultural commentators in fostering a particularly British understanding of American sectionalism that informed reactions to the conflict.[2]

It is remarkable the extent to which studies that set out to understand British responses to the Civil War have been confined to the period of military conflict. Such a restricted chronology is difficult to justify since, as Martin Crawford notes in his analysis of the *London Times* newspaper in the 1850s and 1860s, “the years 1861 to 1865 reveal no independent identity for [British] attitudes towards the United States.” A failure to examine a broader time period of British engagement with US sectionalism partially explains the problems evident in many seminal studies of British reactions to the Civil War. Scholars have often struggled to explain the stances taken by particular individuals because they have considered the period between 1861 and 1865 in isolation. Gladstone represents a classic case in this regard, but he is not alone. Against the backdrop of the Civil War, it is difficult to explain the pro-Confederate positions taken by the radical MP John Arthur Roebuck or the Liberal William Schaw Lindsay. The tendency to overlook the history of British interactions with US sectionalism has permeated much of the scholarship dealing with British and American political history during the period and resulted in claims such as that made by Bill Cash. In his biography of John Bright, Cash contended that before 1861 “the level of knowledge in Britain of the diversity of culture in America was fairly basic. The people had no real understanding, nor a compelling reason to understand, the differences between the 'Yankee' North and the slave-owning South."[3] This was simply not true.

Going beyond the chronological boundaries of the war allows us to see the extent to which such statements are misconceived. While scholars of the antebellum United States are familiar with the development of sectional identities, their British colleagues have been content to view the Anglo-American connection in national terms. This oversight is particularly surprising when the issues at stake in the US sectional dispute are placed in a transnational context. Slavery, free trade, nationalism, industrialization, and ethnicity were debated by Britons just as they were by Americans. Consequently, when the British observed and commented on the United States, they identified a range of familiar issues dividing the North and South. As a result, they constructed a peculiarly British understanding of prewar American sectionalism which drew on developments and ideas from both sides of the Atlantic.[4] Considered in these terms, an examination of British ideas of American sectionalism over this longer period provides the opportunity to refine our understanding of the Anglo-American connection by incorporating debates about sectional identity, while also problematizing traditional views of the British response to the Civil War. This does not, of course, mean that work on British perceptions of the United States as a coherent nation is valueless. The United States clearly possessed a national identity from a British point of view. Yet this British sense of American identity ran parallel to (and occasionally collided with) a discourse of sectionalism. Even if this discourse was not entirely coherent, it nevertheless provided a vocabulary on which later commentators were able to draw when they discussed the Civil War. By unpacking and engaging with this discourse, we can begin to refine our understanding of Anglo-American history as a whole.

Fundamental to a study of the discourse of British sectionalism is a coterie of nineteenth-century cultural commentators. By this I mean the British novelists, travelers, scientists, social critics, and journalists who published popular texts that dealt with the United States. They were invariably drawn from the upper echelons of British society and therefore provide insights into the views of the middle classes and aristocracy. However, the cultural commentators around whose work this study is built were far from a homogenous group. They held diverse views on politics, society, economics, class, and race and published their ideas against the ever-shifting backdrop of antebellum Anglo-American relations. Yet all of these commentators were united by an interest in the sectional divisions between the North and South. By reading their works, literate Britons became familiar with the United States as both a national and sectional entity.

While potentially offering a window on British attitudes, assessing the public reception of printed texts in this period is a notoriously difficult task. The nineteenth-century publisher and author Charles Knight reported that the price of a complete book fell from 16s (shillings) down to 4s. 41/2d (pence) between 1828 and 1832, which, although continuing to limit books to a minority of the population, increased the size of this minority. Quantifying the shift in readership is almost impossible since, as Richard Altick points out, Victorian census data on literacy is deeply unreliable. However, most scholars agree that the size of the reading public increased during this period, and while the price of literature put it beyond the reach of many, a distinct class of literary consumers existed in Britain. This literate class not only possessed the income to purchase the works of writers such as Charles Dickens and Thomas Carlyle but also had the leisure time to read and engage with their content. As a result, writers of the period became important contributors to the public sphere. As Brent E. Kinser concisely puts it, "whether or not people agreed with Carlyle, they listened." Furthermore, many of the most prominent commentators of the era had indirect access to the halls of power, since "politicians and men of letters mingled in the same clubs, the same salons and the same country house parties."[5] This dual role of public intellectual and political confidante meant that writers like Carlyle played a crucial role in British discussions of the United States in Westminster and in the country at large.

Given this book's explicit focus on the emergence of a British discourse of sectionalism among the literate public, its emphasis (in terms of sources) is on texts produced by cultural commentators. As Raymond Williams has noted, the term *culture* is notoriously ambiguous. I have considered fiction, travel narratives, and published political pamphlets, as well as general sociopolitical philosophy, to be the products of cultural commentators in the sense that they were not written with the expectation of immediately altering government policy. In this way they can be distinguished from cabinet documents or parliamentary debates. Rather than distinguishing between sources purporting to be factual and those recognizably fictive (novels and short stories), this work treats them interchangeably. As the literary scholar Christopher Mulvey noted in his 1990 book *Transatlantic Manners,* "travel literature, is in many respects, a form of fiction," a view this book accepts. Despite an emphasis on cultural commentators, the analysis does not simply disregard politics; on the contrary, political discourse is integral to the project. Instead of examining politics in microscopic detail for underappreciated elements of policy, however, the aim here is to reconstruct the public debate around the United States by focusing on the works of those who provided literate Britons with much of their information about that nation—prominent intellectuals.[6]

It would be difficult to overstate the significance of cultural commentators in the development of the image of the United States in Britain in the years before the Civil War. Intellectual heavyweights of the period—such as the novelists Charles Dickens, Frances Trollope, and William Makepeace Thackeray; the scientists Sir Charles Lyell and George Combe; and the political reformers Joseph Sturge and Harriet Martineau—all published works that were eagerly consumed by the rapidly expanding British literate classes. Through the pages of these books, readers became accustomed to viewing the United States as a nation characterized by divisions. These authors typically included detailed descriptions of the distinctions between North and South over slavery, yet this was rarely the only division they identified. Differing attitudes to politics, society, and economics were commonly noted, as were the apparent ethno-cultural divisions within the nation. Furthermore, authors did not simply distinguish the North from the South. They frequently incorporated the identities of smaller regions (for example, New England or the Old South) into their analysis. Readers often found that they were presented with positive images of one section at the expense of another. The precise nature of the images may have altered over time to reflect changes in the Anglo-American relationship, as well as domestic shifts in both nations, yet they contributed to a basic understanding of US sectional disharmony. In establishing this distinctly British discourse of American sectionalism, these prewar cultural commentators provided a lens through which Britons viewed the American Civil War, and therefore their work profoundly influenced responses to the conflict.

Despite this fact, and with the notable exception of Crawford's *The Anglo-American Crisis of the Mid-Nineteenth Century,* little effort has been made to understand the influence of prewar British ideas on reactions to the conflict. This oversight reflects the lack of interaction between scholars of the global Civil War, such as R. J. M. Blackett, Duncan Andrew Campbell, Howard Jones, and Don H. Doyle, and those who work on Anglo-American intellectual history, including Michael J. Turner, Frank Prochaska, Jon Roper, Leslie Butler, Paul Giles, and Sarah Meer.[7] By breaking down the artificial barrier between these groups, we can begin to comprehend the complexity of British reactions to the Civil War and the effect of the conflict on the Anglo-American relationship more broadly.

Work on British reactions to the US Civil War has tended to center on popular opinion about the belligerents and debates over how close the British government came to recognizing the Confederacy as a nation. Whether concerned with high-level diplomacy or working-class opinion, almost all studies in the field examine these issues in some form. After the work of pioneering scholars, including E. D. Adams, Joseph Park, and Frank L. Owsley, two schools of thought regarding British reactions developed. On the one side, figures like Park and Philip Foner claimed that the working classes and political reformers favored the North and came up against a prosouthern British aristocracy and political establishment. Others, such as Mary Ellison and Joseph Hernon, rejected this claim and suggested a high level of sympathy for the Confederacy within working-class communities. More recently, Blackett has provided a corrective to the blunt class analysis that characterized these early books. For Blackett, class played a role in determining views of the war, but so did other factors, including religion and location. Campbell's 2003 analysis led him to conclude that the war was actually of limited interest for most of the British population. Only a committed few, such as John Bright, Richard Cobden, James Spence, and William Schaw Lindsay, consistently and vocally advocated the cause of a side. More recently, Doyle's research has attempted to understand reactions to the war with reference to ideas of international liberalism and the need to defend the American republic as a global progressive icon. Doyle's contention that the Union cause lacked clarity from an international perspective and his claim that "Southern diplomats crafted an appeal that evoked widely admired liberal principles" are both convincingly demonstrated. In addition, his recognition that native writers "translated" the meaning of the war to their respective European populations is a vital observation.[8] By failing to engage sufficiently with the prewar, however, Doyle misses the significance of this final point. Public figures during the Civil War were translating the conflict into a prewar language that was rich with ideas of American sectionalism. By examining how this language was created and deployed, we can begin to get a more coherent understanding of the Anglo-American connection before and during the Civil War.

For all of the strengths of his work, Doyle reasserts the claim that the Union was a symbol of progressive republicanism, which made it popular among radicals and liberals in Europe. In the case of Bright (Doyle's main British case study), this is undoubtedly true, but such a view of Union support in Britain fails to explain why other reformers, such as Lindsay and Roebuck, passionately supported the Confederacy. Doyle's contention does, however, fit with the broader literature on Anglo-American relations in the period, which frequently emphasizes the emergence of a transatlantic liberal tradition. A network of middle-class reformers, united by ideas of abolition, free trade, and republicanism, undoubtedly existed in the Atlantic world during the nineteenth century. With their roots in the campaign to abolish slavery, this group incorporated Americans—such as William Lloyd Garrison, Charles Sumner, George William Curtis, Thomas Wentworth Higginson, James Russell Lowell, and Charles Eliot Norton—as well as Britons, including Bright, Cobden, Goldwin Smith, and Leslie Stephen. These Anglo-American notables were central to the development of transatlantic liberalism during the nineteenth century, yet the Britons listed represent only a portion of the nation's liberal community.[9] To gain a coherent understanding of transatlantic Victorian liberalism, it is necessary to reinsert apparent outliers (such as Lindsay) into the story. How do we explain his decision to break from long-time collaborators Bright and Cobden and support the Confederacy? By providing a history of British interactions with American sectionalism before and during the Civil War, this book explains why figures such as Lindsay embraced the South, and in doing so raises questions about the nature of transatlantic liberalism.

The debate over liberalism also raises important questions regarding terminology. Wherever possible, I have allowed my subjects to speak for themselves by accepting their self-identification as liberals, conservatives, or radicals or their public allegiance to political groups (the Liberal Party, the Tory Party, the Chartists). In cases when a figure failed to publically label themselves, I have considered the extent to which their social, political, economic, and cultural views fit with the broad ideology evinced by one of these groups. The distinction between British and Irish is central to this work as a whole, and the labels themselves are chosen advisedly. As the historian Michael De Nie has shown, nineteenth-century writers and politicians often defined Britishness and Irishness in contrast to one another. At the most basic level, Britishness in this period implied anti-Catholicism, Anglo-Saxon ethnicity, and a belief in the need for social stability. Consequently, Englishness, Welshness, Scottishness, and Anglo-Irishness were all reconcilable with a broader sense of British identity.[10]

The first three chapters of this book are dedicated to concepts that sat at the heart of the British understanding of US sectionalism, and they trace how prewar cultural commentators disseminated and debated these ideas. Chapter 1 examines the issues of race, slavery, and labor, and seeks to undermine the idea that British commentators provided readers with a clear North/South distinction when they discussed these subjects. The chapter challenges the work of scholars who have implied that Britons conflated the North with abolition. Instead, it demonstrates the complexity that characterized British perceptions of slavery in a US sectional context. While most British people disliked slavery as an abstract idea, they often claimed that the slavery of the US South represented a relatively benign form of the institution. Conversely, their descriptions of the treatment of free blacks in northern cities such as New York and Philadelphia were often a catalogue of brutality. Thus, on the eve of the Civil War, the British intellectual mainstream was not accustomed to viewing US sectionalism in terms of a stark distinction between freedom and slavery. They certainly recognized the labels "free states" and "slave states" but failed to see a clear moral distinction between the sections. This ambiguity proved a godsend for pro-Confederates and anti-Unionists and ensured that the struggle to clarify the role of slavery became a key Civil War battleground.

Chapter 2 concentrates on the ethnic and cultural connections across the Atlantic during the antebellum period. It focuses on the development of a British geography of US ethno-cultural regional identity during the antebellum period. Through an analysis of the works of cultural commentators, the chapter demonstrates the emergence of three ethno-cultural regions (New England, the mid-Atlantic, and the South) in British discourse. It considers the development of distinctive identities for the regions, with an emphasis on the way each was held up to a standard of "Britishness" and censured when it fell short. It also considers the relationship each of these enclaves seemed to have with the Anglophobia that characterized American public life. The chapter concludes that New England and the South were commonly presented as ethno-culturally British and prone to outbursts of Anglophilia. At the same time, however, the perceived influence of Puritanism in New England and Cavalier culture in the South allowed commentators to differentiate between them. The mid-Atlantic states of New York and Pennsylvania were consistently described as non-British and aggressively Anglophobic. The focus here tended to be on the influence of Irish and German migrant communities, who many Britons believed had significant political power in the region.

Chapter 3 examines prewar British ideas about the politics of American sectionalism. The chapter focuses on three key areas (political policy, political culture, and states' rights) and illustrates how, as the antebellum period progressed, the British populace developed an awareness of the sectional aspects of these issues. In terms of specific policy priorities, the chapter explores how the nullification crisis of 1833 familiarized Britons with the idea that the sections had antithetical positions on free trade. The chapter also highlights how the British perception of differing policy demands was associated with a belief that the South was dominated by agriculture and the North by industry. The legacy of nullification is also explored through an analysis of British discussions of the states' rights doctrine across the antebellum period as a whole. Furthermore, the chapter considers British discourse on US political culture and notes that, while this culture was commonly seen in national terms, a number of key tropes (the mob, party politics, the press, and tyranny) were increasingly associated with the North. As a whole then, the chapter highlights the British public's familiarity with the politics of sectionalism before the Civil War. It demonstrates a long-standing awareness of the states' rights doctrine and a belief that the sections had distinctive policy priorities that could be used to explain (and potentially justify) secession. It also explains how the association between negative aspects of US political culture and the North led some to express sympathy for the South on the basis that it seemed to have been unwillingly drawn into the democratic system.

The purpose of Chapters 4 and 5 is to examine British responses to the Civil War in the light of the more complex discourse of sectionalism set out in the previous chapters. The idea is not to offer a comprehensive analysis of the levels of sympathy for one side or the other within Britain. Instead, the focus is on understanding the nature of the public debate over the Civil War by analyzing the issues that prominent propagandists and nonpartisan commentators discussed. These two chapters highlight the fact that, by examining British debates over the Civil War as part of a long-standing conversation about US sectionalism, it is possible to gain a more nuanced understanding of why certain individuals committed themselves to the Union or Confederacy. Such an understanding also helps to account for the widespread apathy of the British population toward the war. In simplified terms, the populace was so accustomed to viewing the North and South as divided that they were prepared to accept southern secession as justifiable. An important coda must, however, be added: The existence of slavery in the South ensured criticism of that section, and as a result, Confederate nationhood was only acceptable in Britain so long as the Union refused to commit to abolition. It is therefore vital that claims of a moral division between North and South had tended to be rejected in prewar British discussions of sectional identity. In essence, the prewar discourse ensured that most Britons failed to associate the Union war effort with abolition during the early years of the conflict. The Emancipation Proclamation, however, altered the situation. It is for this reason that the analysis ends in 1863 rather than 1865. For the most part, British sectional discourse had been built on the foundational idea that the moral division between the free and slave states was not a clear one. Most of the British discourse that emphasized the differences between the sections had taken this as a starting point. As a result, the Emancipation Proclamation fatally wounded the cause of the Confederacy in Britain, and it also began a process in which the British understanding of US sectionalism as a broader phenomenon was reformulated.

The final two chapters deal with the opening years of the war. Chapter 4 examines the period from the outbreak of the conflict through to the major diplomatic crisis created by Union captain Charles Wilkes's decision to board HMS *Trent* in November 1861. It follows the attempts made by partisans from both sides to exploit antebellum British ideas about the nature of sectionalism. In particular, it highlights the struggles of pro-Federal activists to convince the British that the Union was motivated by a desire to end slavery. It also considers the extent to which their problems in achieving this aim were the result of the existence of earlier British ideas about the place of slavery in sectional relations. Furthermore, the chapter examines the ways in which pro-Confederates exploited the ambiguity around slavery and deployed the language of ethnic and political sectionalism to validate the right of the South to secede. It also foreshadows some of the fundamental flaws in this discourse, which was never compelling enough to spur either politicians or the general public into recognizing the Confederacy.

Chapter 5 takes this story from the resolution of the *Trent* affair through to the official announcement of emancipation in 1863. It analyzes how the vocabulary of prewar sectionalism was deployed during the diplomatic dispute and public outcry over the *Trent* before moving on to the announcement of the provisional proclamation in September 1862. It considers the reception of the Emancipation Proclamation and highlights how debates over the decision to issue it were conducted within a prewar framework. Finally, the chapter demonstrates the increasing acceptance among the British public that the North was now fighting a war to end slavery and the effect this had. In basic terms, it explains how the Emancipation Proclamation redefined how sectionalism was viewed in Britain. Both anti-Union and pro-Confederate discourse had relied on the ambiguous position of the North on slavery. The lack of public clarity on this issue allowed propagandists the space to play down the role of slavery and justify Confederate nationhood as a natural result of the political and ethno-cultural divisions between North and South. Supporting the South after 1863, however, brought with it connotations of endorsing slavery as a "positive good." This was a moral line that the majority of Britons would not contemplate crossing. In international terms then, the significance of the Emancipation Proclamation stemmed from its ability to recast the war as a moral contest. The complex prewar discourse of sectionalism, which had been exploited by Britons who had sympathy for the South in order to justify secession, lacked the moral weight to counterbalance this shift in perspective on the war.

Seen as part of a broader history, these changing British views of the Civil War and the effect of the Emancipation Proclamation become subjects that need to be examined through a new lens. With all this in mind, we can return to Gladstone standing behind a podium in Newcastle-Upon-Tyne on 7 October 1862, announcing to the world that Jefferson Davis had "made a nation." In a sense, Gladstone's sentiment cannot be traced simply to the *Trent* affair or the tariff policy of the Confederacy. Rather, its roots went much further back, to when, at twenty-three years old, Gladstone settled down to read Frances Trollope's *Domestic Manners of the Americans.*[11]

CHAPTER ONE

"A BLIGHT OVER EVERYTHING"

Race and Slavery in British Views of the American Sections

That William Gladstone had read Frances Trollope's *Domestic Manners* when he was twenty-three and recently graduated from Christ Church College Oxford is peculiarly pertinent to his later views of the Confederacy. A cursory understanding of this archetypal liberal statesman's ideas would suggest that he had no sympathy with the cause of the South after its secession from the Union. Certainly, the position of the millions of African Americans held in bondage in the South profoundly influenced how Gladstone, and many like him, saw the region both before and during the war. The importance of abolition to British identity was something almost all observers noted, with the first Confederate commissioners to Britain, William L. Yancey, Dudley Mann, and Pierre Rost, contending that "antislavery sentiment [was] universally prevalent in England." That Gladstone's Newcastle speech of 7 October 1862 encouraged the recognition of the slave-holding Confederacy, however, suggests that Yancey, Mann, and Rost failed to appreciate the complexity of British opinion. Explaining the views of the British liberals and abolitionists (such as Gladstone) who rejected the northern states during the Civil War requires us to recognize the complexity that characterized British ideas about race and slavery in the context of American sectionalism.[1]

Reconstructing British discourse on the relationship between race, slavery, and sectionalism before the Civil War allows us to identify a number of interlocking ideas that shed light on the lack of popular support for the

Union between 1861 and 1863.[2] In the first place, it is evident that cultural commentators did not see slavery as a purely southern problem. The institution was national, and while it may have been only southerners who held slaves, much of the northern population was violently racist and cared little about abolition. Many northerners even profited financially or politically from the existence of the system. Secondly, a significant number of Britons saw southern slavery as being mitigated by the paternal attitude of slaveholders. Although they rejected slavery as an abstract system, the idea of a paternal connection between slave and slaveholder made southern slavery seem like an acceptable "short-term" arrangement. It also provided a contrast with the treatment of free blacks in the North who suffered violence and social exclusion. Furthermore, the work of these prewar writers also highlights the British belief in the existence of regional variations in terms of attitudes toward race and labor across the United States. Commentators recounted tales of antislavery southerners and pro-slavery northerners, as well as noting the existence of a greater commitment to abolition in New England than in other parts of the free North. This understanding of slavery and sectionalism undermined the idea of a clear distinction between the pro-slavery South and antislavery North. This lack of distinction proved a major problem for pro-Union propagandists during the early Civil War and contributed to the development of a discourse that allowed a number of British commentators to claim that they were both antislavery and pro-Confederate.

Fundamental to bridging the apparent chasm between these two views was a peculiar understanding of the relationship between slave and slaveholder in the South. One of the first observations Trollope made upon arriving in New Orleans in December 1827 (which she later recounted in *Domestic Manners of the Americans*) provides insight into the complex relationship between British views of slavery and sectionalism during the late 1820s and early 1830s. Almost immediately after stepping off the boat in the Crescent City, Trollope commented on the "gentleness" she saw exhibited by a master to his slave, and later she observed that domestic slaves in general were "tolerably well fed, and decently clothed." Although prior to her arrival in the United States she had made clear her revulsion toward slavery in the abstract, Trollope was not particularly harsh about the institution in the published account of her travels. Her descriptions were so mild that in a later edition she added a preface and footnote in which she explained that she had not been critical enough of slavery in the original text. Implicit in Trollope's descriptions of the "gentleness" of New Orleans slaveholders, and absolutely integral to the downplaying of the evils of slavery in British discourse on the South, was the paternal connection between master and slave that the southern system of "care" could apparently offer.[3]

For Trollope, however, it was not just that southern slavery was not always as bad as her abstract conception of the system. Freedom, just as desirable in principle as slavery was objectionable, could be underwhelming in a US context. Trollope visited a freed slave community established by the British radical reformer Frances Wright at Nashoba, Tennessee, and found the successes of the settlement to be limited at best. Consequently, she concluded that "to emancipate them [the slaves] entirely throughout the Union cannot, I conceive, be thought, consistently with the safety of the country."[4]

While abolition was still her long-term aim, Trollope conceded that practical problems would come with ending slavery too quickly. For this reason, her proposed solution was not immediate abolition but the amelioration of the slaves' condition. As a result of this rejection of immediatism, Trollope evinced considerable interest in the comfort and safety of slaves in the South. For her, the most benign treatment stemmed from the existence of a paternal connection between slave and master, and she admitted being impressed by the "gentleness" exhibited by a number of southern slaveholders. Implicit in this view, and absolutely central to the British image of southern slavery as being in some way mitigated by paternalism, was the notion of racial hierarchy. While it would be over a decade before "scientific" labels were widely adopted, British commentators from the 1820s and 1830s were already rooting their ideas about race in their "observations" of the British West Indian colonies. In the 1770s, British planters had begun to develop the negative "Quashee" tropes, while abolitionists of the 1820s and 1830s constructed their own stereotype of "the black Christian man and woman," figures who were "childlike . . . but also able to accept guidance."[5] While intended to be benign, this abolitionist racial stereotyping bled into the works of commentators like Trollope and was repackaged by later writers who saw a form of responsible, paternalistic slavery as the most appropriate social system for the American South.

Works of the 1830s also tended to reject the idea of a clear division between the North and South when it came to attitudes toward race and slavery. One commentator noted that "in *every* [my emphasis] part of the

United States, there is a broad and impassable line of demarcation between every man that has *one drop of African blood in his veins* [original emphasis]." This assertion that northerners were unsympathetic about the plight of African Americans in general was often extended and connected to the belief that abolitionism had just as little support in the North as the South. An editorial in the *Edinburgh Review* in 1833 explained to readers that "the great majority of the white inhabitants and legislature seem all but insensible to the existence of this tremendous evil [slavery]." Some went even further and specifically emphasized the role northerners played in the slave trade. In a discussion of the controversial work of the American Colonization Society (ACS) in Britain during the 1830s, a speaker in Hull informed his audience that it was "well known that the free citizens of America were the vilest slave-dealers on the face of the earth."[6]

To explain the lack of a clear antisouthern campaign in Britain during the height of the abolition movement in the 1830s, it is necessary to appreciate the distinction that was drawn between the act of slaveholding and the decision to positively endorse the system. Certainly, southerners held men, women, and children in bondage, but, as was evident in Trollope's work, the British rarely saw the northern states as committed to abolition. In fact, the treatment of free blacks in the region was frequently highlighted and critiqued by British observers. In March 1832, for instance, the *Leicester Chronicle or Commercial and Agricultural Advertiser* informed its readers that, "in New York, any barber who should shave or dress a *black man* would be sure to lose the custom of all white ones." This same anecdote was printed in the *Morning Chronicle,* a popular national liberal newspaper, while later in the year another edition of the same publication noted that, "in the free states, the colored people are by no means exempt from the effects of the most unjustifiable prejudice." The apparent national hypocrisy and racism of the United States was described in stark terms by the ultra-Tory periodical *John Bull,* which in 1833 claimed that an American always viewed any amount of "negro blood," as tainting a person.[7] Although only the southern states actually held slaves, British commentators presented the North as an area in which racial violence and social exclusion characterized relations between black and white.

The lack of a definite sectional division on the subject of slavery developed into a key touchstone of British commentary during the 1830s and tended to level the moral playing field when North and South were contrasted. Writing in his 1833 book, *Sketches of the United States and Canada,* William Lyon Mackenzie concisely summed up the lack of distinction between the sections. Mackenzie himself was a Scottish-born migrant to Canada who went on to publish a reformist newspaper out of York, Toronto. When traveling in the United States, he concluded that "in all parts of the Union, and by all classes of white society, their ebony brethren are treated as a degraded caste, inferior by nature, whether learned or unlearned, rich or poor, virtuous or vicious." More broadly speaking, Mackenzie emphasized the lack of a coherent division between North and South on the subject of slavery; neither section possessed the sort of thriving abolition movement that Britain boasted at that time. Indeed, as historian Seymour Drescher has noted, the abolitionism that flourished in Britain during the late 1820s and 1830s did not have an American equivalent until the 1850s, and British observers of the early 1830s were patently aware of it.[8]

For some of the more active British reformers (in particular those who had a high level of regard for American democracy), the complex relationship between race, slavery, and sectionalism raised awkward questions. Nowhere is this clearer than in the work of the novelist, abolitionist, and early feminist, Harriet Martineau. As a committed advocate of abolition, Martineau was uncompromisingly negative about southern slavery. In some sense her work was typical of the abolitionist literature produced by her contemporaries (including Frances Trollope, whose *The Life and Adventures of Jonathan Jefferson Whitlaw, or Scenes on the Mississippi* had been published the previous year). Martineau deployed familiar tropes and focused on the violence of the slave system and the perversion of sexual relations that rendered the wives of slaveholders "as much slaves as their negroes." Overall, her antipathy to American slavery was unequivocal. Interestingly, however, when it came to culpability for the system or attitudes to race, even Martineau did not draw a distinct division along the Mason-Dixon Line.[9]

Martineau went well beyond simply rehashing familiar images of American slavery in her travelogue. Her treatment in her work of the slaves themselves was particularly compelling and underpinned her subsequent critiques of the claim that southern slavery was a paternalistic system. Like many other travelers, she visited the slave quarters on a plantation and reported to her readers "their small, dingy, untidy houses, their cribs, the children crouching round the fire, the animal deportment of the grown-up."[10] In addition, and again like many other travelers, she also identified instances of kindness and mercy shown by masters and mistresses toward slaves. It is on this point, however, that her views diverged from those of Trollope, at least as they had been originally presented in *Domestic Manners*. Martineau criticized paternalism as "mercy, made a substitute for justice," and reported being "heart-sick of being told of the ingratitude of slaves, and weary of explaining that indulgence can never atone for injury: that the extremest of pampering, for a life-time, is no equivalent for rights withheld." Through these sentiments Martineau attempted to undermine the claims of British apologists for southern slavery by rejecting the argument that paternalism excused the short-term continuation of the slave system.[11]

Furthermore, Martineau took issue with the political and economic viability of American slavery. From the point of view of economics, Martineau explained to her readers not only that the "shoe-business of New York State" was "of itself larger and more valuable than the entire commerce of Georgia" but also that slave agriculture reduced soil fertility, forcing slaveholders to be aggressively expansionist. From this premise, Martineau moved her argument into the political sphere. Working from the assumption that slavery required an expansive foreign policy, Martineau tied US demands for the annexation of Texas to the slaveholders' need for virgin soil. Similarly, in an electoral sense, she saw expansion as a result of the need to ensure a slaveholding majority in the national government, a view echoed by the prominent liberal newspaper the *Leeds Mercury*. For Martineau, therefore, slavery created a sectional division in the political sphere, as the interests of slaveholders drove an expansive foreign policy.[12]

Martineau's mention of Texas here would have had particular resonance for readers of the 1830s and 1840s. During this period, the fate of the small republic was seen as vital not only to US politics but also to British interests in America and to the progress of global antislavery. As a result, British policy makers and the public demonstrated considerable interest in the subject. The secession of Texas from Mexico in 1836 and the debate over whether the region (with its significant population of slaveholders) should join the American Union provided the immediate backdrop to Martineau's commentary. Some Britons expressed concern that Texan independence or statehood might help to secure the spread of slavery. At the same time, however, a number of abolitionists envisioned an Anglo-Texan alliance, which might facilitate the end of the institution in the new republic by piling diplomatic pressure for emancipation on Washington. The latter development would have required the involvement of the British government, which had little desire to become embroiled in such affairs. Nevertheless, the existence of this debate over Texas during the later 1830s focused Britons on the possible expansion of slavery across North America.[13]

In Martineau's view, most of the ills of the contemporary United States could be traced back to the existence of slavery. When discussing protective tariffs in America, she explicitly rejected the association that many Britons made between free trade and the South. She claimed (incorrectly) that the original impetus behind the tariff came from slaveholders, who, only after its consequences were clear, "became infuriated against the tariff, not only on the reasonable ground of its badness of principle, but on the allegation that it was the cause of all the woes of the south, and the prosperity . . . of the north." She then concluded, "It has always been the method of the slaveholders to lay the blame of their sufferings upon everything but the real cause."[14] The tariff issue was particularly significant since, for Martineau and many other British reformers, protective duties were not simply bad economic policy but also morally wrong. More than almost any other prewar commentator, Martineau was critical of slavery in the South. She used the existence of the system as a catchall explanation to underpin any aspect of the section she interpreted negatively. She also failed to emphasize the mitigation of conditions though the paternalistic system, which, for other writers, differentiated southern slavery from slavery as an abstract institution.

Although Martineau's version of American slavery was liberally sprinkled with illustrations of the institution's sectional nature, it would be incorrect to conclude that her readers were provided with an absolute division between the slaveholding South and the abolitionist North. One of the most striking ideas running through *Society in America* was the notion of slavery permeating and receiving implicit support from groups all over the nation. In political terms Martineau cited the fugitive-slave laws as evidence that northern politicians acquiesced to the slave system. It was not only in the legislative process that slavery was a national issue: Martineau also saw the close commercial relationship between Boston and Charleston as an explanatory factor for the riots in the former city. By making this connection she essentially conflated both places in the slave economy. Similarly, Martineau drew on her own experience in New York to emphasize a related point by highlighting "a public meeting on behalf of the Texan adventurers, where high-sounding common-places had been played off about patriotism, fighting for the dearest rights of man, and so forth." Martineau had personally connected slavery and the annexation of Texas, so her association between this cause and New York was particularly significant. Furthermore, her description of anti-abolition mobs in Boston and Cincinnati, as well as Charleston and Vicksburg, leave no room for doubt as to how she interpreted the views of white Americans on both sides of the Mason-Dixon Line.[15]

While slavery may have been presented in national terms in Martineau's account, the abolition movement in the United States seemed to lack the scope to combat the system. Unlike its British counterpart, American abolition was not a national movement with mass appeal. Instead, it was composed of a core group, described as a moral aristocracy, whose task involved combating the views of "the mass of common men and women" who disliked and feared "the coloured race." Martineau gave something of a regional complexion to her moral aristocracy, describing New England as a particular hub of American abolition. This did not, however, mean that she saw a clear distinction between the North and South as sections. On the contrary, she contended that there existed "certain timid slave-holders of the south, who send money for the support of abolition publications, and an earnest blessing."[16] For Martineau, therefore, the sectional division in relation to slavery was not absolute. Even though southerners held men in bondage, the North, with the exception of a committed group of abolitionists (focused in New England), had passively accepted the situation.

In some cases, northerners were not simply associated with passive acquiescence in southern slavery but became a target for criticism because of the widespread repression faced by free blacks within their own borders. This repression was something that a number of Britons suggested made the lives of African Americans at least as difficult in the North as the South. In his 1839 travel account, Martineau's fellow novelist (and later diplomat) Charles Augustus Murray highlighted the attitudes of northerners toward blacks, noting that "if they [slaves] by any accident acquire their liberty and wandered [*sic*] into New York, or other of the free states, the curse of colour still clings to them; and not only are the doors of liberal employment and society closed against them, but even in theatres, churches and other places of public resort, they find themselves separated."[17] The Tory novelist Frederick

Marryat, who also published a travelogue in 1839, echoed Murray on this point, describing "the . . . degree of contempt and dislike in which the free blacks are held in all the free states" before offering an incredulous description of seeing the body of a black man in the water after an accident in New York and being told by a disdainful New Yorker that "it's only a nigger."[18]

Where these commentators differed from Martineau was on the issue of paternalism. Murray in particular drew his readers' attention to the possibility of a paternalistic bond developing between slave and master, noting "the comparative comfort and good usage enjoyed by their slaves."[19] Crucially, Murray made this point without the coda critiquing paternalism that Martineau had offered. For Murray then, the southern slave system was not as bad as he had been led to believe, since the paternalistic attitude of the slaveholder offset the demands of the system. On the other hand, the treatment of free blacks that Murray saw in the North was considerably worse than he had anticipated. In a sense this should have collapsed the distinction between the sections. It did not, however, and the nomenclature of free and slave states endured, even though the meaning of the labels was not as clear as we might assume. The ideas expressed by Murray and his contemporaries were vital to the establishment of a platform upon which later pro-Confederates could build their case. Their observations lent credibility to the image of the paternalistic, benevolent planter, while at the same time eroding the moral high ground from the Union's cause.

The attitudes toward slavery and sectionalism outlined to this point were not limited to those from specific political persuasions. The cases of Martineau, Murray, and Marryat are evidence of this, as is the writing of the radical British democratic reformer Thomas Brothers, who had resided in the United States for fifteen years before becoming disillusioned with the nation. As a result of his discontent, Brothers returned to Britain and soon after his arrival decided to publish *The United States of North America as they are; Not as they are generally Described: Being a Cure for Radicalism* in 1840. Brothers presented his book as a series of letters to prominent Britons, with one chapter entitled "to D. O'Connell, M.P., Joseph Sturge, Esqrs., and the other English Abolitionists of Negro Slavery." The timing and addressees of the "letter" are worthy of some attention here. Between the end of the apprenticeship system in the West Indies and the 1840s, British abolitionists (including Sturge) published a host of books claiming to show the success of emancipation. As a result, Sturge provided a useful target for Brothers as he attempted to question the value of immediate emancipation with reference to the United States. In his "letter," Brothers gave considerable credence to the paternalism myth and the idea that it contributed to a mitigated form of slavery. His experience of slavery led him to conclude that "from what I have seen in America . . . to free those who were born slaves, and who were fortunate enough to have for their owner a kind man, would be to inflict a curse, rather than bestow a blessing."[20]

Brothers also rejected the idea that northerners had any interest in abolition or the fair treatment of African Americans. He claimed that in Philadelphia, "if a man is only suspected of sympathizing with the blacks, whether free or slaves, such a man finds it necessary to plead, in the most earnest manner, for his life and property." In terms of the treatment of the free blacks in the same city, Brothers reported having seen "mobs march in order down to that part of the city of Philadelphia, which is principally inhabited by coloured people, and deliberately set about to murder them, destroy their houses, break up their furniture, steal their money, or other valuable things that the poor creatures might possess."[21] This was certainly not the image of the North that the pro-Union propagandists of the Civil War era wanted to evoke when they described the free states.

By the early 1840s, a template had been set for an understanding of slavery and sectionalism in the United States which allowed British commentators to maintain an abhorrence of slavery and a public desire for abolition while treating the South relatively sympathetically. Murray's publication was typical in this regard, as was the work of the noted phrenologist George Combe, who published a three-volume collection of his experiences in the United States in 1841. In it he collapsed the assumed distinction between North and South on the subject of slavery. When he discussed the topic with a former Virginia planter who had freed his own chattels, Combe was told that they "had not profited by their freedom; the incapacity for self-action and self-control which slavery en genders [*sic*], renders emancipated Africans, in general, unfit to struggle successfully with the difficulties which surround them." Although an active advocate of what he called "universal emancipation," Combe concluded that the current social system was unable to support individual or small groups of freed slaves.[22]

Combe's work is worthy of particular attention because of the distinctive attitudes toward abolition he noted in different regions of the North. He found that the "Abolition of Negro Slavery excites much interest among the

New Englanders," while, in contrast, in Pennsylvania, "persons of colour resident in the State, although free, and assessed, and paying taxes, are denied the privilege of voting." The comparison between New England and Pennsylvania is not direct here yet the idea that attitudes toward race and abolition differed significantly between New Englanders and other northerners became something British observers frequently asserted. Understood in these terms, the debate over abolition in the United States was not one between North and South; it was national in scope, and only New England could claim any sort of regional identification with abolitionism.[23]

The extent to which this view of slavery and sectionalism influenced all areas of British society is neatly demonstrated by the experience of William Rathbone. As a member of a prominent family of merchants and abolitionists, Rathbone was brought up in a world of antislavery activism reaching back to the 1820s. When his later business career took him to the United States during the late 1830s and early 1840s, he had the chance to study slavery up close. In his correspondence with his brother, Rathbone made clear that he had no sympathy with slavery—rejecting the effect the system had on labor as a "blight over everything." Even as he criticized slavery, however, he expressed little confidence in freedmen in the event of immediate emancipation and balked at the notion of freed slaves gaining political rights.[24] The language Rathbone used in his descriptions invoked the scientific theories of race and natural selection deployed by prominent contemporaries, including Samuel George Morton, Dr. Robert Knox, and Thomas Arnold. The development of racialized scientific language by these figures was crucial, not just in the specific case of Rathbone but for British views of slavery in the United States more broadly. In essence the discourse of scientific racism allowed political progressives to embrace a worldview rejecting racial equality and (potentially at least) justifying southern slavery.

During the following year, Rathbone wrote another letter from Richmond, Virginia, to his mother in which he claimed the southerners themselves disliked slavery. The idea that Virginians rejected slavery as a positive good developed into a broader understanding of southern slaveholders that dissociated them from the immorality of the system. In a sense this understanding performed a similar function to scientific racism by allowing British abolitionists to excuse the short-term use of the system. For an abolitionist like Rathbone, a positive endorsement of the slavery system by the slaveholders would have made it essentially impossible to evince any sympathy for southern planters.[25] Crucially, however, if the slaveholders were seen as prepared to accept slavery as a temporary evil until such a time as emancipation could be safely achieved, they could be potentially sympathetic characters. Furthermore, the idea that slavery was resented in the South also helped to undermine any clear moral distinction between North and South on the issue, even among British abolitionists.

Rathbone's fellow abolitionist, James Silk Buckingham, offered a similarly murky depiction of the relationship between the sections regarding slavery in his account of his time in America. Buckingham was a novelist, abolitionist, and liberal MP for Sheffield who traveled extensively and produced five volumes (split over two books) on the subject of the United States during the early years of the 1840s. His reputation as an abolitionist preceded him, and shortly after arriving in Washington on 5 March 1838, Buckingham received a letter warning him against venturing south of Pennsylvania. The existence of this missive (which Buckingham reprinted) conveyed an explicit sectional division, yet he did not see anything like a clear distinction on the slavery issue while he traveled across the United States. Quakers in Saratoga, New York, informed him that "besides the southern planters, who might be expected to speak ill of the abolitionists, and the rich merchants of New York and Philadelphia, who fancy they have a pecuniary interest in speaking well of the South, and excusing, if not justifying slavery, because their connexions in that quarter are too profitable to be endangered by appearing to side with the abolitionists; there were many clergymen here from different parts of the Union, who were as free in expressing their disapprobation of the course of the abolitionists, as any Southern person could be." There was, of course, more than a modicum of truth to this statement. Northern politicians had frequently bowed to the demands of slaveholders under pressure from bankers and merchants whose affluence rested on the continuation of the Union and who were (as British critics noted) heavily implicated in slavery. The only region in which Buckingham found sympathy for abolition among a significant proportion of the population was New England. He took care to note, for example, that in Massachusetts "negroes are not only free, but enjoy the electoral suffrage . . . with all the freedom and independence of their white fellow-citizens." Buckingham concluded, "It is hardly to be wondered at, therefore, that in this State [Massachusetts], the public sentiment in favour of abolition should increase, both in intensity and extent."[26]

While abolitionist sentiment may have been growing in Massachusetts, the overall impression Buckingham gave of the attitudes of northerners toward both abolition and the fair treatment of free blacks in the northern section was extremely negative. In New York, Buckingham did note the existence of "a large though not an influential body of abolitionists." This group's positive effect on his attitude toward New York was, however, undercut by reactions to the killing of the abolitionist Rev. Elijah P. Lovejoy by a mob in Illinois. Buckingham pointed out that "the greater majority of the Whig papers, and some even of the Democratic, in New York and elsewhere, condemned the pertinacity and obstinacy, as they called it, of Mr. Lovejoy." Furthermore, he gave an account of an open-air meeting held at Vauxhall Gardens in New York "to express sympathy with the Canadian revolutionists" in December 1837. He noted how, after one of the speakers, Dr. Callaghan, had mentioned the name of the prominent politician Daniel O'Connell, "a scene of great uproar ensued, with cries of 'No O'Connell! No O'Connell! he's an abolitionist!' 'And so,' exclaimed Mr. Callaghan, 'am I an abolitionist'; upon which the uproar was increased, and mingled with cries of 'Turn him out! Turn him out!'" This rejection of abolition as a political aim in New York was twinned with a rejection of social equality even for free blacks, something Buckingham noted after visiting a house for juvenile delinquents and finding that "the coloured are separated from the white delinquents; for even among criminals, this distinction of colour is rigidly observed."[27]

Buckingham's observations need to be understood in the context of Anglo-American antislavery activism during the period more broadly. As historian Maurice Bric has pointed out, the 1840s saw a rise in international tensions over abolition despite also seeing increasing levels of international cooperation. British abolitionists (and we can certainly include both Buckingham and Rathbone under this heading) had a tendency to censure the United States as a whole, which naturally led Americans to defend aspects of their nation. Nowhere was this clearer than at major antislavery meetings, such as the 1840 Anti-Slavery Convention in London. This was a significant international event that brought together key figures ranging from O'Connell and Sturge to US activists William Lloyd Garrison and Lucretia Mott. Despite the hopes of the organizers, however, the meeting soon descended into patriotic squabbling.[28] In a sense then, Buckingham's text needs to be seen as not only a travel account but an assertion of the status of Britain as the leading light of international abolition. Yet, its long-term implications remain the same. It presented a complex portrait of slavery and abolition in the United States which discouraged readers from viewing the issues in a stark North vs. South way.

Nevertheless, Buckingham was certainly aware of the centrality of slavery to sectional identity and noted the significance of the institution to the South. He drew particular attention to southern politicians' use of the "positive good" thesis and highlighted a speech given by John C. Calhoun against a bill to abolish slavery. In this speech the South Carolinian "introduced a long series of resolutions, which embraced the whole subject of slavery, defending it as an institution favourable to the welfare of the country and the people it embraced." Buckingham similarly pointed to a resolution by the Georgia Conference of the Methodist-Episcopal Church, which claimed that "slavery, as it exists in the United States, is not a moral evil." This sort of endorsement of slavery was so reprehensible to the British that even West Indian planters had shied away from it during their attempts to prevent abolition in the 1820s and 1830s. Yet despite highlighting these examples of southerners embracing slavery in positive terms (which could have provided him with the scope to undertake a full-blooded critique of the South), Buckingham drew his readers' attention to the system as an institution with supporters across the nation. He cited, among other things, "the [anti] abolition riots of New York and Boston, and the still more recent burning of the Pennsylvania Hall at Philadelphia."[29] The northern states were clearly no bastion of abolition for prewar Britons, even though certain Union propagandists would attempt (with limited success) to claim an antislavery heritage for northerners during the conflict.

In historical terms Buckingham noted that, at least for a time, abolition had been a popular measure in Maryland and Virginia. He then went on to compare the attitudes he had found toward the institution in Baltimore and New York. In the former city Buckingham claimed that he had "never heard the institution of slavery defended or excused"—something he'd known New York merchants to do. He believed that in Baltimore the majority of people "admit it [slavery] to be a great national evil; all appear anxious to see it abolished." Buckingham's conclusion highlights the lack of sectional clarity in British writing on the subject: "It seemed remarkable to us, and was not less agreeable than unexpected, that we should thus meet, in the populous capital of a slave-state, more toleration of opinion on the subject of slavery, and a more general sympathy for its removal, than with a large number of those residing in the free state and populous city of New York."[30]

The ideas Buckingham subsequently put forward in his second book on the United States, *The Slave States of America,* echoed those in *America,* but provided a more comprehensive analysis of the South. The second book's dedication offers compelling evidence that the travel narrative played a key role in popular and political debate in Britain. In this dedication Buckingham noted that his "former work has had the honour to be appealed to, as an authority, on the subject of Free-trade, by the two great leaders of the House of Commons, Lord John Russell and Sir Robert Peel." He hoped this second text would prove useful for politicians arguing in favor of the abolition of slavery and for free-produce advocates. In another portion of the dedication (and in his preface), Buckingham made clear his own view, and that of his countrymen, toward slavery. He recognized "the moral influence of England" and expected "my full share of censure from a large section, at least, of the people of America, for daring to speak, as truth compels me to do, of the wretched condition of the great body of the African race throughout the South, and of the reckless indifference to human life, and human obligations of every kind, which the very system of slavery engenders in nearly all the white population."[31] In the text, Buckingham presented himself and the British populace as a whole as being committed to abolition. At the same time, he invoked the nationalistic abolitionism that had undermined earlier Anglo-American antislavery cooperation and continued to prevent the development of a coherent international abolition movement.

Considering the manner in which Buckingham began his account of the South, it is unsurprising that *The Slave States of America* was, at certain points, a catalog of the evils of southern slavery. Buckingham, however, noted a number of ways in which southern slavery was mitigated in practice, contending that "there are many kind masters and mistresses, who do much to make the condition of their slaves easy and tolerable." In the case of New Orleans specifically, Buckingham discovered that "the negro and coloured population are here, as everywhere else throughout the United States, the proscribed class. On the whole, however, they are better off at New Orleans than in the cities of the North." As part of his analysis, Buckingham distinguished between field slaves and domestic slaves. While in Macon, Georgia, he found that the latter were "well fed and as well clad as the free domestic servants of many countries of Europe," while the former were maintained with as "little cost as possible." In contrasting the situation of slaves in the South with that of European workers, Buckingham concluded that "the condition of the slaves is far from being miserable; they are upon the whole as well fed, better clad, and have much more leisure and less severe labour than the Irish peasant or the English hand-loom weaver."[32]

For all of these mitigating factors, and in a manner typical of almost all British commentators on southern slavery, Buckingham was galled by the "positive good" defense of slavery that he found some southerners using. He described the justification of the system provided by a group of slaveholders after they heard his wife sigh as she watched a gang of slaves head to work. These southerners described the slaves as "among the happiest of human beings," a claim Buckingham made very clear he doubted. The "positive good" argument in favor of slavery in the South was often combined with a campaign to discourage abolition. As evidence of these twin pillars of the South, Buckingham quoted the work of the South Carolina academic Thomas Cooper. Buckingham further expanded on the "positive good" theory by highlighting an oration given at a December 1838 meeting of the South Carolina Society for the Advancement of Learning, during which slavery had been described as a "cherished institution." Buckingham's overall conclusion about southern abolition was that "the prejudices of the whites all over the South, appear to me to be so rooted and so strong against even entertaining any proposition on the subject of emancipation, that one might as well attempt to still the tempest by reason, as to move them even to discuss the question . . . all support each other in the assurance that 'the slaves are far better off than the working population of Europe,' and all contend 'that they are so happy that they would not have their freedom, if offered to them.'" Buckingham was clearly no pro-southerner and mercilessly criticized slavery in *America* and *The Slave States*. In the second book, he essentially stated that traveling around the United States had confirmed his belief that slavery was fundamentally evil.[33] Even so, however, Buckingham failed to recognize an absolute division between North and South. The southern section held slaves, while the North did not, and much to his disgust some eminent southerners claimed that this was a preferable social arrangement. Yet the North was no abolitionist paradise. The section had a population that turned a blind eye to the institution of slavery and, in some cases, actively prevented abolition.

The apparent lack of abolitionist sentiment in the northern states was similarly noted by one of the most popular of the British commentators on the United States—the novelist Charles Dickens. In 1842, Dickens published his infamous travelogue *American Notes for General Circulation,* a searing attack on the United States; however, his most striking observations on the subject of slavery were found in his later novel *The Life and Adventures of Martin Chuzzlewit* (1844). Attempting to begin a new life, the novel's title character and his servant, Mark Tapley, move from New York to the western settlement of Eden (based on Dickens's own observations of Cairo, Illinois), then become wholly disillusioned with the United States and return to Britain. While not one of Dickens's best sellers, *Martin Chuzzlewit* still averaged sales of 23,000 parts per month. In the novel Dickens made it clear that he saw slavery as an example of American national hypocrisy, with the key term here being *national,* as opposed to sectional. In New York, the only sympathetic character Martin and Mark meet is Mr. Bevan. Bevan is a Bostonian visiting New York City on business, and he cautions Martin about expecting New Yorkers to have progressive views on issues like race and emancipation just because they are residents of a free state. The lack of toleration in New York is made explicit during a meeting between Martin and the purportedly antislavery Norris family. After discovering the abolitionist views of his hosts, Martin "expressed his sympathy with the oppressed and wretched blacks" but the Norris family roundly derides this view.[34] The case of Dickens provides another example of a vocal and popular liberal who rejected the image of the United States as being neatly divided by slavery.

This sense that the North lacked a commitment to abolition was echoed in the 1844 travelogue of the social and political reformer John Robert Godley. Godley observed, "The mobs in the northern states are very much divided upon this subject [abolition], but the majority (including all the Irish) are in most places anti-abolitionist." New Englanders, however, were genuinely committed to ending slavery: "I had no idea of the strength of feeling which exists upon this subject in New England; the number of those who even go to the length of advocating a dissolution of the Union upon this ground is considerable." The problem that Godley identified was that "the more the abolitionists exert themselves to disseminate their principles, the farther 'the Southrons' commit themselves in a contrary direction." As an illustration, Godley pointed to "Mr. Calhoun, who may be called the head and representative of the slave-holders, and who will be one of the 'first favourites' for the next presidency," noting that he had "gone the length of saying lately that he considered slavery as a 'glorious institution,' the corner-stone of a free and democratic government, and that he hoped and prayed it might endure forever." Godley believed that this speech "would not have been ventured upon twenty years ago" and explained to his readers "that, considering the ground which has been taken, and the means which have been employed by the abolitionists, I neither wonder at nor blame the jealousy and soreness felt by the South upon this subject: it is with them a question, not simply of property, but of life and death."[35] Godley's point was not simply that slavery was an acrimonious sectional issue but also that the North failed to provide coherent resistance to the institution. At the same time, he noted how southerners were increasingly seeing their labor system under attack from the North, despite the fact that (from a British point of view) American abolition was relatively ineffective.

Although Godley found little to commend in the southern slaveholder and rejected the view of his peers that paternalism mitigated the institution, it was the gradual-abolition doctrine of Henry Clay, as opposed to immediatism, which Godley believed would result in successful abolition. He noted that Clay "acknowledges that slavery is a great evil, that a country can hardly prosper under its influence, and that interest as well as morality would counsel its extinction, if a practicable and safe method for effecting it could be discovered." Godley concluded his thoughts on slavery with a quote from Thomas Jefferson, who "said, many years ago, 'nothing is more clearly written in the book of destiny than the emancipation of the blacks,' it may be so, but at present it appears as far off as when he spoke; nor do I see any prospect of it, except through the agency of foreign invasion, or a dissolution of the Union."[36] Godley's analysis of American slavery in a sectional context provides yet more evidence of the nuances in British discourse on the topic. Godley was explicitly antislavery and had little positive to say about the South, yet he saw a level of indifference on the topic among northerners, and (crucially in hindsight) speculated that the division of the Union offered the best chance for abolition—an argument vocally utilized by antislavery supporters of the Confederacy in Britain during the Civil War.

Increasingly during the 1840s, discussions of sectionalism and slavery in Britain reflected a subtly changing understanding of race. One element in this change relates to the popularization of the "Quashee" tropes that had developed in the 1770s. The application of this racial language is typified by the work of the geologist and diplomatist G.W Featherstonhaugh, whose 1844 travel account echoed the ideas of figures like Godley while aggressively deploying racial stereotypes. Featherstonhaugh's attitude was encapsulated in his assertion that "the poor negro slave is naturally a cheerful, laughing animal, and even when driven through the wilderness in chains, if he is well fed and kindly treated, is seldom melancholy . . . it is only when he is ill-treated and roused to desperation, that his vindictive and savage nature breaks out." In a conversation with a southern slaveholder, which Featherstonhaugh recounted at length, he was informed that "the working of the institution of slavery . . . was not understood outside of the slave states; that it elevated the character of the master." This same southerner also contended that "the slaves were not an unhappy race of men; they were well fed, well clothed; and if there had been a necessity for it in the late dispute with the United States government, the slaves would have shown to a man their well-known fidelity to their masters." Featherstonhaugh was, however, skeptical of these descriptions, just as James Silk Buckingham had been before him.[37] Nevertheless, the nature of the debate between Britons about slavery and sectionalism provides a powerful illustration of the complexity of British sectional discourse. No simple moral dichotomy between North and South existed and consequently the precise views of the people in each section were not easy identifiable for the British. Furthermore, growing disillusion with West Indian emancipation resulted in an increased belief in the innate inferiority of blacks and the use of the "Quashee" stereotype. This belief, in turn, provided a valuable racial framework within which the paternalistic relationship between slave and master seemed like an obvious way to mitigate the excesses of the system until the groundwork could be laid for successful abolition.

Even as he discussed the southern commitment to slavery, however, Featherstonhaugh highlighted a clear antislavery impulse in the section. He specifically discussed the views of Virginian and former president James Madison, who had hoped for eventual abolition across the nation. Featherstonhaugh reported that Madison "had assembled all his slaves—and they were numerous—and offered to manumit them immediately; but they instantly declined it, alleging that they had been born on his estate, had always been provided for by him with raiment and food, in sickness and in health, and if they were made free they would have no home to go to, and no friend to protect and care for them. They preferred, therefore, to live and die as his slaves." Featherstonhaugh decided that Madison's position was indicative "no doubt . . . [of] the situation of many humane right-thinking proprietors in the Southern States" and therefore accused "the Abolitionists of the Free States, when they denounce slavery and call for its immediate abolition," of ignoring "the conditions upon which alone it could be effected." When it came to the subject of sectional animosity over abolition and slavery, he maintained that "the uncompromising obloquy which has been cast at the Southern planters, by their too scrupulous adversaries, is therefore not deserved by them."[38]

In his own analysis of the northern position on slavery, Featherstonhaugh's fellow geologist, Sir Charles Lyell, highlighted the region's hypocrisy. He emphasized the contrast between the nominal equality offered to free blacks and the practical oppression they faced, giving as an example the case of a black Philadelphia businessman, whose two sons had been unable to speak at a public meeting on a topic directly relevant to the family trade. Lyell also discussed at length the contrast between racial attitudes among whites in the North and South. Not only were free blacks in the North politically and economically at a disadvantage, they were social pariahs. Furthermore, Lyell maintained, southern whites were more comfortable interacting with blacks on a regular basis than their northern counterparts.[39] For this eminent and influential scientist, as for so many other commentators from Britain, the difference between North and South did not lend itself to a simple division into good and evil. In many ways the North was no better than the South, and while the latter might preach slavery and the former equality, hypocrisy undermined the North's claims to moral superiority. This powerful observation could be used to negatively characterize the whole United States before the conflict, and during the Civil War it had the sectional potency to undermine Union claims that slavery was at the heart of their cause.

Regardless of his experiences in America, Lyell was still a committed abolitionist, although he had serious reservations about the efficacy of immediate abolition in the United States. Particularly important for Lyell, in terms of understanding slavery as an institution, was the British experience in the West Indies, which he discussed with reference to the practicality of altering the conditions of slaves in the short term. By the mid-1840s both the British public and policy makers were abandoning their previous high hopes for emancipation in the Caribbean. This shift was accompanied, as we saw in Featherstonhaugh's text, by the more frequent usage of "Quashee" racial tropes in discussions of emancipation.[40] Increasingly, then, the case of the West Indies became a warning about the potential pitfalls of badly planned abolition, rather than a model that the Americans should follow. Crucially, this warning did not imply a rejection of abolition as a fundamental good. It did, however, help to justify the short-term continuation of slavery as long as it occurred under a regime that mitigated its worst features.

These characterizations influenced those who helped to form British opinion on the United States. The North was usually seen as somewhere between well meaning (but flawed) and downright hypocritical, while the South, though objectionable in theory, was often considered more sympathetic in reality. Lyell, for example, concluded that "the negroes [in the South], so far as I have seen them, whether in domestic service or on the farms, appear very cheerful and free from care, better fed than a large part of the labouring classes in Europe." He also identified a strong paternalistic relationship underpinning slavery, which the slaves themselves reciprocated. He described how "we asked a woman in Georgia, whether she was the slave of a family in our acquaintance. She replied merrily 'Yes, I belong to them, and they belong to me.'" Anecdotes of this sort were meant to suggest the material contentment of some slaves living below the Mason-Dixon Line, and in recounting them Lyell added his voice to those who rejected (at least in the context of the South), the brutality so frequently associated with the slave system. In this version of slavery, violent compulsion to labor was replaced with something at least vaguely paternalistic.[41]

The attitude of the slave population as described by Lyell (with its emphasis on childlike contentment) would have resonated with the significant proportion of the British public who were exposed to increasingly popular "nigger" minstrel acts during the 1840s. From the first appearance of the form in London in 1836, these blackface acts quickly spread across the nation and developed a particular flavor that differentiated them from their US counterparts. As scholars have noted, they were often a medium through which Britons criticized American society; yet, as Frederick Douglass pointed out while in Britain in the 1840s, the portrayal of African Americans in simplified terms in the shows made them as much a subject of ridicule as white Americans. In a sense, minstrel acts utilized elements of the "Quashee" stereotype but deployed them in a different form and consequently familiarized a new audience with the image. Descriptions such as Lyell's are indicative of the racial ideas of "Quashee" and minstrelsy permeating "factual" accounts. Furthermore, because Britons lacked exposure to alternative models, they increasingly saw these tropes as representative of African Americans as a whole.[42] As a result of the use of the childlike slave model in travel narratives, it seemed almost natural for some Britons to believe that the paternalistic relationship between an idealized master and slave was the appropriate one, given the racial makeup of southern society.

This view of racially defined intellectual capacity was vital for those, such as the novelist Charlotte Matilda Houstoun, who maintained that slavery was evil but that the worst excesses of the system were mitigated in the South. Houstoun made her distaste toward slavery clear in her 1844 travelogue, *Texas and the Gulf of Mexico,* in which she criticized "the almost absolute dominion which a slave-owner, at least in the plantations, possesses over his human property." Nevertheless, her depiction of slavery was not simply a catalogue of misery. She described areas of the South in which, "during our drives through the streets, especially on Sundays, the display of negro finery and taste was very remarkable . . . I saw such persecuted negro slaves frequently; they appeared to have no other occupation than that of flourishing about their gold-headed canes, and fixing a glass in their eye." The sarcastic use of the term "persecuted" and description of slaves apparently living in luxury were obviously intended to undermine the image of the desperate slave, a longstanding feature of abolitionist literature. The paternalist connection was integral to this mitigated slave system. As Houstoun described it,

> the owner of a slave, when he purchases him, enters into an agreement, understood though not expressed, that his services will be repaid by food, lodging, and decent clothing; that he will be allowed sufficient intervals of rest, and a certain portion of time in which he may work for himself; and also he may look forward to eventual independence if he is able to earn it, or if his own good conduct may render him deserving of the boon. The life of the slave is protected by the laws, and his good treatment is to a certain degree secured by the powerful argument, that it is contrary to his owner's interest to ill-use him.[43]

This paternalism was contrasted to the plight of the freed slave: "If there is any truth in the supposed degrading, and enervating influence of slave-owning, there is still more reason for believing that the forced servitude in which he is kept, together with the strong prejudice which exists against his race and colour, render the freed slave, in his present state of mind, education, &c., incapable of valuing his free position properly."[44] In a sectional context, therefore, Houstoun's descriptions contributed to the British belief that, for all its faults, US slavery was not simply a system of mindless violence but a complex social system in which white and black played "appropriate" roles.

In the account of his second visit to the United States, Lyell offered further evidence for the existence of a paternalistic, mitigated form of slavery in the South. While in Virginia he noted that "the negroes . . . have certainly not the manners of an oppressed race" and found on one plantation that "when I inquired if, in reality, there were hundreds of runaway slaves in the woods, everyone laughed at the idea. As a general rule, they said, the negroes are well fed, and when they are so, will very rarely attempt to escape." Lyell even contested the common critique that slavery broke up families. He saw little evidence of this, "owing to the kind feeling of the southern planter toward their 'own people,' as they call them." He presented two cases as evidence, including one in which a judge in Richmond had accepted a price below market value so that his slaves could be sold to their preferred location. Later, upon seeing a group traveling from Alabama to Texas, Lyell described "the cheerfulness with which these slaves are going they know not where with their owners, notwithstanding their usual dislike to quit the place they have been brought up in, [which] shows a strong bond of union between the master and 'his people.'"[45]

Lyell was informed by "an Abolitionist in Massachusetts" that "great pains must have been taken by the planters to conceal from me the true state of things," but he was confident that his own experiences had given him an accurate impression of slavery. At its most romanticized, the labor system described by Lyell possessed a quality akin to feudal paternalism:

> During a fortnight's stay at Hopeton [Georgia], we had an opportunity of seeing how the planters live in the South, and the condition and prospects of the negroes on a well-managed estate. The relation of the slaves to their owners resembles nothing in the Northern States. There is an hereditary regard and often attachment on both sides, more like that formerly existing between lords and their retainers in the old feudal times of Europe, than to anything now to be found in America. The slaves identify themselves with

> the master, and their sense of their own importance rises with his success in life. But the responsibility of the owners is felt to be great, and to manage a plantation with profit is no easy task, so much judgment is required and such a mixture of firmness, forbearance and kindness.[46]

Contemporary readers likely contrasted this description with the situation in the North, where Lyell claimed to "have heard apologists . . . endeavouring to account for the degraded position which the negroes hold, socially and politically, in the Free States, by saying they belong to a race which is kept in a state of slavery in the South." As far as Lyell was concerned, however, "if they really desired to accelerate emancipation, they would begin by setting an example to the Southern States, and treating the black race with more respect and more on a footing of equality."[47]

It is important not to misconstrue Lyell's argument. He was intending to highlight the hypocrisy of the free states rather than launch a crusade for racial equality. For the majority of the British population, total racial equality was a flawed ideal. Most saw fine gradations between races, which in turn meant each racial group was suited to a particular form of labor. Nowhere was this thesis more prominently expressed than in Thomas Carlyle's *Occasional Discourse on the Nigger Question.* Carlyle had risen to the top of Victorian intellectual life in Britain after the publication of his satirical novel *Sartor Resartus* in 1831. The "sage of Chelsea" (as he became known) counted among his disciples Dickens, the political philosopher John Stuart Mill, and John Ruskin, and one of his biographers shrewdly noted, "it is impossible to understand the Victorians without understanding Carlyle first." Although concerned primarily with the effects of West Indian emancipation, Carlyle's *Occasional Discourse* and Mill's response to it provide an insight into the complexity of racial attitudes in Britain and what this meant for views of the American sections.[48]

Carlyle's philosophy of race and labor posited the existence of appropriate labor roles for members of different ethnic groups. He even went as far as to suggest that if those at the bottom of this hierarchy (Africans) refused to work, then violent compulsion could be justified. In his view, social relations should be characterized by a similar sort of racial hierarchy. Carlyle addressed American slaveholders directly in his pamphlet, assuring them "that your relation to the Negroes, in this thing called slavery . . . [is] actually fair, just and according to the facts;—fair, I say, not in the sight of New-England platforms, but of God Almighty." This particular line merits attention because it locates the movement for abolition in New England, an association frequently made by popular commentators discussing the United States in the period. More broadly speaking, Carlyle's text focused heavily on a combination of the "Quashee" stereotype and criticisms of West Indian emancipation. While Carlyle was an extremist, his voice was respected among the British literate classes and in Westminster itself. As Brent E. Kinser succinctly puts it, "whether or not people agreed with Carlyle, they listened."[49]

Mill's rebuttal is illustrative of the intellectual divisions that existed between British thinkers on the subject of slavery. Furthermore, that such a prominent philosopher issued a response reminds us how much attention Carlyle's work garnered. Mill, whose text *The Negro Question* set out explicitly to undermine Carlyle's racial and political argument, was a key liberal thinker of the era and may well have spoken for many of his intellectual kin when he rejected Carlyle. Yet, it would be a mistake to believe he spoke for all liberals. The radical reforming MP for Sheffield, John Arthur Roebuck, for instance, expressed annoyance at British abolitionists who he believed ignored domestic working-class problems. In essence, Mill spoke for a particular set of middle-class liberals such as John Bright and Richard Cobden. While they might cooperate with figures like Roebuck over the issue of franchise reform, they were not in sync when it came to abolition. Conversely, despite drastically different political views, both Roebuck and Carlyle critiqued middle-class abolitionism and maintained that the traditional rural gentry could act as a paternal force with a sincere desire to help the poor. While neither explicitly made the connection, it is possible to see how this relationship might have been analogous to that of the southern planter to the slave in its mythologized, feudal form.[50]

Carlyle's publication was simply the most prominent and extreme illustration of a general British disillusion about West Indian emancipation. This disillusion was increasingly expressed through the sort of racial language used by Carlyle, which in turn had consequences for the way Britons understood race and slavery in the United States. A belief that blacks would not work without compulsion had been a staple claim of West Indian planters during the 1830s and had been hotly disputed by the architects of abolition. With the ending of the apprenticeship system, it was hoped that former slaves would engage with the imperial economy as wage laborers and guarantee the prosperity of sugar plantations. The 1840s, however, brought serious economic difficulty in the West Indies, which (despite evidence to the contrary) was commonly blamed on the refusal of former slaves to work for wages. This understanding of the situation increasingly characterized debates in the public sphere and among policy makers. In his *Occasional Discourse,* then, Carlyle simply vocalized these opinions about racial characteristics at a time when popular views regarding the success of abolition were at a low ebb. The significance of his work stemmed from his ability to shift the terms of the debate on the West Indies and essentially normalize certain racial views to such an extent that even his primary critic (Mill) failed to dispute many of Carlyle's caricatures.[51] In the context of the United States, the British experience of emancipation in the West Indies (when viewed in Carlylean terms) seemed to raise questions about the desirability of the rapid abolition of slavery in the South; even if it did not lead to a rejection of abolition as a desirable long-term goal.

Furthermore, the racial typology Carlyle deployed was utilized by British travelers discussing race and slavery in a US context. In her 1850 travel account, *Hesperos,* Charlotte Houstoun claimed that "the negro race when left entirely to their own resources, and solely dependent on their own intelligence and industry, instead of rising, will rather retrograde . . . in the social scale." She believed "that the blacks [would not work] unless compelled to do so." That this was true, she claimed, was "sufficiently proved by the present state of our possessions in the West Indies, where, though the accessaries [*sic*] of life are not half so abundant as in the United States, it has been found impossible to induce the blacks to labour." Her experiences in the United States, combined with her analysis of the results of West Indian emancipation, led Houstoun to conclude that slavery "is not only the main source of wealth of America, but that the advantages derived from it render the Northern States and those of the South so dependent on each other, that a separation would be the ruin of both."[52]

Despite these reservations, and like most British observers, Houstoun evinced a desire for abolition in the long term. While southern slavery still existed, however, she maintained that it was not as brutal as some critics had presented it. Upon entering Kentucky, Houstoun took the opportunity to explicitly compare white attitudes toward enslaved and free blacks in North and South: "The people of Kentucky are so fully awake to these advantages [of long-term abolition], that they are now, I believe, quite unanimous in their desire that slavery should be abolished in their state."

She also claimed that, in the short term, Kentucky slaveholders ameliorated the position of their chattels and that "the Kentucky slaves are, at length, beginning to understand that their condition is not so bad but that it might be worse, and that even in their fancied paradise, the Free States, they might find cause to regret [leaving] the land of their bondage." Houstoun's account was permeated by similar descriptions of slavery showing the mitigated form of the institution that she believed characterized the South and emphasizing that many southerners aimed to abolish slavery in the long term.[53]

Houstoun also pointed to the close personal relationship between slave and master which she believed underpinned southern slavery. Her descriptions of the time she spent in Natchez, Mississippi, are particularly telling in this regard. Upon arriving in the town, Houstoun commented on "the genuine and heartily-expressed joy of [enslaved] negroes, who, being most of them old retainers of the family, came down in numbers to the river side to greet the return of their masters, and to be received by them with looks of pleasure, and by a hand cordially and kindly extended." Later observations of plantations along the Mississippi River, on which she saw a "granary, storehouses, and workshops" and "the hospital for sick negroes," seem to have confirmed her earlier suppositions about the importance southerners attached to slave welfare. Houstoun also noted the kitchen gardens the slaves kept and the time given over for slaves to tend them. She even claimed that "their produce is generally bought by their masters, who are certain to pay them twice as much as it is worth." Here again the planters were portrayed as a benevolent class patronizing their social and racial "inferiors." Houstoun concluded that the slaves' "bondage is not so irksome, or their situation half so unhappy as it is represented to be." All of these examples led her to reassert the division between slavery in the abstract and the southern slavery to which most British readers would have been accustomed:

> During this, and my former visit to the United States, I have passed nearly a year in the South, and have had good opportunities of ascertaining the true condition of the negro race in this country. This being the case, I have come to the conclusion that the evil exists here in its most modified form, and that the domestic slaves are the least unhappy menials in the world; moreover, I am convinced that they are very far from being so severely worked as most of the servants in free countries. The accounts of the atrocities committed

> in the plantations are, I have reason to believe, greatly exaggerated: that a great many shocking acts of cruelty and oppression are perpetrated by some of the slave-owners in the out of the way parts of Arkansas and the Red River Plantations, cannot, I fear, be denied; and moreover, that the lax state of morals is, in many parts of the South, painful to think upon; but these instances are the exception to the rule, and I have no hesitation in asserting that the universal public feeling in the South is on the side of humanity.[54]

Houstoun's explicit rejection of any systemic cruelty in the slave South, in favor of a characterization of the slave owner as a figure with a clear sense of morality, posited a social relationship between black and white that mitigated a potentially objectionable labor system. Through this claim she contributed to the British understanding of American sectionalism by grounding her ideas in preexisting literature on the United States and current British debates regarding race, slavery, and labor.

British views of American slavery were constantly shifting throughout the antebellum period in response to domestic and international developments. As a result, there remained scope for continued debate in Britain right through the 1850s. Writing in 1851, for instance, the poet and travel writer Lady Emmeline Stuart-Wortley, unlike most other commentators, described instances of free blacks receiving equal and compassionate treatment in the North in her narrative *Travels in the United States*. It is worth noting, however, that these free blacks were still servants and that she also claimed to have found instances of a paternalistic relationship mitigating the condition of slaves in the South. After spending time on the plantation of President Zachary Taylor in Natchez, Stuart-Wortley concluded that "the slaves themselves were . . . well fed, comfortably clothed, and kindly cared for."[55]

Despite the claims of figures like Stuart-Wortley, the idea that free blacks in the North suffered violence and social exclusion continued to feature heavily in British commentary. Writing in 1851, the agricultural scientist James F. W. Johnston drew his readers' attention back to an 1834 Philadelphia riot during which mobs had physically driven free blacks out of their traditional role as the cities' unskilled labor force. Such ideas about free blacks being persecuted were so pervasive that they even entered into the vocabulary of high politics. Following a discussion of the Negro Seaman Laws, British ambassador John F. Crampton wrote on 20 February to the Charleston consul George Buckley-Matthew, explaining that opposition to the act could stimulate a violent response "not only in the South, but all over the United States."[56] By the early 1850s, the British understanding of the relationship between race, slavery, and sectionalism was clearly more complex than has previously been recognized. The British experience of emancipation in the West Indies had created a context in which slavery could be accepted as a short-term expedient, as long as the slaves' condition was ameliorated and a long-term commitment to abolition existed. At the same time, British commentary on the United States had rejected a clear North/South division in terms of both slavery and the treatment of blacks. Abolitionism and equitable treatment may have existed in New England, yet the North as a whole was commonly associated with racial violence and the financial and political support it provided to the slave system. At its very worst, then, the North actively perpetuated slavery—profiting from the institution while failing to offer the necessary paternalistic care to either southern slaves or its own free black residents.

Writing in 1852, the lawyer Edward Sullivan provided further evidence of the absence of a clear division between North and South when it came to slavery and race. Sullivan was clearly aware of the concept of mitigated slavery in the South and conceded that the slaves "seemed very happy . . . and chatted away like so many monkeys; the thoughtless happiness, however, of the American slaves, that is always in the mouth of the free and enlightened citizen as an argument in favour of slavery, is not the happiness of a human being, but that of an animal." In a tone reminiscent of Martineau, however, Sullivan also expressed concern that this mitigated form of slavery was not underpinned by a sense of moral responsibility, since "profit, and profit at any cost, is all the slave-owner thinks of, and to that he will, if necessary, sacrifice the health and comfort, and even the life itself of his slaves." Sullivan also emphasized the violence of slavery, noting that "a slave can get no protection from the cruelty of his master; the law, and what is of much more importance, public opinion, countenances the corporeal punishments of slaves." Despite this catalogue of criticisms, Sullivan made it clear that the situation was hardly better in the free states and that even though "in the northern free States . . . he [the free black] has the legal position of a citizen, the right of voting . . . if he dared to avail himself of his privilege . . . he would be turned out as sure as possible." Overall, "his social position in the south is better than in the north; he is treated equally as a dog in both, with this difference, that in the south he is sometimes a pet dog, whereas in the north he is always a cur, kicked and hooted on every occasion."[57]

Despite rejecting a clear sectional division on the subject, Sullivan was a critic of slavery as a national institution and was particularly vocal about the 1850 Fugitive Slave Law; he described it as "the most iniquitous bill ever framed by human beings." The precise provisions of the bill, which demanded the arrest of anyone thought to be a runaway in any state of the nation, combined with the fact that it had been accepted (albeit grudgingly in some cases) by northern politicians, seemed to further enmesh the supposedly free states in slavery. Interestingly, the novelist Charles Kingsley claimed that the Fugitive Slave Law should have provided the impetus for the dissolution of the United States. In making such a claim, Kingsley may have been invoking the ideas of earlier writers (such as John Godley) who had suggested that breaking up the United States would be the simplest way for northerners to disentangle themselves from the slave system. The refusal of the free states to follow this course contributed to a belief among some in Britain that American abolitionists lacked sincerity. From a British point of view, dissolving the Union provided an obvious way to end slavery with no risk. Gradual abolition might be needed for the South, but the North could rid itself of the slave states and set up as an entirely new nation. That northerners did not attempt to leave the Union following the passage of the Fugitive Slave Law seemed to suggest a preparedness to accept the existence of slavery. For Sullivan, the Fugitive Slave Law itself was "proof of the feeling of the country against the negro," for "the abolitionists are quite as much to blame as the southern men."[58] Rather than severing the ties of union and ridding itself of slavery, the North had simultaneously annoyed the South (by criticizing slavery) and reinforced the slave system.

A review of Sullivan's work in the December 1852 edition of *Blackwood's Edinburgh Magazine* is illustrative of the response to the ambiguous treatment of slavery in the work of popular commentators. The reviewer bemoaned the brutality of slavery and maintained that the system must be abolished, despite the potential intellectual differences between black and white. However, in terms of the attitudes displayed toward free blacks in the US North and South, the *Blackwood's* writer did not give his readers a neat division, instead noting (in a manner consistent with Sullivan) that "in the northern states, it is true, slavery does not exist; but in those states the social condition of the negro is hardly better than in the south."[59] These sentiments may well have been a product of anti-Americanism, and it is certainly true that throughout the antebellum period a significant proportion of Britons found the existence of slavery and the treatment of blacks a valuable stick with which to beat their transatlantic rivals. Nevertheless, observations like this were crucial in constructing a British understanding of sectionalism in the United States, regardless of the purpose of their author.

The consistent rejection of a close relationship between the North and abolitionism, combined with the claim that the condition of southern slaves was mitigated by paternalism, continued to feature in much of the British commentary of the 1850s. Such claims were often underpinned by distinctive racial ideas then entering the public lexicon. The novelist William Makepeace Thackeray, whose reputation was second only to Dickens in the period, provides an illustration of how sectionalism and British racial ideas could be tied together. Thackeray visited the South in 1853, and although he didn't publish a travelogue recounting his experience, Thackeray's correspondence reveals the connections he saw between race, slavery, and sectionalism. He specifically rejected racial equality, and even though he maintained the evil of slavery in theory, he explained that "the sum of unhappiness is as great among our wretched poor as it can be here; controversy has this good in it that it will pique black & white man-owners into generosity & I dare say better the labourers' condition in Dorsetshire as in Virginia."[60] Although this was partly a critique of working and living conditions at home, by comparing southern slavery with poverty in Britain, Thackeray rejected the idea of the southern slaveholder as exceptionally immoral (or at least placed British industrialists on the same level).

The more complex morality of the slaveholder, at which Thackeray appeared to hint, was an idea with currency beyond the British literati. Even those in the highest echelons of the government often failed to make the moral division between free and slave states which Union supporters later would be so keen to convince the public had been at the root of the Civil War. The British ambassador, Crampton, wrote in 1853 that northern "social prejudice against negroes is just as strong as that of the South, and their hatred of the Southern Slavery rests upon other grounds than ours." This distinction, which Crampton made in passing, is highly significant. Britons' pride in their own abolition movement stemmed from their belief that it had been moral and selfless. US abolitionism, however, was presented as something utilized for political leverage, which made it fundamentally different from its British counterpart.[61] For Crampton, the US debate over slavery illustrated a difference between the sections that was based on political posturing rather than a moral division. At least as late as 1853, therefore, key British politicians flatly rejected the notion that the northern states had committed to moral abolitionism, an understanding that would influence initial reactions to the Civil War in the corridors of power.

This lack of equitable treatment for free black Americans was emphasized once again in the 1854 travelogue of the noted physiologist and social reformer Marshall Hall. He described how in Pennsylvania "no one of this persecuted race may drive an omnibus," and in New York "an African gentleman . . . may not take his seat in that public conveyance." Hall considered this treatment of free blacks in Pennsylvania a "second slavery of prejudice and oppression," a telling indication of the apparent lack of difference between the lives of blacks in the North and the South. He provided a particularly detailed account of free African American communities in New York before noting that "Connecticut, Ohio and Illinois, of the free States, have most disgraced themselves in their legislation against the African race." This did not mean, however, that Hall endorsed slavery. Instead, he contended that "when he [the slave] has escaped from the slavery of the land, he finds himself bowed down by a slavery of prejudice and oppression. One thing, and one alone can nobly emancipate him: it is a well-combined plan of education, discipline, elevation and wealth." As evidence he cited various examples of former slaves excelling in the right circumstances. Hall's text offers a concrete example of the influence of the apparent failure of West Indian emancipation on British ideas of abolition in the United States. Hall was explicit about the "utter and melancholy failure" of Jamaican emancipation and seems to have formulated his plan for the United States with the hope of avoiding the repetition of this scenario.[62]

Particularly interesting in terms of the different attitudes Hall found evinced toward African Americans across the United States was an account he provided of the places where he believed it was least desirable to be black.

> Maryland enjoys what I deem the proud pre-eminence of being, of all the States, the first in friendliness towards the African. Next comes Louisiana, with its mild 'code noir.' Then follow Virginia and the Carolinas; and next, Rhode Island, Pennsylvania, Connecticut and New York. Then come Kentucky, Ohio, Indiana, and Massachusetts; and then, at a considerable distance, Tennessee, Illinois, Georgia, and Alabama; then, at a still greater distance, Mississippi . . . lastly, strange to say, Maine, New Hampshire and

Vermont. I trust, the unfriendliness of the last three is more that of climate, than of the people.[63]

That this list implies little connection between the slaveholding status of an individual state and the overall condition of African Americans shows the extent to which Britons were not presented with a simple geography that could be mapped onto the Civil War by pro-Unionists.

Hall juxtaposed his descriptions of the North with images of slavery in the South that highlighted the mitigated nature of the system. Interestingly, Hall published his travelogue almost two years *after* the appearance of a novel that might have been expected to stimulate a clear antisouthern reaction in Britain, *Uncle Tom's Cabin,* by Harriet Beecher Stowe. This explicitly abolitionist book was written, at least partially, as an indictment of the Fugitive Slave Law and followed the lives of the slaves Tom and Eliza as the latter was sold down the river to a brutal Louisiana slaveholder and the former attempted to escape slavery with her child. A prominent reviewer (the economist Nassau William Senior) published an analysis of *Uncle Tom's Cabin* in the *Edinburgh Review,* which he later extended and reprinted in the form of a pamphlet. Senior drew on a number of typical themes relating to slavery in the United States, but he did so without sugaring his criticisms with the positive interpretation of the southern slaveholder some writers had used. He also drew a distinct line between North and South on the basis of slavery in a way that would be reflected in some British Civil War propaganda. Unsurprisingly, he claimed that, "for the first two years after the passing of the Act [Fugitive Slave Act], the lower classes in New York and Boston enjoyed the excitement of a negro hunt as much as our rustics enjoy following a fox hunt." According to him, Stowe's work had had a major influence on popular opinion. Though he conceded "that the mere reading of the novel would [not] have much affected them," the fact that "it was dramatized and acted in the Bowery theatre in New York" had helped to bring about a change in northern popular opinion.[64] Senior's account, with its relatively clear distinction between North and South on the basis of slavery, allows us to glimpse the roots of the sectional division pro-Union writers would attempt to emphasize during the Civil War. Crucially, however, and despite the later claims of John Bright to the contrary, this vision was contested and never unanimously accepted.

Uncle Tom's Cabin was a publishing sensation in Britain and sold a million copies in its first year. Reaching the highest levels of government, it was read by Queen Victoria and Prince Albert. Despite the book's popularity, however, the literary scholar Audrey Fisch has noted that some reviewers (Senior notwithstanding) had reservations about it. Many felt that its ideological foundations were flawed and that it lacked literary merit. While Dickens commended Stowe on her intentions, he criticized the work's "overstrained conclusions and violent extremes." The *Times* expressed reservations about the novel's practical consequences, noting in September 1852, "We have little doubt at all . . . that the very readiest way to rivet the fetters of slavery in these critical times is to direct against all slaveholders in America the opprobrium and indignation which such works as *Uncle Tom's Cabin* are sure to excite."[65] While it was a popular and influential indictment of slavery and a capable piece of abolitionist propaganda, Stowe's work also raised serious questions about American abolition for British readers. Furthermore, it made readers wonder whether the movement was helping or hindering abolition in the South.

The complex reactions to *Uncle Tom's Cabin* in Britain provide context for physician Marshall Hall's contention that "the African in the slavery of the United States is . . . well cared for." Part of the reason Hall was still able to draw this conclusion two years after the publication of Beecher's novel was that he had found free blacks in the North "crushed by State legislation and popular prejudice," in contrast to the close social relationship he believed existed between black and white in the South. He also drew his readers' attention to the apparently paternalistic nature of the master/slave relationship, describing having "witnessed [it] myself with the utmost satisfaction" and recounting how "at Richmond, I was kindly invited to visit a gentleman, the hospitable owner of a plantation on the James River. I visited the 'cabins' of the negro-slaves, and saw them at their daily occupations in the farm-yard and in the corn-fields. Their physical comfort and well-being appeared to me to be perfect."[66]

For all of these apparent examples of the condition of slaves being mitigated, Hall maintained that he was no apologist for the system. He likened the treatment of southern slaves to the maintenance of cattle's physical well-being and conceded that the power that the slave owners possessed over the lives of their chattels meant that cruelty and exploitation were always possible. As far as Hall was concerned, however, the solution to the problem of southern slavery would not come about as a result of northern abolition, since "the case of the poor slave has been aggravated by the violent but vain efforts of the abolitionist." Hall here evoked Godley's earlier contention that any abolitionism that did exist in the North was having a detrimental influence on the lives of southern slaves. This was not intended as an assertion of the power of northern abolition. Instead, the claims of Hall and Godley reflected the perceptions of southerners, who became more defensive of slavery as a result of feeling threatened by what was (at least from a British point of view) a weak abolitionist movement.[67]

The claims of Hall and his contemporaries (that the condition of slaves was not as bad as might be expected) continued to feature in the works of British commentators and ensured that the image of southern slavery as mitigated by paternalism endured through the end of the 1850s. This was evident in the 1857 travel narrative produced by the writer Amelia M. Murray, entitled *Letters from the United States, Cuba and Canada*. In her work, Murray quoted a text, published in the South, that presented slavery as the most appropriate labor solution based on the social makeup of the South. The image of the paternalistic southerner that had had such a significant history in British discourse on the South ran throughout Murray's work, beginning with her description of her first exposure to slavery in Baltimore. Her later experiences were typified by the notion of slaves and masters being deeply attached to one another, with slaves described as "well clothed, merry and content," and "good-natured, and easy in their manner." She observed a group of slaves in New Orleans who considered "Mr. L. more in the light of their father than their master." Murray's most extensive experience came while staying on a plantation in Darien, Georgia. Her account of Darien combined various racial tropes, which drew on the "Quashee" model, with the conclusion that "a happy attached negro population surrounds this abode; I never saw servants in any old English family more comfortable, or more devoted; it is quite a relief to see anything so patriarchal, after the apparently uncomfortable relations of masters and servants in the Northern States."[68]

Murray's criticisms of master-servant relations in the North and of the abolition movement were characterized by concerns over a combination of ideas and methods. Given the continued British antipathy toward positive endorsements of slavery, Murray's contention that abolitionists such as Stowe and Henry Ward Beecher were pursuing a desirable end was predictable enough. She also claimed, however, that such activists were unaware of the practical difficulties of emancipation. She even went so far as to imply that *Uncle Tom's Cabin* was "a libel upon the slaveholders as a body." One of the few northerners with whom Murray appeared to be in agreement on the issue of slavery was the New York Democrat Horatio Seymour, who envisioned a plan for gradual emancipation, "not by stringent laws and ill-judged prohibitions, but by the introduction of free labour."[69] This gradualist approach to abolition saw the end of slavery coming as a slow process—a method that had considerable appeal for Murray.

In her descriptions of traveling around the Charleston area, Murray offered her own version of the paternalistic southern slaveholder and explained to her readers how she believed the British should treat these men and women.

> I begin to mark cotton plantations, and my compassionate feelings are rapidly changing sides. It appears to me our benevolent intentions in England have taken a mistaken direction, and that we should bestow our compassion on the masters instead of the slaves. The former by no means enjoy the incubi with which circumstances have loaded them, and would be only too happy if they could supersede black labour by white; but as to the negroes, they are the merriest, and most contented set of people I ever saw; of course there are exceptions, but I am inclined to suspect that we have as much vice, and more suffering, than is caused by the unfortunate institution of Slavery [*sic*]; and I very much doubt if freedom will ever make the black population, in mass, anything more than a set of grown-up children.[70]

Murray's Charleston slaveholders were apparently, therefore, fulfilling a necessary role in a paternalistic social setting. They were not involved in the buying and selling of slaves based on a belief that the system was morally right. Instead, they were attempting to work within the social and labor structure that they had inherited until "safe" abolition could be achieved.

Murray's commentary was typical of that produced by British figures in the sense that she distinguished between abstract slavery and the mitigated form of the institution that she identified in the South. A particularly comprehensive analysis of this same division was provided by James Stirling in his 1857 travel book *Letters from the Slave States*. Stirling described slavery itself as "an accursed thing" and claimed that he pitied "the white men who labour under this affliction." Despite his avowed abolitionism, however, Stirling conceded that "on the whole, and taking the slave population of all the States, statistics prove incontestably that the treatment of the slaves must be reasonably good," while also reporting that slaves themselves had found their conditions improving in recent years. This improvement was the result not of northern abolitionism but rather of changing attitudes in the South. Nevertheless (and regardless of these potential forms of mitigation), Stirling flatly rejected any suggestion that the slaves could be described as happy in their bondage.[71]

The condition of slaves seemed particularly objectionable to Stirling because of his experiences in Boston. Like a number of his forebears, Stirling characterized this city as being "in the van of American civilization," particularly when it came to the equitable treatment of African Americans. He informed his readers that free blacks "are treated much more as equals than formerly, and in some respects are comfortable. They are not now excluded from public conveyances in New England, and in some States are even allowed to exercise the franchise, as well as to possess it." While admitting the range of continuing challenges for free black Americans, Stirling still provided a relatively rosy image of emancipation in the free states (albeit with a clear focus on New England).[72]

Stirling expressed concern about the debate over the expansion of the Union leading some southerners to endorse the slavery system as fundamentally good. Despite that concern, though, Stirling went further than many of his peers and claimed to have identified pro-abolition sentiments in the South. He noted that "a not inconsiderable class of men in the Southern States, especially in the more northern ones, and in all the commercial cities . . . see clearly the evils of slavery, and would fain see it done away with." He further expanded upon this, explaining that "symptoms are not wanting of anti-slavery feeling in the frontier Slave States," before describing how "in Missouri and Kentucky, Abolitionist movements have already taken place; and perhaps, ere long, the grand 'Old Dominion' [Virginia] herself will re-assert the noble abhorrence of slavery that yet breathes and burns in the words of her wise men of olden time." On the topic of long-term prospects, Stirling confidently concluded, "Slavery cannot continue in the South. The governing class of the South is too highly-civilized to co-exist with slavery."[73] The crucial overarching point here is that, as late as 1857, British ideas about sectional disputes in the United States were fundamentally different from those around which Civil War propagandists for the North would try to construct their arguments. Public commentators such as Stirling presented the Mason-Dixon Line as a permeable boundary between the sections and rejected the idea of an absolute division between freedom in the North and slavery in the South.

This rejection of a clear division was echoed in William Chambers's *American Slavery and Colour* (1857). In his travelogue, Chambers reinforced to his readers that blacks suffered serious mistreatment in the free states: "It is not possible to speak without indignation of the contumelies to which free coloured persons are exposed throughout the United States; and what is most offensive of all is, that more flagrant cases of maltreatment occur in the North than the South." Chambers went on to give further illustrations of the attitudes he saw evinced toward free blacks and described how "nothing is more common in the northern states than to hear the free people of colour spoke of disparagingly." Similarly, he contended that "it was no unusual occurrence for an inoffensive man of colour, particularly if he was decently dressed, to be openly assaulted by white persons" before going on to describe "riots of the most frightful nature [which] occurred in New York, Philadelphia, Boston and Cincinnati."[74]

Despite these sweeping criticisms, Chambers did find evidence of abolitionist activity and the social acceptance of African Americans in the North. While in Boston, he reported coming across a number of black lawyers, physicians, lecturers, and industrialists. He contrasted this situation to New York and Philadelphia, where he found social exclusion of African Americans to be more engrained. In terms of abolition, Chambers highlighted the activities of the Massachusetts Anti-Slavery Society and American Anti-Slavery Society. He found both groups to be relatively small but noted the spread of abolitionism across the North as a whole. Interestingly (particularly given what would occur during the Civil War), Chambers also drew his readers' attention to the ideology of disunionists who maintained that dissolving the Union was the only route to abolition. Chambers was not alone in discussing disunion as a mechanism to end southern slavery. Many other British observers speculated on the potential effect of secession and concluded that once the political pressure of the North had been removed southerners would be more open to abolition or that the northern states would be able to rid themselves of the stain of slavery by leaving the Union.[75] In the context of British ideas of slavery and sectionalism, these observations on the likely consequences of disunion and the lack of support for the cause in the North suggested an absence of abolitionism in the section. In short, it seemed that retaining the Union as a political arrangement was more important to the majority of northerners than ending slavery.

In Chambers's analysis the North was not simply complicit in slavery because it lacked an effective abolitionist movement. The free states were also legally and politically implicated in the continuation of the slave system. To illustrate his point Chambers reached back to the Missouri Compromise, which he described as an example of northerners "seeing slavery fortif[ied] and extend[ed] . . . provided it keep within a certain limit." He then moved on to the Fugitive Slave Law and noted that even the clergy of New England had failed to offer any meaningful resistance to the legislation. Speaking about slavery in sectional terms more broadly, he informed his readers that, "but for the selfish compromises of the North, slavery must long since have been extinct"; however, northerners "seek to conciliate the South, for the sake of selfish interests." These selfish interests included the need for southern raw materials and the political compromise by which "the South votes for Protection, and the North in return votes for Slavery," all of which meant that "the question of slavery had never, as a general rule, been seriously entertained by the great northern orators in congress. The thing which was really fought for . . . was political power."[76] The idea that slavery and abolition were primarily political questions for northerners took on particular resonance during the Civil War. As a result of the belief that northern abolition lacked sincerity, the British public—which was accustomed to viewing slavery as a political rather than a moral question in the American sectional struggle—cast a skeptical eye over any Union antislavery activities.

The rejection of an association between the free states and abolitionism (at least as the British understood the term) endured until the outbreak of the Civil War, even among those who actively advocated emancipation and might be expected to publically censure the South. The example of the cotton manufacturer and free-trade activist Henry Ashworth is particularly telling. In 1860, at the Bolton Mechanics Institute in Lancashire, Ashworth gave a series of lectures in which he discussed American affairs. While clearly opposed to the institution, he failed to draw a moral distinction between North and South on the issue of slavery. He was personally shocked by his experiences while traveling in the South, but his description of southern slavery was not simply of list of brutalities. On the Sea Island plantations, he found "hospitals, with well-trained nurses in attendance [being] regularly provided by the planters," an arrangement he found replicated in Mississippi.[77] Overall, Ashworth did not present slavery simply as an exploitative labor system characterized by violence but as a reciprocal social arrangement based on a paternalistic model.

To speak, then, of a dominant discourse neatly dividing the northern and southern states when it came to the topic of slavery before the American Civil War is an oversimplification. A close examination of the works produced by some of the period's most prominent intellectuals highlights that any assumption of this sort is unsustainable. Rather, it is apparent that the antebellum distinction between the North and South on the issue of slavery was not interchangeable with the division that pro-Federals claimed existed between the Union and Confederacy during the Civil War. At the same time, the terms *slave states* and *free states* were evidently common among British commentators describing the North and South. Yet the dividing lines and the actual implications of the terminology were complicated. Certainly, as far as most Britons were concerned, slavery was a central pillar of southern identity. This did not, however, automatically result in widespread British sympathy with the northern states. In the first place, even though slave owning was central to the southern divergence from the North, it was not the sole difference from a British perspective. For the thirty years prior to the Civil War, the British public had read about southern abolitionists and pro-slavery northerners. Secondly, and intimately related to the above, was the belief that the North was heavily implicated in the slave system and that the free black population of this section was subject to widespread mistreatment. The notion of northern free blacks being treated appallingly, despite the region's claims to social equality, subverted the argument that the North was morally superior to the South. For these reasons, when British commentators placed slavery, race, and abolition in a sectional context, they were often cast in terms of political expediency and as part of a northern attempt to force its social, economic, or political vision on the South. As a result, the British remained unconvinced that their own, morally motivated, abolition movement was being replicated in the United States. The image of "the good North" was also subverted by the common division of the section into subregions, with New England presented as the only area with a moral commitment to abolition. In the longer term, describing northern abolition in this way undermined any sense that northerners were committed to end slavery, which in turn damaged the Union cause in Britain.

Along with elaborating this more nuanced view of the American sections and slavery, the work of British intellectuals of the period also played a role in undermining the use of slavery to single out and condemn the American South. R. J. M. Blackett has correctly noted that racism in Britain gradually increased between the 1830s and the 1850s. The perceived "failure" of West Indian emancipation, combined with the growing popularity of biological, anthropological, and ethnographical theories of racial hierarchy, contributed to the change. As the idea of a clear racial hierarchy developed, it was increasingly related to a belief that certain social and laboring roles were appropriate to different races. Frequently, this idea was linked to the notion that paternalistic relationships represented the ideal linkage between those in different racial groups. Thomas Carlyle might have taken this view to its extreme in his justification of violently compelled labor in *Occasional Discourse,* but the underlying idea influenced the thinking of many mainstream intellectuals from various political persuasions. Crucially, it had clear implications for the understanding of sectional relations in America. For somebody like William Makepeace Thackeray, who rejected the use of violence in labor relations but also rejected the idea of racial equality, the South had the potential to represent a form of slavery that mitigated the worst effects of the labor system by embracing paternalistic responsibility.[78]

Qualifiers of this sort do not mean that many in Britain actively advocated slavery or did not frequently criticize the South. Instead, the work of these commentators demonstrates that for the British the relationship between slavery and sectionalism was complex. Between 1832 and the firing on Fort Sumter, the British public were bombarded with descriptions of the United States that offered images of the various interactions between race, slavery, and sectionalism. Southern slavery was commonly seen as being mitigated by its paternalism, which rendered it a pragmatic social system in the short term. Conversely, the North was seen as being both implicated in the system (still objectionable in the abstract from a British perspective) and as treating its free black population at least as badly, if not worse, than slaves. By the outbreak of the Civil War, there was, therefore, no popular consensus that the Union was launching a crusade to rid North America of slavery. As a result, when the Lincoln government remained silent on the topic, few in Britain had any reason to believe John Bright's claim that "the conscience of the North [had never been] satisfied with the institution [of slavery]."[79]

CHAPTER TWO

"SPECIMENS OF THE OLD ENGLISH GENTLEMEN"

Seeing Britain in the American Sections

Debating whether or not the northern states had been, to use John Bright's words, "satisfied with the institution of slavery" during the antebellum period engaged Britons of the 1860s as much as it has scholars ever since. Nevertheless, just as a scholarly examination of US sectionalism concerned solely with slavery would prove inadequate, any attempt to understand British views of sectionalism through the same lens is similarly flawed. Bright's version of sectionalism, with its emphasis on slavery, is undoubtedly worthy of attention, but it was only one of the many interpretations offered during the Civil War. One significant alternative approach focused on ideas of ethnic and cultural division in the United States. The pro-Confederate propagandist D. W. Mitchell, in his 1862 work *Ten Years Residence in the United States,* which recalled its author's life in America in the wake of the 1848 revolutions in Europe, considered these divisions in some depth. Mitchell described how "to this day Old Virginia is more like Old England than is any part of New England or the true Yankeedom" and noted that "there were few Irish in the South" in comparison to urban areas of the North. This was particularly true of New York, a city in which "the Celtic Irish form a large [part], probably more than a third."[1] In making these associations, Mitchell was not providing readers with an unfamiliar version of sectionalism. Ideas of an "English" South and an "Irish" New York predated the war and had been subjects for popular comment for a number of decades. These were just some of the examples of sectional and regional differentiation based on ethnicity and culture that had existed in the public sphere before the conflict.

This chapter traces the development of what I term the British mental geography of American ethno-cultural regional identity before the American Civil War, and in it I analyze the ethnic and cultural tropes that British cultural commentators associated with particular regions of the United States. By examining the literature produced by these commentators prior to the Civil War, we can identify three distinct American ethno-cultural regions: New England, the South, and the mid-Atlantic. Each possessed a set of identifiable characteristics that were primarily discussed with reference to their apparent similarity (ethnically and culturally) to an ideal of "Britishness." Frequently, this connection to Britishness was, in turn, tied to a broader understanding of American Anglophobia. In its most simplified form, this association led observers to conclude that Anglophobic ideas were most dominant in areas that seemed to lack ethnic and/or cultural British credentials. Through their prewar engagement with American ethno-cultural geography the British populace developed a complex understanding of sectionalism, which they could relate directly to Anglo-American relations and which offered a framework for them to engage with the Civil War after 1861.

British writers were relatively consistent in their descriptions of New England, the South, and the mid-Atlantic and drew on a combination of personal experience and the work of their forebears to reinforce the characteristics of each region. New England and the South tended to be presented as ethnically British, yet a distinction was made between the two, based on a set of assumptions about the Puritan inheritance of the former and the Cavalier inheritance of the latter. These differing cultures (meaning in this context a shared set of ideas and/or behaviors) helped to explain the divergent characteristics of these two groups. The mid-Atlantic states of New York and Pennsylvania provided the counterpoint to the "British" regions of New England and the South. In both states there was an emphasis on ethnic and cultural diversity, which was frequently tied to German and Irish migrant communities.

The significance of the Irish presence as an influence to British perceptions of a region cannot be overstated. Criticism of the Irish as an ethnic and cultural group increased considerably in Britain during the first half of the nineteenth century. As a result, by the 1830s the idea of Irishness brought with it a range of negative associations. In his 2004 book, *The Eternal Paddy: Irish Identity and the British Press, 1798–1882,* Michael De Nie makes the convincing claim that for most Britons of the period, Irishness was shorthand for social, racial, and religious inferiority. In essence, Irishness denoted Catholicism, Celtic ethnicity, and poverty. More often than not, this broad idea of Irishness was directly contrasted with a similarly general notion of Britishness. In religious terms, Britishness was most closely associated with Anglicanism, but, as Linda Colley has highlighted, the gulf between Catholicism and Protestantism was so wide that dissenting groups could be comfortably accommodated under the British umbrella. In fact, Colley goes so far as to suggest that it was the power of anti-Catholicism that welded together the union of England, Scotland, and Wales. This idea of Britishness (combined with related associations, including Anglo-Saxon ethnicity and a belief in the need for social stability) even allowed the Anglo-Irish to viably describe themselves as British. What is more, the negative stereotyping of the Irish was not solely the preserve of Tories. Even an advanced liberal like Richard Cobden was prepared to vocally critique the Irish in general and Irish Catholicism specifically. Furthermore, the connection between Irishness and Anglophobia transcended the British Isles. In a US context the association led to British observers blaming Irish migrants (at least in part) for the Anglophobia which they believed characterized life in the mid-Atlantic states.[2]

Understanding the importance of these debates over the ethno-cultural geography of the United States, in general, and the place of the Irish, specifically, requires recognition of the significance of the "Irish problem" for Britons of the period. Despite the Acts of Union in 1800, the relationship between Britain and Ireland remained strained. From the British point of the view, Ireland, populated by an obstinate people, continued to be a potential source of rebellion. Following a campaign spearheaded by the charismatic activist Daniel O'Connell during the 1820s, the British parliament passed the 1829 Catholic Relief Act as a way to quell calls for Catholic Emancipation. The act allowed Catholics to be MPs and opened up a range of political offices to them. More importantly, however, the campaigning surrounding it also provided a model for the mobilization of ordinary Irish Catholics in support of political causes. The 1830s, therefore, saw a sharpening of denominational struggles in Ireland and ensured continuing British interest in the "Irish problem." These developments were accompanied by increased British concerns about the power of Irish Catholics as an Anglophobic force.[3] This peculiarly sensitive combination of issues provided the context in which the British debated the role of ethnicity and culture in the United States during the early 1830s.

The development of a distinctive sense of American ethno-cultural geography among British writers required more than just the disparagement of the Irish (or German) influence in certain regions. Even during the 1830s, commentators were ascribing "British" characteristics to particular areas of the United States. Harriet Martineau made a typical association in her 1837 travelogue, *Society in America,* noting the British influence on and the Anglophilia of New England. She told her readers how, in that area, "the veneration of England is greater than I think one people ought to have for any other." The way that Martineau contrasted New England with New York and Pennsylvania was typical of British commentators of the period. In one sense, however, her views were outside of the intellectual mainstream. Unlike almost all of her peers, Martineau embraced ethnic heterogeneity as something that would act as a motor for social, economic, and political progress in the United States.[4] In the context of this study, the significance of Martineau's work stems from the regional divisions she emphasized rather than the conclusions she drew. Many other commentators would have balked at the idea of ethnic diversity contributing to the success of a nation but would have agreed with the ethnic geography she set out. In short, Martineau unwittingly contributed to a growing awareness in Britain of the various ethnic and cultural regions in the United States, which would go on to have a profound impact on Anglo-American relations during the Civil War.

Prewar British commentators often used New York as a negative proxy for the North. While in New York, Martineau was disconcerted by the machinery of an election in a city containing a significant population of Irish migrants. She described "the atrocious corruption of the New York elections, where an Irishman, just landed, and employed upon the drains, perjures himself, and votes nine times over." She claimed, however, that this was "chargeable, not upon immigration, nor yet upon universal suffrage, but upon the faults of the machinery of registration." While Martineau's criticism was explicitly directed toward New York politics, her emphasis on the Irish placed her descriptions within a British discourse critical of the influence of non-British migrants on American politics. For many commentators, the electoral power of these migrants was a contributing factor in the aggressive Anglophobia of American political discourse.[5]

Despite personally eschewing mainstream British Hibernophobia, Martineau used language to describe US politics which later commentators would exploit to criticize the Irish. Particularly important to this rhetoric were ideas of mob rule, party, and political mismanagement. Even during the 1830s the suggestion that the Irish were central to corruption in the United States had a receptive public in Britain. Daniel O'Connell's continued agitation resulted in a popular British view of the Irish as being prone to the influence of demagogues and likely to resort to mob violence. One journalist specifically highlighted the political activities of the Irish diaspora in January 1835, suggesting that the Irish "seem likely to become as troublesome in America as they have long been in their own country." Shortly after the publication of this article, O'Connell secured a significant political victory by offering the Whig administration of Lord Melbourne support to form a government in exchange for Irish reforms (the so-called Lichfield House Compact). In Britain the alliance led to widespread dismay over the power O'Connell could now exert, as well as fears that his success might encourage more large-scale political activism in Ireland. Many Irish were also disappointed with the arrangement, and by the following year popular discontent over the concessions gained through the Lichfield House Compact led to a spike in disillusion with the Act of Union. This antipathy to the union with Britain would become a key cause around which many Irish reformers united during the subsequent decade.[6] The connection between regions of the United States and the Irish must be understood against the backdrop of the Anglo-Irish political tension that dominated the prewar period. Descriptions of the preponderance of the Irish in New York, and the apparent turbulence of urban politics in the state, meshed with the British understanding of Irish political activism at home. Consequently, commentators' claims about the Irish in the United States seemed consistent with British ideas about their capacity as political actors.

While the relationship between New York and Irishness became increasingly important for British writers, the ethnic complexion and culture of Pennsylvania also developed into a major subject for analysis. Criticism of Pennsylvania tended to be less intense than that directed toward New York. Nevertheless, a rich tradition of anti-Pennsylvania sentiment developed in this period. In his 1839 work, *Travels in North America,* Charles Augustus

Murray discussed at length his experiences in and around Philadelphia. He concluded that "this part of the country was chiefly settled by Germans; indeed, many of them can speak little English," while also noting the existence of German-language newspapers further west in Ohio.[7] While Murray was not explicitly critical of these groups, his emphasis on ethnic and cultural heterogeneity in Pennsylvania became part of a coherent discourse that presented the mid-Atlantic states as distinctly "non-British."

Murray's discussion of the different characteristics of the British areas of the South and New England provides a fascinating insight into the way these two regions were differentiated despite their ethnic Britishness. After recounting his experiences in both areas, Murray remarked that "there are many features of character in which the Carolinian planter bears as much resemblance to a Boston or Salem Merchant, as a Spanish grandee does to a Flemish burgomaster." However, even as he appeared to set up a fundamental division between the regions, Murray still suggested that both groups were essentially British. To perform this sleight of hand, Murray drew on his own Scottish identity and suggested that, "with due allowance for exceptions, I should say that the Carolinian character is more akin to that of England; the New England, to that of the lowland Scotch," before going on to make a general comparison between the English country house and the Virginia plantation. In attempting to account for the peculiarly "English" South, Murray noted how, "before the year 1770, almost every planter sent his boys to Oxford or Cambridge, where he himself had been educated; the necessary consequence of this custom, was a partial adoption of the manners, tastes, and perhaps, too, the faults of the British youth of the higher class."[8] Crucially, both Scottish and English identity could be comfortably accommodated under the broad heading of "British" in a way that Irishness never could. Both had positive associations that gave scope for New England and the South to be seen as distinctive but equally sympathetically by British observers.

Murray's mention of country houses and Oxbridge educations seems to imply that the Old South was an outpost of romanticized Britishness and appears to evoke the "Cavalier myth" of the area. The Cavalier mythology of the South centered on a fictionalized southern past built on the belief that Royalist refugees had originally settled the region.[9] The factual accuracy of the claim was rarely a major concern for British observers, and not all travelers even discussed the subject. Nevertheless, it is striking that antebellum British commentators never applied the Cavalier image to the northern states. As a result, the myth provided a distinctive southern heritage, which would later be integrated into British discussions of Confederate nationalism. When taken as a whole, Murray's work made a clear contribution to a sectionally accented British understanding of the ethnic geography of the United State. This geography became central to British ideas about the different areas of America and, after 1861, developed into a key feature of Civil War propaganda when pro-Confederates attempted to portray the entire North as an ethnically heterogeneous area hostile to British values and interests.

Tory novelist and naval office Frederick Marryat also discussed at length the emphasis on ethnic and cultural diversity across the United States. In the opening remarks to his *Diary in America* (published in the same year as Murray's book), Marryat offered a brief overview of US regional differences, which he conjectured stemmed, at least partly, from the alternative cultures of "the puritan of the east, the Dutch descent of the middle states, [and] the cavalier of the south." The mythology of the Cavalier South was again invoked here to suggest a clear three-way division in the United States. For Marryat, as for other observers, the historical roots of each area had contemporary resonance when it came to accounting for regional peculiarities. In Marryat's account, for example, New England was still enthralled to its Puritan heritage. He specifically highlighted the Connecticut "Blue Laws" to demonstrate this point about cultural inheritance. These laws were essentially a legal framework intended to regulate society and morality. Marryat, however, attacked them in no uncertain terms before concluding that the "pilgrim fathers were fanatics and bigots."[10]

Though Marryat was unequivocally critical of Puritan ethics, he was not wholly negative about New England. He gave glowing descriptions of the pro-British attitudes of the people in Massachusetts and noted the ethnic homogeneity of the area. He described the people of Boston as being "more English than in any other city in America" and noted how, in the state of Massachusetts, the people were "fond of comparing their country with that of England." Marryat tied this cultural sympathy to the claim (common among British observers) that there was "less intermixture of foreign blood in this city than in any other in America."[11] The New England of Frederick Marryat represented something of a curiosity. The apparent contradictions in his depiction are, however, indicative of the tensions that characterized the way many British people saw the identity of the region. The people of New England were unequivocally ethnically British and had inherited many of the manners of their forebears. Yet many had also inherited the harsh Puritan morality believed to have characterized the early British inhabitants of the area. This stern morality was an element of their identity that some Civil War writers attempted to exploit in order to subvert the otherwise peerlessly British credentials of New England. In turn, pro-Union partisans frequently endeavored to play down the Puritan connection and to assert the close ethno-cultural relationship between New England and Britain in their own writings.

The problem for those who attempted to trumpet the British credentials of the northern states during the Civil War was the prevalence of a discourse emphasizing the power of non-British ethnic and cultural groups in areas outside of New England. Marryat contributed to the development of this discourse through his published account of the mid-Atlantic states. In a discussion of Albany, New York, he told his readers that it "may even now be considered a Dutch city," while he noted that the numbers of Dutch and German settlers in Cincinnati, Ohio, gave them such an influence that the local government were considering printing city regulations in multiple languages. Like others, Marryat saved his most pointed critiques for the Irish communities of the North, specifically highlighting the detrimental effect he believed they had on political affairs. He reported that, "not long ago, an Irishman, who had murdered his wife, was brought to trial upon the eve of an election." Despite the evidence against the man, he had been acquitted, a verdict that was a result of the power of "the Irish party." Similarly, while classifying the German migrants as "contented and well behave[d]," Marryat was highly critical of the Irish influence.

> We have been accustomed to ascribe the turbulence of the Irish lower classes to ill-treatment and a sense of their wrongs, but this disposition appears to follow them everywhere. It would be supposed that, having emigrated to America and obtained the rights of citizens, they would have amalgamated and fraternized to a certain degree with the people; but such is not the case; they hold themselves completely apart and distinct, living with their families in the same quarter of the city, and adhering to their own manners and customs. They are just as little pleased with the institutions of the United States as they are with the government at home; the fact is, that they would prefer no government at all.[12]

The anti-Irish rhetoric utilized here is, itself, no surprise. It is simply an illustration of the sort of ideas De Nie has identified in Britain being transferred across the Atlantic. In a sectional context, however, this language was significant, as certain areas of the United States (New York specifically) became increasingly connected with Irishness and the negative implications the term possessed.

It is difficult to identify the precise influences at work on figures like Marryat when it comes to their conclusions regarding the Irish in New York and Pennsylvania. Certainly, Anglo-Irish relations and the negative implications of Irishness must have played a part. Yet the American context may have also contributed. The 1830s and 1840s saw Americans themselves spending more time discussing the growing Irish population of the urban North. In some places this discussion was accompanied by the growth of nativist and anti-Catholic movements such as the Protestant Association and the American Protestant Reformation Society. In isolated cases, urban mobs actually attacked and burned down Catholic convents. As Matthew Jacobson has pointed out, the growing nativist movement of the period tended to be expressed in terms of anti-Catholicism rather than anti-Irishness, yet the two causes frequently overlapped. This close connection certainly helps to explain the widespread rumors about a papal plot to undermine America through the power of Irish migrants.[13] It would be reasonable to assume that British travelers in the United States were aware of this rising tide of nativism (if only via newspaper reports), and popular accounts of the period seem to support this assumption. Interestingly, most of the British writing on the subject tended to neglect the activities of the nativists themselves and concentrate on the "Irish problem" that the urban North faced. Consequently, the political and social turbulence of the era was commonly presented in terms that reinforced preexisting British ideas about popular Irish activism.

The negative connotations of Irish political activism and the concentration of Irish in the urban North were reinforced in the travel literature produced by the liberal politician and abolitionist James Silk Buckingham. In his first book (published in 1841), Buckingham spent time discussing the large Irish population of New York City and the electoral process of the state. He then yoked these two ideas together by contending that high levels of immigration to the area had given the Irish a major influence in state politics. Buckingham also noted that "no proof of citizenship is demanded beyond [the elector] swearing to the fact," which meant that "many Irish labourers, who have not been six months in the country, and who have no legal claim whatever to citizenship [*sic*]," were "voting as Americans." Buckingham's criticisms were partly intended as an indictment of the corruption in New York politics, yet they also reinforced the perception that the Irish possessed considerable political influence in certain areas of the United States. Buckingham's comments are even more powerful when understood in their historical context. The early 1840s were a period of heightened Anglo-Irish tensions. The fall of the Whig ministry of Lord Melbourne in 1841, and his replacement by the Conservative (and aggressively anti-Irish) Robert Peel, caused O'Connell to publically push for the repeal of the Union in earnest.[14] When viewed through a contemporary British lens, which tended to equate Irish political activism with social upheaval and Anglophobia, the power of Buckingham's comments on New York take on increased resonance. The New York Irish were seen as either a threat to good governance or a natural consequence of democracy, while also being viewed as a potentially powerful anti-British force that could shift US policy.

The Irish, according to Buckingham, were not the only non-British group with major influence in areas of the United States. He also provided detailed descriptions of the ethnic diversity of the mid-Atlantic. Buckingham highlighted, for instance, the existence of Pennsylvania towns such as Reading, Bethlehem, and Bethany; in the latter two, "the English language is literally an unknown tongue." In Buffalo, New York, "Dutch and German emigrants abound and the Irish are not less numerous." Yet even in his depictions of areas characterized by a broad ethnic heterogeneity, the Irish tended to be mentioned as a negative influence. In Albany, for example, Buckingham quoted from the local *Temperance Recorder* on the subject of immigration to illustrate the detrimental effect the Irish population had on the morality of the town.[15]

While Buckingham presented Pennsylvania and New York as non-British, he simultaneously emphasized the close relationship he believed existed between the South, New England, and Britain.

> The old men, from the south, and from Carolina and Virginia especially, are what would be called perfect gentlemen of the old school with us,—precise, yet elegant in their dress—courteous and affable in their manners—high toned in their politics and taste—lax in their morality, while fashion sanctions their conduct—warm in their attachments—fierce in their resentments—and

> punctilious in all points of honour and etiquette. The remains of the feudal system in Virginia, where the laws on entail existed, and where large estates descended hereditarily from father to elder son, sustained the manners and feeling; and Virginia is still called "The Old Dominion," as if to preserve the recollection of its ancient condition as a colony of the British crown.[16]

This passage appears to evoke the Cavalier mythology of the South, along with the existence of an aristocratic social system and, potentially at least, a lingering sense of Anglophilia among southerners.

On the subject of New England, Buckingham found evidence of both the positive and negative aspects of Britishness, which Marryat had previously highlighted. He wrote that "there is no portion of the United States in which the character of the inhabitants has been more extensively influenced, if not almost wholly formed, by the institutions and conduct of their ancestors, than in New England." Despite criticizing the Puritan morality that he believed underpinned this character, Buckingham still contended that Boston "more resembles England, than any other city of America." These sentiments were echoed in the work of the scientist Charles Daubeny, whose travelogue (published in 1842) included a discussion of Boston high society. After a meeting with the prominent Otis family, Daubeny explained that "Mr Otis [was] a thorough English gentleman of the old school." After visiting a theater in the same town, Daubeny decided that "the manners and appearance of the audience [was] quite English."[17]

Contradictions were, however, at work in Buckingham and Daubeny's books. Buckingham, for instance, noted the existence of a close ethnocultural connection between Boston and Britain: "The New Englanders, and the Bostonians in particular, pride themselves upon the purity of their descent from English blood, and trace . . . their origin to English families, with all the pride of ancestry that characterises our nobility and gentry at home [*sic*]." Even so, Buckingham suggested that "there is perhaps no city in the Union where the jealousy of the English is greater."[18] As he saw it, the Old South and New England could claim a distinctive English heritage, but the ways this heritage played out in contemporary politics varied considerably.

After having dealt with the North in detail during his first travelogue in 1841, Buckingham's 1842 sequel (*The Slave States of America*) saw him examine the ethnic and cultural relationship between Britain and the South in similar depth. While not as critical as Martineau's, Buckingham's depiction of the South was far from positive. Unlike the majority of his peers,

Buckingham recognized the early influence of Puritanism in the South (specifically focusing on Charleston), while also noting the legacy of "the disappointed Cavaliers," and of "rakes, gamblers and persons of profligate habits." Furthermore, Buckingham also noted the development of migrant communities in areas of Georgia, Carolina, and Mississippi. He provided a particularly in-depth portrait of the ethno-cultural and political life of Baltimore which focused on the influence of migrant groups on the society and politics of the city and which echoed his observations about New York.[19]

Despite its wide-ranging criticisms of the South, Buckingham's text was not simply a multivolume critique of the section. On a number of occasions, he decided to focus on the Anglophilia that he had found in the region. While in attendance at a temperance meeting in Charleston, for example, he observed, "At the close of the meeting, a second anthem was sung by the choir, to the British national air of 'God save the King,' which I was afterwards told was done in compliment to the nation to which I belonged. I had been announced, indeed, to the meeting by the judge as 'the distinguished foreigner'; which sounded strangely in my ears and all around me—the place, the people, the language, and even the object of our meeting seemed so thoroughly English that I could scarcely think I was in a foreign land."[20] While the extent to which this reception was intended as an illustration of passionate Anglophilia on the part of southerners might be questioned, less ambiguous is his earlier contention, "Virginia is still called 'the Old Dominion,' as if to preserve the recollection of its ancient condition as a colony of the British."[21]

Buckingham identified a similar sort of cultural affinity between Britain and the South. When discussing the town of Norfolk, Virginia, he informed his readers, "I should think [it] resembles much more the old Colonial state of society, in feelings and manners than any place in the North, and may fairly rank with Charleston and Savannah, which resemble it in this respect." These positive assessments of the manners and society of Virginians, Georgians, and South Carolinians fed into a more general respect that Buckingham evinced for residents of the Old South. He found these men and women an amiable middle ground between "the coldness and reserve of the New Englanders, and the boldness and recklessness of the Louisianans and Mississippians."[22]

For Buckingham, as for previous popular commentators of the period, the United States offered a variety of cultures and differing degrees of ethnic homogeneity, which were increasingly definable in regional terms. From a British perspective, a clear mental geography of the United States was beginning to emerge, and although it did not present the nation as split along the Mason-Dixon Line, it had obvious sectional implications. Ethnically and culturally, New England and the Old South had British roots. They were, however, starkly divided as a result of their Puritan or Cavalier morality. In a sense, then, they represented the opposing poles of Britishness. Both were distinctly Anglo-Saxon, Anglophone, and anti-Catholic but were divided by divergent ethical systems and social norms—a divergence that most British commentators explained with reference to Puritan or Cavalier mythology. New York and Pennsylvania, however, represented a definite "other," with New York the center of the ethnically non-British and politically Anglophobe United States. Despite variations from commentator to commentator, these divisions remained relatively consistent. As a result, the British populace became familiar with the idea that America lacked national unity and was composed of a variety of regions with distinctive ethnic and cultural characteristics.

The relative consistency of the cultural and ethnic identifiers associated with particular regions may have resulted in some commentators actively searching for evidence of the Cavalier in the South or the Puritan in the North during their visits to the United States. Charles Dickens's *American Notes for General Circulation* (1842) offered readers a version of New England Puritanism that would have resonated with the earlier account of Frederick Marryat. This should not be surprising since Dickens had prepared for his trip by devouring travel accounts and was likely to have been familiar with Marryat's work. He was undoubtedly a more talented writer than Marryat, and there is no reason to believe that he was consciously drawing on his colleague's work. Even so, it is reasonable to conclude that when Dickens used the term "Puritan" to describe striking aspects of northern life—such as a law in Hartford, Connecticut, that stated that a man could be placed in the stocks for kissing his wife on a Sunday—he was drawing on ideas imbibed during his preparatory reading.[23]

Commentators consistently went beyond simply identifying the ethnic and cultural characteristics of New England, the mid-Atlantic, and the South and often discussed the prevailing attitudes toward Britain in each region as well. Writing in 1843, Charles Daubeny reported a conversation with a group of southerners that included a number of veiled references to the political dimensions of ethno-cultural sectionalism and its relationship to views of Britain. He reported how, in a discussion of the American union, a southerner had told him that they were "losers by this national compact" before writing that "it is surprising how much more fond they seem of talking on English politics than their own; Brougham, Canning, Melbourne, and the little Queen, were the principal themes of our after dinner conversation, and I must say, seemed as familiar to them, as they are to us." Daubeny also took note of some specifically Anglophile southerners, including Bishop Moore of Richmond, who, according to Daubeny, "spoke with great affection of Old England," and a judge named Porter who professed "undiminished love for the Old Country."[24] The significance of these exchanges was clear. At one level they demonstrated that Anglophile southerners had a deep interest in British political affairs. In addition, they highlighted a southern sense of alienation from Washington politics and suggested a possible connection between Anglophilia and southern sectional political identity.

The subsequent power of southern Britishness and/or Anglophilia during later debates over Confederate identity relied on contrasts with the ethnically heterogeneous North. Luckily (at least from the perspective of pro-Confederates operating in Britain), the groundwork for this version of the North had been put down well before the war. John Robert Godley, for instance, explored the theme of ethnicity in New York in his two-volume 1844 work *Letters from America.* In both the city and state, Godley noted the significance of the Irish and German populations. He reported that in Albany he "heard a good deal of German talked in the streets, and saw German inscriptions over the shop-doors," while in Buffalo "one third of the population of the town is composed of Germans." In addition, Godley commented on the large Irish population of New York, criticizing their influence over the political and social life of the state.[25]

Godley expanded his analysis of the politics of sectionalism to include an examination of the relationship between contemporary North/South disputes and the historical cultures of the Puritan and Cavalier. He traced the development of sectional identities from the Puritan/Cavalier root, through the era of Federalism and Jeffersonianism, before ending with an analysis of the tensions he observed in American political life during the 1840s. He also noted the enduring power of the Cavalier myth in Virginia: "They even seem to like talking of themselves as the 'cavaliers' of the Union, and of recalling the origin of their States' sobriquet of the 'old dominion.'"[26] Through his text, Godley offered readers a version of US sectionalism that linked ethnicity, cultural practices, and politics with reference to a familiar sense of American ethno-cultural geography. Although Godley's account contained unique aspects, it provides a useful illustration of the complexity that characterized the British understanding of US sectionalism before the Civil War, as well as a specific example of the ways in which ethnicity and culture could be related to the discourse of sectionalism more broadly.

Outside of the non-British mid-Atlantic region, questions of cultural and ethnic regional identity in the United States were more difficult for British observers to address. A broad acceptance of the British credentials of New Englanders and southerners meant that neither population could be conveniently "othered," yet the two regions were clearly different. As we have already seen, attempting to explain this difference led many commentators to utilize the model of the Puritan and Cavalier. In his 1844 travelogue, George Featherstonhaugh offered readers a short history that he claimed accounted for the differences between the South and New England: "The original colonists of North America may be divided into two classes,—those enterprising and speculative adventurers who went to Virginia in pursuit of wealth, and the Puritans, who left their native country for the sake of enjoying freedom of opinion. The southern, or Virginian colony, became in all material circumstances a copy of the mother country."[27]

As the colonies developed, "dissatisfaction was evinced [toward Britain] in Virginia at an early period, yet the first germ of American aversion to monarchical government is to be traced to the Puritans who settled the northern colony of Massachusetts."[28] In this analysis then, while the revolution had been a national movement for self-determination, American democracy was rooted in the Puritan North. Featherstonhaugh's distinction requires some attention, as it reveals the simultaneous consistency and instability of the Puritan/Cavalier model. Those who used the terminology maintained that southern identity had derived from Cavalier ideals and New England identity from Puritanism. The specific implications of each of these categories were, however, not always the same. Generally speaking, the Puritan was associated with an unnecessarily strict morality, while the Cavalier tended to be seen as Anglophile. As a result, for British readers, the Cavalier represented the more sympathetic characterization. Yet there was not necessarily agreement among British commentators over fundamental issues: Were Puritan New Englanders more democratic? Did southern Cavaliers respect contemporary British culture more? These points remained up for debate. Consequently, the precise parameters of what made each region British, yet distinctive, remained flexible.

One of the most consistent hallmarks of Cavalier mythology (and in some cases of the South as a section) was a general sympathy for England and English social structures. Sir Charles Lyell, the eminent geologist and close friend of Charles Darwin, certainly conveyed this view of the South to the readers of his 1845 *Travels in North America: With Geological Observations on the United States, Canada and Nova Scotia.* Just as Charles Daubeny had done two years before, Lyell expressed great respect for Virginia, where "to be an Englishman engaged in scientific pursuits was a sufficient passport, and their servants, horses and carriages, were most liberally placed at my disposal." Even further South in Charleston, Lyell explained that among the planters "the usual style of living is that of the English country gentlemen. They have well-appointed carriages and horses, and well-trained black servants."[29]

For Lyell, however, Virginia and South Carolina seemed to be islands of Britishness in a nation more generally diluted by immigration. Lyell, much like Frederick Marryat, expressed particular concern about the effect that high levels of migration might have on the US political system. As he saw it, immigration was likely to undermine democracy, which led him to warn his readers: "Any foreigner who has hastily embraced the notion that a suffrage virtually universal must be incompatible in the U.S. with order, obedience to the laws, security of property a high degree of civilization, and the most impeachable public credit, has only to make himself acquainted with the present condition of the New-England States, especially Massachusetts, and he will feel wholly satisfied that the charge may be refuted."[30] Lyell was making a clear division in the United States on the political process itself and offering something of a defense of democracy in doing so. Nevertheless, his point was underpinned by ethnicity: "It is a wholly different question whether so democratic a constitution is equally fitted for the exigencies of many other parts of the Union, where the mass of the people are less advanced in knowledge and wealth, where the forces of public opinion and sympathy is checked, and free-communication impeded by *distinctness of race* or language" (my emphasis).[31] New England was apparently only able to operate as an effective democracy because of its ethnic homogeneity.

Consequently, Lyell treated very differently the areas of the nation that lacked this ethno-cultural base.

In order to emphasize his point about the political consequences of ethnicity and culture, Lyell drew his audience's attention to areas with more heterogeneous populations. He noted, for instance, that "Pennsylvania labours under the disadvantage of being jointly occupied by two races, those of British and those of German extraction [*sic*]" and that in Ohio "an influx of illiterate Irish, Welsh, and Westphalian settlers has tended to lower the educational qualifications of her electors." For Lyell, as for so many others, the Irish connection proved particularly unsettling. He drew on contemporary British concerns regarding the potentially subversive undertones of Irish political action in the United States by drawing attention to "an endless procession of Irish parading through the streets with portraits of O'Connell." The parade Lyell described here was connected to the Repeal movement and its leader back in Ireland, who had formed his Loyal National Repeal Association in Dublin in 1840. For British observers, the existence of a Repeal movement in the United States was worthy of comment because of the controversial nature of the cause in British domestic political life. In a US context, however, Britons soon began to associate the Anglophobia of American political discourse with the efforts of Irish activists (such as the Repealers).[32]

That a number of prominent politicians in major northern cities publically came out in favor of Repeal further reinforced the perceived connections between the Irish, the urban North, and Anglophobia. An 1844 edition of the *Freeman's Journal and Daily Commercial Advertiser* provided an account of a speech given by New York governor William Seward to a group of Repealers in Utica. Seward's speech, and the fact that it was reported in Britain, highlights the ways in which developments in Ireland played a role in US political life and demonstrates British awareness of the importance of the "Irish problem" in a transatlantic context. As part of an attempt to woo Irish voters, Seward came out in favor of Repeal in this address and liberally seasoned his sentiments with Anglophobic rhetoric. From a British perspective, the speech seemed to call attention to the close relationship between three of the key features that commentators had associated with New York political culture—the Irish, mass activism, and Anglophobic language. The idea that these features dominated mid-Atlantic politics became engrained in Britain during the antebellum period. As a result, these aspects of ethnicity and politics became vital matters for debate during the propaganda battles of the Civil War, particularly when well-known New York Anglophobes such as Seward appeared to be at the forefront of Union policy making.[33]

With the growth of the Repeal movement, Anglo-Irish and Anglo-American concerns became increasingly fraught, and British commentators increasingly devoted their attention to them. After a slight lull following the Lichfield House Compact and the relatively stable liberal administration of Lord Melbourne (1835–41), O'Connell decided to push for the repeal of the Union more aggressively when the Conservative Robert Peel assumed office in 1841. As a result, Repeal came back into the foreground of British and Irish politics. Crucially, however, the issue was not simply a matter for Britain and Ireland. As Seward's address at Utica demonstrates, it was a rallying cry that had the power to mobilize elements of the Irish diaspora in the United States. Of course, the increasing prominence of Repeal agitation did not go unnoticed by other Americans, and nativists began to tie Repeal to reports of a papal plot against US politics and society. From a British point of view, American Repeal activism and the nativist response to it seemed to confirm existing fears about US democracy and the political influence of the Irish in the urban North.[34]

Anglo-Irish tensions continued to increase during the 1840s and reached fever pitch in 1843. O'Connell declared this to be the Repeal year and planned to organize fifty "monster meetings" across Ireland that would push the British government to act on the issue of Repeal. The climax would come in October with a meeting to be held at Clontarf in County Dublin. Increasingly coercive British legislation led O'Connell to withdraw from the Clontarf meeting, yet the government opted to arrest him. The decision to incarcerate O'Connell was a political misstep by the Peel administration, and even though it did not develop into the major controversy that might have been expected, O'Connell's arrest reduced sympathy for the British in Ireland. The arrest also helped to radicalize many Repealers, despite Peel's attempts to pass legislation to appease them. Furthermore, the treatment of O'Connell provided an impetus for the development of the Young Ireland movement, which would subsequently attempt to overthrow British rule in Ireland in 1848 and whose legacy would further enmesh the United States in Anglo-Irish affairs.[35]

The aggressive Anglophobia of US politics (which many British commentators explained as a result of the influence of the Irish) became increasingly shrill during the mid-1840s, as diplomatic tensions over Oregon increased. In 1818 the territory had been declared "free and open." As the number of British and American settlers to the area grew, however, it became clear that it would be necessary to split Oregon. The fate of the territory was a key talking point for the Democratic presidential nominee, James K. Polk, who, during his 1844 election campaign, promised the public no compromises with Britain over the border. As American statesmen and journalists continued to ratchet up the rhetoric in 1845 and 1846, the British responded in kind. Foreign Secretary Lord Aberdeen dangled the prospect of war in front of Ambassador Louis McLane, and the *Times* announced that Oregon had become a matter of national honor over which the British would fight to uphold their rights.[36]

Polk had consistently utilized Anglophobic language to secure public support for his belligerent stance. This approach proved to be particularly effective in mobilizing non-British groups in the United States. On his second visit to America, Lyell learned from Daniel Webster details about how this Anglophobic rhetoric was used with reference to the Oregon question. According to Lyell, Webster had not only urged peace but "rebuked the blustering tone of defiance, in which the demagogues and newspapers in some parts of the Union were indulging against England." A South Carolinian offered Lyell a similar analysis of the tensions over Oregon, explaining that the reason for political support for potential war was the existence of a "set of demagogues," who "in this country . . . trade on the article called "hatred to England." The language of popular political Anglophobia, particularly in the press, was—in this instance at least—national. Yet the idea of an Anglophobic rallying cry in American politics developed a distinctly sectional edge against the backdrop of the Civil War. The connection between Anglophobia and sectional identity seemed particularly strong during the *Trent* crisis, when the image of Union politicians and the press whipping up the Anglophobia of non-British urbanites became central to Confederate propaganda in Britain.[37]

Lyell discussed at length the specific connection between the urban North (in particular New York) and ethnic heterogeneity, considering the implications of the connection for both the political process and the popularization of Anglophobia. At one point, Lyell mockingly recounted a conversation with an American friend who had informed him that the pigs could not be removed from city streets because of the likely response of their Irish owners. Similarly, in a discussion of Philadelphia, Lyell explained that the development of an Irish enclave in the city had necessitated a more expensive and active police force. Boston, despite being frequently associated with "British-Americans" by commentators, also had a strong Irish community. Lyell reported on a Repeal meeting there, during which an artisan had informed him, "We hope that we may one day be able to do for Ireland what France did for the United States in our great struggle for independence." Crucially, Lyell's point of emphasis when discussing Boston and New York was the Irish who, as Lyell's discussion of mass politics and Repeal demonstrated, had close associations with Anglophobia and mob rule.[38]

A New York friend of Lyell's later described the electoral consequences of the ethno-cultural heterogeneity that his British acquaintance had outlined. In recounting the conversation to his readers, Lyell described how, in New York, the "Irish . . . turn the scale in the elections for mayor and other city officers," and he repeated the accusation of his American friend that, if not for the often-fraudulent immigrant vote, Henry Clay would have been the victor of the 1844 election. The success of Polk, according to Lyell's acquaintance, came about because "the Romanist priests feel, or affect, sympathy with this political party [the Democrats] and in the last election they instructed the Germans and Irish to vote for Polk against Clay." The relationship between migrant groups and Catholicism alluded to here further highlights the connections between certain ethno-cultural areas in the United States and powerful tropes of non-Britishness concerning ethnicity and religion. Lyell's account of the 1844 election specifically centered on the claim that the political power of the Germans and the Irish in America had contributed to the electoral success of a notoriously Anglophobe president. The assertion, however, also fed into a more general British discourse that emphasized the influence of non-British groups on political life in the United States.[39]

Lyell utilized well-established images of the ethnic and cultural makeup of different regions to describe his travels. His New Englanders were marked by their "strict morals," while he found that the white population of Massachusetts was "more educated than elsewhere, and more Anglo-American, having less of recent foreign admixture." Religion provided Lyell with another chance to discuss the identities of particular regions. He noted the influence of Catholicism in New York and the historical significance of Anglicanism to Virginians. Lyell appears to have found southerners somewhat affectionate toward Great Britain, although he did suggest that abolition was, at least to some extent, increasing anti-British feeling in the slave states. This idea that the South held an Anglophobe position because of the close association between Britain and abolition was recognized by a number of travelers and was later exploited by British pro-Unionists during the Civil War. Yet, as Peter Onuf has noted, the end of the Mexican War (1846–48) convinced most southerners that Britain had no interest in interfering with slavery, which reduced the use of Anglophobic rhetoric in the slave states. Although it would be incorrect to contend that the perceived relationship between British abolition and southern Anglophobia was irrelevant, the connection should not be exaggerated.[40]

In many ways, the potential Anglo-southern antipathy over slavery, which could have masked Anglo-northern tensions, was obscured (although not obliterated) by the consistent "othering" of the mid-Atlantic. In 1849 the journalist and free-trade advocate Archibald Prentice delivered a set of lectures that included suggestions about the influence the German population of Pennsylvania could wield. Prentice also explicitly rejected Dickens's view of Hartford as puritanical and even went as far as to suggest that "Mr. Dickens, in his notice of Hartford, had adopted a little of [the] southern imputation of hypocrisy."[41] Prentice's sentiment illustrates the place of the travel narrative as a key point of reference for the British literate classes' view of America, and it is also indicative of the growing appreciation of northern and southern identity among Britons. Although Prentice clearly overstated his case with regard to Dickens's sympathy for the South, his comment highlights a growing sense in Britain that a travel text could present the United States from a sectional perspective. Furthermore, his critique of Dickens demonstrates the importance of the Puritan/Cavalier mythology and the negative associations the term "Puritan" often brought with it.

While connecting Puritanism with New England associated the region with a number of negative characteristics, it also implied a close connection to Britain. As a result, critiques of New England tended to be relatively muted. Writings on the mid-Atlantic, on the other hand, were often more trenchant and rarely included the sort of positive comments about British heritage often featured in discussions of New England. The Irish connection was typically drawn upon to differentiate between the regions of the North and, as we have seen, brought with it a range of negative associations that were increasingly presented as synonymous with the mid-Atlantic. A letter sent by an American resident in Britain to the liberal *London Daily News* in June 1848 is indicative of the strong Irish connection to New York and the consequences critics suggested it had for the region. This correspondent opened his account by noting that "among the thousands who emigrate to the United States, the Irish are conspicuous for their number and peculiarities." They were also very active in politics and had a negative effect on the city's political system. The letter's author referred specifically to Seward's attempt to court the New York Irish by noting that he "advocated repeal, and became the intimate friend of the leading priests and bishops of the Romish church." The connection made here between the Irish and Catholicism would have resonated with many Britons, not simply in terms of New York politics but as part of a broader set of concerns regarding the role of priests as political actors in Ireland itself. The nature of Irish political activism in the United States (and in New York specifically) disgusted the *Daily News* correspondent and led him to conclude that "one thing is certain, that the freedom of Ireland, if achieved by the present generation, would present a most revolting spectacle of government."[42]

The 1848 Irish rebellion provided a particularly clear illustration of the close connection between Ireland, the United States, and popular British discourse regarding the ethnic and cultural geography of the United States. The uprising was led by a group, known as Young Ireland, who had broken away from Daniel O'Connell and who, led by William Smith O'Brien and Thomas Francis Meagher, attempted to spark off a revolution in Ballingarry (County Tipperary). The uprising was quashed by the British government, resulting in two deaths and the arrest of many of the leaders of the movement. A level of sympathy apparently existed among Americans for the cause of Young Ireland, a sympathy that seemed to be localized in the ethnically heterogeneous regions of the United States. The Philadelphia correspondent of the *Morning Chronicle* outlined various meetings in support of the Young Ireland rebellion, describing how, in Philadelphia itself, "another Irish sympathy meeting was held," while in Reading, Pennsylvania, "a Society of the Friends of Ireland was formed." Young Ireland support seemed strongest in New York. A newspaper correspondent described "a meeting of the Brooklyn Republican Society of Friends of Ireland" in which "an address and resolutions were voted to Mrs. Mitchel [wife of Young Irelander John Mitchel], and [a] resolution tending support and protection."

Other meetings were held in different parts of the city, including one "at the large space near Broadway," chaired by a member of the prominent Irish Emmett family. Most disconcerting of all, however, were the descriptions of various Irish brigades who, according to one speaker, were "ready to go and fight the battles of Ireland."[43]

One of the most interesting responses to US support for Young Ireland was a sketch published by the *Hampshire Advertiser and Salisbury Guardian* in September 1848. The writer of the piece invoked Elijah Pogram (Charles Dickens's fictional American Anglophobe journalist) to emphasize to readers the ridiculousness of reports circulating in the United States which claimed that the uprising had killed six thousand British soldiers. The writer then shared an ominous appeal that supposedly had been made by the Irish: "People of America, Ireland stretches her hands out to you for assistance. Do not let us be disappointed."[44] This article provides a concise but effective illustration of the power of cultural commentators such as Dickens in constructing a popular British understanding of the United States. As we can see, the ideas of figures like Dickens became so engrained in public discourse that a local journalist felt comfortable invoking a character from *Martin Chuzzlewit* when commenting on current affairs. The article is equally indicative of the extent to which Anglo-Irish developments influenced British ideas of the United States and the significance many Britons believed the Irish diaspora had in American politics.

With the exception of Harriet Martineau's text, these illustrations of the British sense of US ethno-cultural geography have been drawn primarily from the political mainstream. Yet the British view of America as ethnically and culturally divided was imbibed by those from a range of social groups and political persuasions. Writing in 1849, the former Chartist and radical reform MP for Sheffield, John Arthur Roebuck, offered a view of the United States that had plenty in common with his mainstream contemporaries. Roebuck's *The Colonies of England: A Plan for the Government of Some Portion of Our Colonial Possessions* was primarily an exploration of possible reforms that could be made to the British Empire. As part of his analysis, Roebuck provided a detailed history of the American colonies, which centered on the Puritan/Cavalier dynamic contemporary commentators had utilized to account for the differences between New England and the South. In describing the development of New England from its Puritan roots, Roebuck mitigated the negative implications of the term "Puritan" by explaining that over time "all the sterner and cruel characteristics of their class [the Puritans] were, by constant collision with their neighbours and the world, so checked and subdued as to seem almost effaced." In contrast to Puritan New England, Roebuck wrote, "the most powerful nobles of the court of Charles [II] united to plant a colony, to which they gave the name of their royal master. Such were the auspices, under which Carolina became a colony."[45]

The writer and Chartist activist Thomas Wheeler offered a similar view of the ethnic and cultural characteristics of the different regions in his 1849 novel *Sunshine and Shadow*. Wheeler's fictional protagonist, Arthur Morton, spent a year and a half in America, during which he "observed its varying traits of character—from the phlegm of the descendants of the early Dutch settlers of New York, to the high blood and bounding spirit of the sons of Maryland and Virginia." Wheeler and Roebuck show that British perceptions of ethnic and cultural regionalism transcended political boundaries and were integrated into a popular British vocabulary about the United States. Yet for all these differences within the nation, Roebuck at least, still found the American people as a whole to be "the same as ourselves," and although "no longer connected by government with us, they, nevertheless, retained characteristics of the race from which they sprang."[46]

Roebuck, therefore, presented the United States as *both* a national entity unified by its British heritage and a sectionalized nation that lacked coherence. His apparently contradictory viewpoint was far from anomalous among British observers. The recognition of certain national American characteristics did not preclude an engagement with sectional differences when it came to the Anglo-American relationship. In essence then, Britons believed that the United States existed as a national, sectional, and regional entity simultaneously. Often, conceptions of American nationalism were concerned with broad political debates over foreign policy and democracy, while sectional identity was frequently constructed with reference to culture and ethnicity. Nevertheless, the national and the sectional intersected in many British accounts. The demands of a particular ethno-cultural region were often used to explain the peculiarities of the political process in an area or the attitudes of that area's population toward Britain.

Roebuck's fellow reformer Sam Rathbone (a member of a Liverpool shipping family with strong abolitionist links) wrote a private letter back to Britain from the United States in 1849 which evoked much of the mythology and many of the historical ideas explored by Roebuck. According to Rathbone, "the southerners were more gentlemanly, pleasant men. They are not the descendants of bigots & Puritans but of gentlemen & this good blood seems to have stuck to them." When this sort of cultural heritage is emphasized, it becomes easier to see how somebody like Rathbone could express so much apparent fondness toward southern slaveholders. As he saw the situation, southerners were not *simply* slaveholders, they had a more complex identity based on strong connections to Britain. The travelogue of Lady Emmeline Stuart-Wortley, published in 1850, expressed similar sentiments. After a meeting with new president Zachary Taylor, she explained to her readers that "he spoke very kindly of England" and that "he continued in this strain and spoke so nobly of England that it made one's heart bound to hear him." Again the slaveholder here was more than a one-dimensional figure and was certainly no straw man.[47] Stuart-Wortley's published account conveniently demonstrates the dissemination of this view of southerners to the British public, while Sam Rathbone's correspondence is testament to the fact that the Cavalier myth and southern Anglophilia influenced private discussions of American identity.

These claims about southern Britishness and Anglophilia continued to be juxtaposed to images of ethno-cultural heterogeneity in the mid-Atlantic to emphasize regional divisions in the United States. In her 1850 travel account *Hesperos,* Charlotte Houstoun built on the ethnic geography she had originally set out in her 1844 work *Texas and the Gulf of Mexico.* She noted the Dutch heritage of Albany, as well as the continuing use of the "Dutch" language in areas of Pennsylvania. (She probably conflated Dutch and German.) Houstoun also described how "a great proportion of the inhabitants of Cincinnati are German; there are many names from Deutschland above the shop doors, and an inn is as frequently a Gast Haus as an hotel." She also continued the British tradition of emphasizing the large Irish population in the Mid-Atlantic region. Criticizing these communities of Irish migrants, Houstoun emphasized the Irish penchant for Anglophobia, as well as their political power, by describing them as being "the first to promote any measure likely to produce war with the old country." This idea of Irish political power was reinforced in an article in the *Belfast News-Letter,* which reported on how, as an election loomed in America in 1851, the Irish "attempted to organise an agitation . . . for the purpose of influencing American politics, and threatening with the vengeance of the 'Irish Vote' the candidates."[48]

These discussions about the ethnic and cultural geography of the United States, and the ways in which this geography might affect politics, were not solely the preserve of public intellectuals. Prominent policy makers frequently used the same language. Sir John Crampton wrote to the Foreign Secretary Lord Malmesbury in September 1852 to inform him that the power behind the election of Franklin Pierce that year had been "the Irish and German emigrants," who were motivated by "hatred of Great Britain and a wish to interfere in the affairs of every other nation in support of rebellion and revolution."[49] The similarities between Crampton's language and the public debate surrounding Polk's election in 1844 are striking, to say the least. Even if we shy away from the claim that Crampton was expressly invoking this earlier campaign, his note is still compelling evidence of the extent to which democracy, ethnic heterogeneity, and Anglophobia were influencing private, as well as public, discourse.

On a similar note, the liberal MP and later pro-Confederate William Schaw Lindsay received a letter on 16 October 1854 from the New York merchant Asa Whitney. In the letter Whitney updated his British friend about the activities of the Anglophobic elements of the American press and informed him how they used Britain as a bogeyman in domestic debates.[50] Unfortunately, the content of Lindsay's papers is such that we can only speculate on exactly why he sided with the Confederacy six years later, but his brush with American Anglophobia in the North may well have been a factor. More broadly speaking, the views of US politics evinced by figures such as Crampton and Lindsay are a testament to the extent to which figures at the center of British political life perceived a connection between Anglophobic politics and ethnic heterogeneity in America. Even if the relationship to the mid-Atlantic region was not always made explicit, the popular discourse that equated non-Britishness with this area provided the scope for other figures to offer an analysis that did integrate regional identity into the equation.

In most cases, commentators brought the issue of regional identity into focus by highlighting the connections between New York, the Irish, and Anglophobia. This tactic, as we have seen, had been common since the 1830s, and general claims about the Anglophobia of the Irish and their influence over US politics continued to feature in the British press throughout the 1850s. Crucially, however, a diplomatic dispute during the first half of this decade added a new focus to British interactions with the American Irish and highlighted the extent to which issues relating to Irishness intersected with ideas of American regional identity. The dispute in question related to the arrival of the Young Ireland leader John Mitchel in the United States following his escape from a transportation sentence. Mitchel had been arrested just before the 1848 rebellion and transported to Bermuda and then later moved to Van Dieman's Land (Tasmania). In 1853 he was able to escape from the island and travel to New York with the help of an Irish American Young Irelander.[51]

Many in Britain believed that Americans, particularly New Yorkers, had received Mitchel sympathetically. In November 1853 the radical *Reynolds's Newspaper* described how "a meeting of the members of the Thomas Meagher Club was held last evening at Hermitage-Hall [New York], John Duffy in the chair, for the purpose of making preparations for the reception of John Mitchel, the Irish exile." In January of the following year, the *Bradford Observer* similarly noted a "complimentary dinner [given] to Mr. John Mitchel in the Broadway theatre, New York." Once settled in the United States, Mitchel began to publish an Irish-nationalist newspaper, the *Citizen* (unsurprisingly out of New York). The British *Era* produced an article discussing Mitchel and the *Citizen*, entitled "Irish Madmen in America," which contended that his publication had "been scandalizing his former confederates by advocating Negro slavery in America." This connection between Mitchel's *Citizen* and pro-slavery once again hints at the lack of a coherent image of the antislavery northern states and did little to rehabilitate Mitchel or the Irish American image in Britain.[52]

During the period more broadly, Britons even claimed that an armed Irish uprising was afoot in the United States which would take advantage of the Aberdeen administration's preoccupation with the Crimean War in order to liberate Ireland. The Anglo-Irish *Belfast News-Letter* reported a conspiracy that had centered on Cincinnati and had been intended to create "hostilities between the American Republic and the Government of this country"; the paper described the conspirators as "a gang of 'fugitive Irishmen.'" The idea of an Irish American invasion turned out to be a rumor, but it gained enough traction in Britain that Lord Crampton requested the US government to break up a number of Irish societies that he believed intended to promote rebellion.[53]

In terms of Anglo-Irish relations, the 1850s are often seen as a period of relative calm. Despite the formation of a number of tenant organizations and the Independent Irish Party, Britons felt relatively secure about their position in Ireland. Even occasional bouts of agrarian unrest did little to shake British confidence that the "Irish question" was less pressing in the 1850s than it had been over the previous two decades. Nevertheless, Ireland and the related issue of Catholicism maintained a presence in British public life. The Oxford (or Tractarian) Movement had culminated in the conversion of a number of prominent theologians to Catholicism, leading many in Britain to feel nervous about the potential spread of the religion. Their concerns were compounded in the 1850s by the so-called Papal Aggression, which many Protestants saw as an attempt by the Vatican to reestablish the Catholic hierarchy in Britain. The popular British response was a reaffirmation of Protestantism as a core element of Britishness via a vocal anti-Catholic crusade.[54]

Against the backdrop of the Papal Aggression, British commentators' criticisms of Irish Catholics in the mid-Atlantic states continued to resonate, even if Ireland itself was no longer viewed as a province in revolt. Lucy Bird, in her 1856 account, *The Englishwoman in America,* discussed her experience with cabbies in New York, noting that "they are generally Irish and cheat people with unblushing audacity." She also suggested that the high levels of political violence in the city stemmed from the contests between the Irish Catholics and the Know-Nothing party. In more specific political terms (and echoing contemporary concerns regarding Catholic influence), she concluded that the Irish were simply "the willing and ignorant tools of an ambitious and despotic priesthood."[55]

While critical of German Americans for their tendency toward socialism and atheism, Bird gave them more sympathetic treatment overall than their Irish counterparts. At one stage she even went as far as to commend the German population "for their genius and industry" and to make a direct comparison to the Irish, whom she felt lacked the skills and drive of the Germans. It was, however, the British population of New England that provided the clearest contrast to the Irish in Bird's text. She described the "English air" of Boston and informed her readers that a thirty-one-gun salute had been fired in the city to celebrate the British victory at the battle of the Alma in 1854.[56]

The same approach of using the Irish population of the mid-Atlantic states as a negative point of reference was utilized the following year by James Stirling. In his case, however, it was the South rather than New England that provided a contrast to the ethnically heterogeneous states of

New York and Pennsylvania. In his travelogue, *Letters from the Slave States,* Stirling observed that "few Irish, comparatively, come to the South." He also made the Irish connection explicitly negative by criticizing the extent to which government in America "resolves itself into the supreme rule of Irish Rowdyism" and claiming that "the Democratic party has very nearly reduced the Republic of the United States to an Irish mobocracy."[57]

Stirling also reasserted the cultural differences between regions: "the North is essentially Puritan; the South, Cavalier. They are so historically, and they are so in all the characteristics of their development." To Stirling, this inheritance meant that "the North, then, was originally, and is yet, Puritan and Plebeian; the South, on the contrary, was Cavalier and Patrician; Virginia and the Carolinas were settled mainly by English gentry, with a sprinkling even of the nobility." In a similarly romanticized account, traveler Henry Murray wrote that the planters' homes along the James River in Virginia reminded "one in many ways of the old country."[58] These sectional characterizations plainly drew on a whole host of preexisting tropes constructing a mental geography of the nation which claimed an English Cavalier inheritance for the Old South in contrast to a Puritan North. The characteristics of both of these regions were in turn contrasted with the "Irish Rowdyism" that apparently dominated New York and Pennsylvania.

The Puritan/Cavalier dynamic was echoed and examined in more depth by the novelist William Makepeace Thackeray, whose 1859 work *The Virginians* centered on the development of colonial America and the Revolution. Thackeray's book was published in the serial format typical of popular fiction in the period, with thirteen to twenty thousand copies printed each month. His narrative follows the fortunes of a Virginia family, the Warringtons, during the 1770s and concludes with the split between loyalists and revolutionaries during the War of Independence. The Warringtons' heritage is traced directly back to Britain through an extensive discussion of family history and is a persistent source of pride for the matriarch. The state of Virginia itself is described at various times as being committed to the king (George III) and the Church of England. Thackeray contrasts the Warringtons with the Van Den Boschs, a family of Dutch merchants from New York. The ethnic dichotomy, combined with the actions of the two families (the landed Warringtons as opposed to the trading Van Den Boschs), provides an obvious distinction between the South and the New York/Pennsylvania region. The specific mention of the Church of England with reference to Virginia echoes the work of earlier commentators who had noted the strength of southern Anglicanism, while also suggesting a contrast with the Catholic other of New York. Furthermore, Thackeray's emphasis on the perceived connection between the established English church and the Old South hints at the existence of peculiarly British values in the region. This observation about the religious relationship between the South and Britain demands particular attention because of the high levels of support for the Confederacy among the Anglican clergy in Britain during the Civil War. Taken as a whole, Thackeray's novel offered readers a clear division between Virginia and New York/Pennsylvania that incorporated many of the key tropes that British commentators had been utilizing for the previous thirty years.[59]

The relatively coherent British understanding of ethnic and cultural regionalism in the United States did not, however, exist wholly outside of the framework of the Anglo-American national relationship. The influence of Anglophobia and Anglophilia provided a vital backdrop for debates over American regional identity. The private diary of Benjamin Moran, the secretary of the US legation between 1853 and 1874, provides evidence of these themes, as well as an indication of the continued significance of the travel narrative for the development of British ideas about the United States up to the eve of the Civil War. After the opening of a transatlantic telegraph cable in 1858, Moran commented in glowing terms that "to-morrow will be the Sabbath; and it will be the first Sabbath upon which the two great branches of the Anglo-Saxon family—mother and daughter—will be within speaking distance of each other." The following year, in a speech to celebrate his seventy-fifth birthday, Prime Minister Palmerston discussed Anglo-American cousinhood and the threads that connected the two nations. The idea of an "Anglo-World" that both men invoked points to a growing conception of Britain and the United States as being two parts of a global Anglo-Saxon family with a shared mission to spread "civilization." The idea was certainly a powerful one. So much so that, according to historian Reginald Horsman, the understanding of the British as "Anglo-Saxon brethren" had acted as a brake on US politicians going to war over Oregon in the mid-1840s.[60]

Yet the concept of an Anglo-Saxon mission uniting Britain and the United States clashed with a more complex understanding of race, ethnicity, and Anglophobia. From a British perspective, the United States was an ethnically and culturally divided nation. As a result, British commentators could not unproblematically apply the concept of an international Anglo-Saxon destiny or mission. Similarly (and despite his romantic familial rhetoric), Moran was no Anglophile. His outlook was consistently anti-British, and only a month after he appeared to emphasize the close Anglo-American relationship in his comments on the telegraph cable, he noted, "England heartily hates America. The hearty manner in which the people of the United States have received the success of the Atlantic cable has been taken up here with jeers and ridicule." He also claimed that the British "lie about us, rob us, and treat us insolently and will so continue to do until we give them another good flogging." Moran even distrusted claims of goodwill toward the United States; he commented in 1859 that "[Charles] Mackay recently wrote a book on the US in wh. [*sic*] he pretended to be very friendly towards us: but the truth is he hates us."[61]

Allowing for Moran's characteristic hyperbole, his insights are still indicative of the love/hate connection between Britain and America. Taken as a nation, the United States was capable of being either passionately Anglophobic or Anglophilic—something Moran typified. Placing this flexibility against the complex backdrop of the regional differentiation so frequently discussed in Britain allows us to see the power and malleability of Anglophobia as a hallmark of American identity. It also helps to explain why Anglophobia became a key pillar of Civil War discourse in Britain. In some senses British wartime propaganda was produced with the purpose of sectionalizing Anglophobia. Commentators and politicians were well aware that doing this effectively could shift public opinion considerably. Consequently, the sort of ethnic and cultural divisions discussed in this chapter were appropriated by pro-Confederates and anti-Unionists to suggest the existence of coherently sectional Anglophobia that incorporated ethno-cultural non-Britishness alongside Anglophobic rhetoric and political policy. The primary tactic to achieve this involved emphasizing the preexisting connection between American Anglophobia and the non-British mid-Atlantic states, while simultaneously asserting the dominant role these states played in the North during the conflict.

In constructing this view of the North as a whole, of course, it was necessary for pro-Confederates to disregard both the reports of non-British areas of the South and positive portrayals of New England. The latter were not easy to ignore since these descriptions had long been a staple of British commentary and continued to be until the outbreak of the war. During 1860, for example, the private secretary of the Prince of Wales, John D. Englehart, published an account of the prince's travels through the United States featuring a number of descriptions asserting the British credentials of New England. Englehart recalled how in Boston "the most enthusiastic welcome greeted the Prince as he drove through the streets." He also noted that in the same city "the feeling towards England [is] as towards a *home,* the home of their forefathers."[62]

The sort of regional variations that Englehart and his predecessors described engrained in the minds of British readers ideas of ethnic disunity in the United States. While the prewar ethnic and cultural map of the nation did not divide the North and South along the Mason-Dixon Line, it did establish a clear geography. The United States could, broadly speaking, be conceived of as three major regions; the ethnically and culturally British Cavalier South, the ethnically and culturally British Puritan New England, and the ethnically and culturally heterogeneous mid-Atlantic. This division in itself had clear implications, given the anti-Irishness that characterized much British thought during the period, yet the division also opened up space for an engagement with broader themes of American identity. Preconceptions about non-British ethnic groups and cultural practices meant connections could be made between the Anglophobia of US political and public life and the geographical areas of the nation that seemed to be dominated by these groups. This is not, of course, to claim the existence of entirely coherent and unchallenged ideas about ethno-cultural sectionalism and Anglophobia in British perceptions of the United States. A range of writers recognized the existence of Irish populations in Boston and the South, while others suggested a level of antipathy toward Britain in the slave states, based on the connection between Britain and abolition. Nevertheless, a number of key ideas can be identified that characterized most accounts. In the first place, the Old South was more ethno-culturally British than New York and Pennsylvania, and was also uniquely connected to the mythology of the Cavalier. Secondly, the Cavalier roots of the region were frequently contrasted to the British Puritanism that seemed to characterize New England. Finally, New York was strongly identified with Irishness and was almost always tied to Anglophobia in the political sphere. This identification contrasted to New England and the Old South, each of which could be described in terms of both Anglophobia and Anglophilia.

Confederate propagandists attempted to exploit these broad-stroke divisions to dissociate their cause from that of slavery during the war. Similarly, their pro-Union counterparts frantically tried to emphasize the values of New England in their own attempts to sell the northern cause to the British public.

CHAPTER THREE

"NO SIR, I AM A SOUTH CAROLINIAN"

British Interpretations of American Sectional Politics

The 1856 *Punch* cartoon entitled "the American Twins, or North and South" offers a glimpse into the complex British discourse about political sectionalism in US democracy during the antebellum period.[1] The illustrator chose to present North and South as two distinct individuals as opposed to showing the traditional "Brother Jonathan" personification of the United States. The Union itself appears as an artificial, possibly even forced connection holding the two unwilling partners together. The tension between unity and disunity in the image is indicative of a broader theme in British prewar discourse—the widespread recognition among the British literate classes that the American Union was not as unified as it might seem. This appreciation of political disunity in the United States had obvious resonance during the Civil War. In essence, most of the British population were accustomed to viewing the United States in terms of political disunity and consequently saw the conflict as the culmination of tensions between North and South.[2] At first glance it might be tempting to see international commentary on US politics during the antebellum period as presenting readers with a practical and ideological monolith. It is certainly true that an overarching idea of American politics developed and seeped into popular consciousness during this period. Yet a level of complexity existed which often undermined the foundations of this monolith.

This chapter identifies three aspects of US political life that dominated British commentary between 1832 and 1861 (political culture, political policy, and states' rights) and chronologically traces how each related to

"The American Twins, or North and South," *Punch* (September 27, 1856). Reproduced with the Permission of Punch Ltd., www.punch.co.uk

sectionalism. As early as the 1830s, British observers were identifying a sectional division over specific political policies (most importantly the tariff). These differing policy demands intersected with a perception of the South as an area dominated by agriculture and in favor of free trade, a perception that was contrasted with the image of a manufacturing and protectionist North. This debate over tariff policy led, in turn, to an increasing British awareness of the states' rights doctrine. This chapter unpacks British discourse regarding states' rights in the wake of the nullification crisis to highlight the extent to which the British populace was familiar with states' rights ideas prior to the Civil War. Finally, the chapter examines British perceptions of US political culture in the period. It identifies the key tropes of this culture (the mob, party politics, the press, tyranny) and suggests that, while ideas of policy and states' rights were seen through the lens of sectionalism from the 1830s, Britons tended to see political culture in national terms. There was, however, a gradual (but incomplete) development of a discourse that associated US democratic political culture with the North and claimed that attitudes toward democracy in the South ranged from ambivalence to antipathy. Moments of Anglo-American tension relating to US territorial expansion often saw British commentators emphasize the national characteristics of US political culture, which prevented the emergence of a clear sectional division on the subject. In summary, the chapter analyzes long-standing familiarity the British had with sectional policy disputes and with the doctrine of states' rights, as well as considering the shifting place of political culture in the British understanding of sectionalism.

Although Frances Trollope's *Domestic Manners* was nominally an examination of the behavioral peculiarities of Americans, it also had considerable political resonance. Crucially, Trollope's book was read by a British public in a state of political ferment as the debate over the 1832 Reform Act convulsed the nation. Popular agitation over the reform of the British political system meant that Trollope's observations on American democracy seemed particularly pertinent to a public being forced to confront the possibility of an enlarged franchise in Britain. Those who examined Trollope's text to understand the consequences of broader political participation were unlikely to be comforted by what they read. Although she traveled to the United States with high expectations, Trollope quickly became disillusioned with US politics—a process reflected in *Domestic Manners*. In some sense her experience of the American political system was an unusually negative one. The electoral contest she observed in 1828 (between John Quincy Adams and Andrew Jackson) was ill tempered even by US standards. Trollope, however, did not treat this election as a one-off. She drew broad conclusions about American politics from the campaign and explained to her readers that "no one in their senses, who has visited their country and known the people can doubt [the appropriateness of American democracy] for them, such as they now are, or its utter unfitness for any other people."[3]

Crucial for those who attempted to use the US example to ward off British electoral reform (before and after 1832) were the twin concepts of the political party and the mob. Both ideas were intimately associated with US democracy in British prewar commentary, and, as early as the 1830s, we find evidence of Trollope sketching out the contours of each, as well as highlighting their place in the US political system. *Domestic Manners* touched on both subjects, but a more telling passage can actually be found in Trollope's 1832 novel *The Refugee in America.* In this fictional companion piece to *Domestic Manners,* Trollope describes a scene in which the doors of the president's home are thrown open to a mob because the servants are "quite aware that they owed more obedience to the mob than to their master [and] yielded to their remonstrances."[4] In a domestic British context, Trollope was clearly warning the public about the extension of the franchise in both of these works, yet her conclusions also need to be understood in terms of British views of American political life. At one level, Trollope's texts are indicative of the negative discourse of American democracy that became an increasingly prominent feature of British commentary during the antebellum. Yet it is important to recognize that the features she identified were gradually integrated into British ideas of American sectionalism. As the antebellum period progressed, certain hallmarks of American political culture (including parties and the mob) began to be associated with areas of the North.

Although the association between the North and democracy was established slowly (and was never entirely coherent), we still find evidence of sectional political distinctions being made during the early 1830s. After she had roundly derided members of the US Congress, Trollope added a subtle but significant codicil: "Among the crowd who must be included in this description, a few were distinguished by not wearing their hats, and by sitting on their chairs like other human beings, without throwing their legs above their heads. Whenever I inquired the name of these exceptions, I was told that it was Mr This or Mr That, of *Virginia.*" The particular emphasis on Virginia may seem like a small detail, yet as a bifurcation of American politics developed through the prewar period, that state (if not the South more generally) was often portrayed as the outsider of American democracy.[5]

Trollope's work even touched briefly on aspects of the states' rights doctrine. Scholars have frequently ignored the extent of British familiarity with the debate over states' rights in the United States before the Civil War, yet many commentators at the time evinced considerable interest in questions of state sovereignty. Even though she did not always grasp the specifics of each dispute, Trollope had been struck by the fact that "if I mistake not, every debate I listened to in the American Congress was upon one and the same subject, namely, the entire independence of each individual state, with regard to the federal government."[6] Reports such as Trollope's contributed to a general belief in Britain that the US political system allowed each state considerable scope to direct their own affairs. This preexisting awareness of a form of states' rights doctrine among the British populace would prove useful for pro-Confederates attempting to justify secession after 1861.

British ideas about states' rights and the lack of a national political culture in the United States became particularly potent forms of sectional commentary when they were discussed with reference to policy disputes. Crucial in this regard was the issue of free trade. The nullification crisis of the early 1830s pushed the issue of protective tariffs to the forefront of Anglo-American relations and helped to familiarize the British public with a vital sectional policy dispute. Nullification also raised the public profile of the states' rights doctrine, since the attempt by the state of South Carolina to nullify federal tariff legislation in 1832 involved a rejection of the right of the national government to enforce measures, alongside an assertion that different sections had distinct policy requirements. The stance taken by South Carolina appeared to demonstrate to the British public the disharmony in the Union and the diverse political and economic demands of the different states.[7]

That the nullification crisis raised questions related to the use of protective tariffs made it a subject of considerable interest in Britain. The free-trade movement was gaining traction in the 1830s, and although it would be another fourteen years before the repeal of the Corn Laws, the stand that South Carolina took over protectionist economics became the basis for a working relationship between British free traders and the South during the subsequent decade. Nevertheless, it would be wrong to think that the British were only interested in nullification in so far as it had implications for the cause of free trade internationally. They also engaged with nullification as a domestic American political dispute. The veteran radical and former resident of Philadelphia, William Cobbett, remarked on the regional dissension over the tariff. In an issue of *Cobbett's Weekly Political*

Register, he explained that the South and West "look upon the tariff as a robbery of them committed for the benefit of the states of the north." Newspapers across Britain echoed these sentiments. The *Aberdeen Journal,* for example, went so far as to raise the specter of secession when it noted that "the United States of America seem to be on the eve of a disruption. The discontent that has arisen among the Southern States—particularly South Carolina and Georgia—has assumed a most alarming aspect. Nothing can now prevent the withdrawal of these two important States from the Union, but the immediate modification, if not repeal, of the obnoxious tariff."[8]

During the nullification crisis, the British press also emphasized the relationship between the tariff dispute and broader sectional divisions. The *Morning Post,* a mainstream anti-reform newspaper, reprinted an editorial that had originally appeared in the *Standard* on 7 September 1832 informing readers that "there is, in fact, little to bind the Carolinians and Georgians to the New Englanders or even the Virginians. Their habits, their domestic systems, their commercial interests, are all diametrically opposed to those of the men of the northern states." The *Essex Standard* made a similar observation in an 1833 editorial, contending that the tariff had placed sectional differences in sharper relief rather than creating them. This article also noted that "the ostensible ground of the breach is the oppression, upon the Southern States, of the tariff on goods imported; but in various particulars it seems that the interests, temper, and habits of these Southern countries [*sic*] do not harmonize well with the laws and government of the general Congress, where Northern interests prevail."[9] Generally speaking, the British saw the tariff issue as an expression of the differences between sections rather than the sole cause of them. Furthermore, even if some observers chose to pay attention to nullification because of the implications it had for free trade internationally, they invariably became enmeshed in a debate about US sectional politics.

Although debates about the fundamental divisions between North and South made up a significant proportion of the British commentary on nullification, plenty of the writing was suffused with selfish economic pragmatism. The idea of an Anglo–South Carolinian or Anglo-southern economic partnership had considerable appeal to those on both sides of the Atlantic. As an editorial in *Cobbett's Weekly Political Register* put it, "All these southern and western men, are commercially speaking, closely connected with Birmingham, Sheffield, Manchester and Leeds . . . have no such connexion with the northern states." This claim chimed with the views of a number of southerners, such as the planter Robert Turnbull, who contrasted the lack of compatibility between the North and South with what seemed a self-evident economic connection between Britain and the section.[10] At its most basic, this relationship involved the South acting as a raw-materials supplier for the industrialized factory towns of Britain, which would, in turn, produce the manufactured goods southerners required.

The idea that the North and South had distinct economic interests became a useful point of departure for Britons who wished to differentiate between the sections even if they were not suggesting a possible Anglo-southern alliance. In 1836, *John Bull* produced an article that looked back on the nullification crisis and reasserted the fundamental economic differences between North and South before going on to highlight more general sectional sociopolitical divisions. The newspaper also prophetically speculated that the differences were so great as to mean that "the federation of States has never, and will never recover" from nullification. When it came to the United States as a whole, "its government is supported by those only who benefit by the tariff." The editorial went on to outline the different sectional perspectives regarding the newly independent Republic of Texas.[11]

The discussion about the fate of Texas, to which *John Bull* alluded, was obviously a major concern for US statesmen, who nervously contemplated the potential sectional implications of their policy following the secession of the republic from Mexico in 1836. This debate over Texas also had significant transatlantic dimensions. A number of American statesmen were concerned that the British might gain a foothold in the region by offering to recognize the republic in return for Texans committing to abolish slavery. While some Britons viewed the scheme sympathetically, the majority of government ministers wished to avoid becoming entangled in Mexican-American relations and potentially drawn into a conflict over the fate of a territory with limited economic and strategic value. Despite the diplomatic realities at work, the continued uncertainty surrounding the republic and the popular clamor in the United States for annexation meant that the Texas problem continued to fester and provided an uncomfortable backdrop for Anglo-American relations in the late 1830s and early 1840s.[12] This issue, in turn, colored British views of American politics and politicians.

The diplomatic situation was certainly not improved by developments in the Northeast during the late 1830s. The Treaty of Ghent (1815) had left unclear the precise border between the Canadian province of New Brunswick and the US state of Maine, resulting in an ongoing dispute within the region. An attempt to mediate a solution between the states had floundered in the early 1830s, and by 1838 the activities of raiding parties in the area had sparked the Aroostook War (1838–39). In May 1838 the death of an American citizen on the ship *Caroline*, after it was burned by a group of Canadians, saw Americans respond with an attack on the British craft *Sir Robert Peel*. By this stage, popular American journalists were adopting an increasingly belligerent tone and attempting to push for war with Britain in the region. Fortunately, the effective working relationship between President Martin Van Buren and Foreign Secretary Palmerston facilitated a diplomatic solution and helped to take the public eye off the area.[13] Nevertheless, the course of events in Texas and the Northeast had focused British attention on the United States and raised questions about the politics of the nation.

While in reality the situations in Texas and the Northeast were driven by distinct issues, it was common for Britons and Americans to yoke the two together as part of a broader discussion of their rivals' foreign policy. One of America's most prominent Anglophobes, the former president Andrew Jackson, certainly believed that developments in both areas were evidence of a coherent British policy to surround the United States in what he termed an "iron hoop." Jackson's claim credits the British authorities with a level of strategic forethought that seems highly unlikely. Nevertheless, his sentiments are telling. His characterization of British diplomacy fed into a preexisting discourse of Anglophobia in the United States that helped to justify continued expansion. For their part, the British saw expansion in Texas and the Northeast as indicative of an American desire for territorial gain, which in turn led to questions about the extent to which US ambition might come at the expense of Britain.[14]

Britons saw the desire for Texas annexation in terms of the expansion of slavery. In her highly perceptive 1837 analysis of the United States, Harriet Martineau noted the dual desire of slaveholders to expand the institution for the purposes of political representation and to increase potential lands for growing export staples. Subsequent writers such as John Robert Godley (1844), Sir Charles Lyell (1849), and James Stirling (1857) essentially echoed Martineau's claims. The precise interpretation of expansion, however, could vary considerable—even if the slave states were seen as the prime mover. Lyell, for instance, placed a particular emphasis on the role played by the states of New England in resisting expansion in Texas and Oregon. Eight years later, James Stirling accused slaveholders of driving the demand for annexation in Cuba and Nicaragua but conceded that the policy was supported by the "Democratic mob" in the North. For her part, Martineau implied that support for Texan annexation might be driven by southerners but had supporters across the nation. She specifically highlighted a meeting in New York "on behalf of the Texan adventurers, where high-sounding common places had been played off about patriotism."[15] The debate over Texas helps to illustrate key features of prewar British sectional discourse. Understood with reference to the nuanced interpretation of slavery outlined in Chapter 1, it is possible to see how Martineau could present expansion in terms of increasing the territory of slaveholders without implying that the cause was only supported by southerners. Essentially, the debate over the fate of Texas provided evidence of national culpability in the slave system. Conversely, in a Civil War context, the Texas case provided potential ammunition to the more sophisticated Union propagandists. Particularly significant in this regard was John Elliott Cairnes, who focused on the expansion of the "slave power" as part of his justification for the Union war effort. The fate of Texas, therefore, provides an invaluable illustration of both the nuance that characterized British ideas of sectionalism before the Civil War and the significance of this understanding for commentators during the conflict.

Often when British writers described the United States as an aggressively expansive nation, they tended to play down the levels of national disunity that had characterized discussions of nullification. This does not mean, however, that sectional political divisions no longer featured in British work during diplomatically tense periods. Even writers who held up the United States as a polity that the British should emulate—and therefore had an interest in emphasizing unity—were forced to recognize the existence of major divisions in the nation. Martineau's 1837 text, *Society in America*, provides a valuable illustration. Despite her sympathy for the American political project, Martineau was forced to concede the existence of distinct socioeconomic systems in the North and South, and to discuss the problem of bringing the sections "into a state of exact conformity of institutions." She also touched on the relative power of the state and nation, warning her readers against "supposing the state governments to be subordinate to the general." Possibly most worrying for Martineau and her readers was her conclusion that this division was becoming more pronounced over time, so "while the north is still fostering a reverence for the Union, the south loses no opportunity of enlarging lovingly on the virtue of passionate attachment to one's native state."[16]

Martineau did not simply consider the underlying debate about the relationship between state and federal government in abstract terms. She engaged explicitly with the tariff, the nullification crisis, and the deeper issues that these disputes had raised. As one would expect, given her wholehearted commitment to liberalism, Martineau conceded that South Carolina had legitimate grievances over the tariff. However, she made it clear that, even though she supported free trade as a cause, South Carolina was mistaken in blaming all its problems on protectionism.

> The curse of slavery lies heavy on the land, and its inhabitants show the usual unwillingness of sufferers to attribute their maladies to their true cause. Right as the South Carolinians may be as to the principles of free trade, no tariff ever yet occasioned such evils as they groan under. If not a single import duty had ever imposed, there would still have been the contrasts which they cannot endure to perceive between the thriving States of the north and their own. Now, when they see the flourishing villages of New England, they cry "we pay for all this." When the north appears to receive more favour from the general government, in its retrospective recompenses for service in war, the greater proportion of which service was rendered by the north, the south again cries, "We pay for all this." It is true the south pays dearly; but it is for her own depression, not for others prosperity.[17]

By creating such a coherent image of sectionalism, and incorporating slavery and the politics of the tariff debate, Martineau was able to maintain a position that was both anti-tariff and pro-northern. Protection made for bad policy, and in this sense the South was right to resist it. Yet southerners did not understand that the socioeconomic issues they faced were a result of internal problems caused by slavery rather than the tariff policy of the federal government. Central to Martineau's thought, therefore, was the assumption that to be pro-northern did not mean rejecting clear sectional differences—for Britons to subscribe to the doctrine of political sectionalism before the Civil War, they were not required to nail their colors exclusively to the mast of the North or the South.

Despite recognizing these fundamental differences, Martineau played down the power of sectionalism, concluding that "sectional hatred, if not an abstraction, is founded mainly on abstractions, and give[s] way at once when the parties are confronted." The closing of national ranks against a common enemy was a particularly relevant illustration of this phenomenon for Martineau and her readers, given the Anglo-American tensions over Texas and the Northeast that provided the backdrop of her publication. Even so, the idea that sectional tensions were of limited significance had been highlighted before this period. Although many British commentators emphasized the gulf between the North and South during the nullification crisis, editorial writers for a number of newspapers, including the *Bristol Mercury, Preston Chronicle,* and *Leeds Mercury,* played down the likelihood of and legal justification for secession.[18]

Martineau had the scope to consider the limits of sectionalism in more depth than journalists did, and she provided specific examples of those who advocated disunity, while also maintaining that they had little chance of success. At one point Martineau described a northern clergyman "who expects and desires a dissolution of the Union, saying that the north bore all the expense," while she later discussed a South Carolinian who "sees no use in the Union, but much expense and trouble." In both cases, however, she decided that these were simply eccentric individuals. For Martineau, sectional disputes featured in American political life, but disunity tended to be subsumed by nationalism, which led her to conclude that "the probabilities of the continuance of the Union are so overwhelming, that no man, not in a state of delusion, from some strong prejudice can seriously entertain the idea of a dissolution."[19] Harriet Martineau had a particular motivation for emphasizing the success (and unity) of the United States to her British readers. She was a passionate Americanophile and lobbied for changes to the British political system to bring it more in line with that of America. It was, therefore, imperative that she present the Union as a political success.

Nevertheless, Martineau's discussion of the United States as a national and sectional political entity highlights the extent to which the two categories were used simultaneously in Britain. It gave scope for later writers to sectionalize aspects of the American political system that had previously been viewed as national. Particularly valuable in this regard were the prominent negative characteristics of US political culture, such as the mob, political parties, and the possible rise of an American despot. Trollope had emphasized the centrality of these features to US political culture in 1832, and later commentators built on her foundations. In 1833, at the height of the tensions over nullification, the newspaper *John Bull* connected the conflict between state and federal government to the descent of the United States into a democracy dominated by the mob.[20] While these comments about the mob were consistent with the overall modus operandi of *John Bull* during the period (to undermine the United States at every turn), they had long-term significance. They accentuated images of America that came to be sectionalized and increasingly associated with the North.

The close association between American democracy and the negative imagery of the mob, party politics, and despotism became an increasingly prominent characteristic of British commentary as the decade progressed. In his 1839 *Diary in America,* Frederick Marryat invoked many of these ideas. At the heart of his analysis of US political culture was the concept of democracy, which he thought defined political life in America and which he criticized as being the rule of an "uninformed majority" over the nation. The power of the mob (at least in Marryat's work) was felt by politicians through both the popular press and the bribery and patronage of the party system. Marryat established a clear distinction between democracy and republicanism, which he characterized as governance by the best and brightest in a society. As with most of the work produced in the period, Marryat's views need to be understood in both a British and an American context. As the author remarked near the end of his text, the movement for political reform in Britain had significantly influenced his discussion of American political culture. He expressed concern that the reforms of 1832 could drive Britain toward democracy and place power in the hands of the mob—something he believed had already occurred in the United States.[21] In this sense, Marryat's work was a warning to British readers. By framing this warning as a critique of American political culture, however, Marryat helped to cement the range of negative associations that US democracy had for many Britons.

When taken to the extreme, these British critiques of American democracy often incorporated comparisons with revolutionary and Napoleonic France. In some cases, authors followed through on the comparison and predicted that a charismatic despot would eventually emerge from the mobocracy that figures like Marryat had discussed. An editorial published in *John Bull* in 1836 suggested that this eventuality had already occurred and that President Andrew Jackson was, to all intents and purposes, a tyrannical despot supported by the mob. The article informed readers that "the United States are evidently reaping not only the fruits of reform and modern mountebankism, that of mob-law and pretended self-government, but of actual despotism. There is no, *nor ever was,* in the Eastern Hemisphere such a practical despot as ANDREW JACKSON." Marryat made a similar claim a few years later, contending that Jackson was the epitome of mob democracy, "raised, as he was, to the office of President by the mob."[22]

The relationship between American political culture and sectionalism remained ambiguous during the 1830s. Nevertheless, the characteristics that the British associated with US political culture cannot be ignored in an analysis of sectionalism. Despite continued ambiguity, Britons intermittently commented on how US political culture intersected with sectionalism during the antebellum period. In essence, the tropes of US political culture that emerged during this period were later sectionalized and integrated into British discussions of northern and southern identity. It is even possible to see the roots of this sectionalization in the 1830s. Marryat's decision to use the *New York Morning Herald* as a case study in his discussion of the press, for example, was likely to have reinforced existing British views regarding the political process in the urban North, even if a coherent discourse of northern mob democracy had not emerged.[23]

Marryat also made a number of more explicit sectional distinctions in his analysis of US political life. In the introduction to his text, he noted that "even on that point upon which you might safely venture to generalize, namely, the effect of a democratical form of government upon the mass, your observations must be taken with some exceptions, arising from the climate, manners, and customs, and the means of livelihood, so differing in this extended country." He then went on to outline the significant socioeconomic divisions between different regions of the United States before explaining how the economic distinction between the sections underpinned their major political differences. Marryat also made it clear to his readers with which side it would be in British interests to remain on good terms. He saw an alliance between Britain and the agricultural South as being perfectly natural and was bullish about southerners themselves recognizing this fact. He explained that "the Southern [are] very anxious to remain at peace with England, that their produce may find a market; while the Northern, on the contrary, would readily consent to a war, that they might shut out the English manufactures."[24] Not only did Marryat invoke the agricultural/manufacturing division, which had previously been highlighted during nullification, he also emphasized that the South could prove to be a valuable economic complement to Britain.

Marryat then proceeded to engage with the debate over the legality of secession and suggested that the sections might eventually be able to divide into different nations. On the topic of ending slavery in the South, he recognized some form of the states' rights doctrine by noting that the only way the national government could act against slavery would be to "trample on the constitution." He then concluded, "By examination into the Constitution of the United States . . . the States have reserved for themselves all the real power, and that Federal Union exists but upon their sufferance. Each State still insists upon its right to withdraw itself from the Union, whenever it pleases."[25] The differences between the sections were not simply pronounced therefore—a genuine legal channel existed for the division of the nation into its constituent parts.

A similar emphasis on the possibility of a state seceding from the Union can also be found in the work of Thomas Brothers, who published *The United States of North America as they are; Not as they are generally Described: Being a Cure for Radicalism* the year after Marryat brought out his book. Brothers had been a radical political activist in Britain and had moved to the United States believing that it would offer him the freedom he craved. The text he produced after returning to Britain was written in the form of letters to major reformers of the period and explained to readers the reasons for his disillusion with the United States. In his missive to the noted penal reformer, Matthew Davenport Hill, Brothers engaged with the nullification crisis explicitly: "That threat, to dissolve the Union, was soon followed by another which at first seemed to be of still greater importance,—it was what was termed the South Carolina Nullification; that is, the state of South Carolina refused to pay any more taxes to the general government, unless the general government would alter the laws, and make them agreeable to their wish. These high-minded, gallant, and honourable men, ever true to their purpose, made a protestation that they would perish to a man before they would longer submit to the tariff [*sic*]."[26] In truth, Brothers had a number of reservations about the stand South Carolina had taken against the tariff, and his text should not be viewed as a wholehearted defense of nullification. Regardless, Brothers still highlighted the tensions over political policy between South Carolina and Washington and in doing so conveyed to his readers the extent of disunity in the United States.

That these depictions of disunity over policy were often deployed alongside descriptions of an apparently unified national political culture is highlighted in Brothers's work. Alongside his missive to Hill, with its emphasis on disunity, Brothers also penned a letter to the Birmingham reformer Thomas Attwood, attacking the American political process as a whole. He concluded this letter in blunt terms by claiming that "the British people never were, are not now, and, I think, never will be, any more like the great mass of the American republicans."[27] The version of US politics Brothers presented to his readers was, therefore, both sectional and national. While seeming to suggest the existence of a national political culture, Brothers drew attention to the existence of sectional animosity over specific policies. This simultaneous emphasis on sectional and national politics was not a unique feature of Brothers's text; rather, it was characteristic of British commentary across the entire prewar period.

The travelogues produced by the liberal MP James Silk Buckingham in 1841 and 1842 provided a more in-depth British analysis of the negative characteristics of the American electoral system. After traveling around the United States and having "an excellent opportunity of seeing the working of the political machine, and the conflict of opposing parties," he recounted in detail the "election for the State Legislature, which occurred, soon after [his] arrival in New York." The subject was clearly of interest to Buckingham, and even after he left the state, he continued to comment on New York electoral politics. Buckingham was particularly concerned about the role played by political parties and the press, believing that both were instrumental in whipping up the passions of the mob through their hyperbolic partisan rhetoric. He believed that "a stranger in the country . . . not knowing anything of the state of parties beforehand, or of the mode of warfare practised on such occasions, would have imagined that the fate of the whole Union depended on the issue of this single election." He similarly noted the extent to which any public controversy was used by the press for partisan ends, meaning that "if a treasury defaulter runs off with a large sum, it is sure to be attributed to his Whig or Democratic politics, neither of them caring a straw about the immorality of the act, but each being anxious to obtain a party triumph."[28]

Buckingham's work on US elections extended far beyond the borders of New York. While the city remained a subject of interest for him, Buckingham also examined Bostonian, national, and southern elections. The descriptions of contests in the South requires particular comment, given the attempts made by some commentators to dissociate the section from democratic political culture. After observing the mayoral contest in Mobile, Alabama, Buckingham was particularly critical of the role played by alcohol. He specifically suggested that the same phenomenon had not characterized the northern elections he had witnessed (despite his criticisms of these contests). Interestingly, however, Buckingham explicitly rejected the idea that the violence and mob activism that he observed in the South had any relationship to democracy. Instead, he claimed that they were actually characteristics of the "aristocratic states" and compared the Mobile contest to British local elections in Liverpool. Explaining Buckingham's views here requires some comment on his political ideals. Buckingham was both a political reformer and a temperance advocate, and he accounted for the riotous conduct of the Mobile election in a way that would serve the cause of franchise expansion and temperance legislation in Britain.[29] Consequently, he presented his readers with a far more sympathetic portrayal of politics in the northern states than the South. Nevertheless, his version of US political culture (with its focus on the aristocratic credentials of the South in contrast to the democracy of the North) validated the view of a divided nation.

When he moved on to the subject of political policies, Buckingham highlighted the debate over protective tariffs and presented it as a case study of the antagonism between North and South. His own view of protectionist economic policy was unequivocal. He noted that "the doctrine of high duties, tariffs, and protection for domestic manufactures [had been] exploded by all the best writers on political economy in Europe." In his second text, *The Slave States of America*, Buckingham developed his analysis of protectionism as a divisive policy issue in the United States, using the nullification crisis to illustrate his point.

> The origin and end of this celebrated controversy may be thus briefly stated. The people of the free states, including all those of the Union north of the river Potomac, wishing to encourage domestic manufactures, and thus to render themselves independent of importations from England, were powerful enough in Congress to establish by law a scale of high duties on almost all British manufactures, ranging from 20 to 50 per cent., professedly with a view to protect the dearer manufactures of their own country. To this the people of the South very naturally objected, as they would derive no benefit

> whatever from the establishment of manufactures, since their States were not likely to establish any; while on the other hand, they would be injured to a considerable extent, by being obliged to pay for every manufactured article of which they stood in need, from 20 to 50 per cent, more than the price at which they could be supplied from England if no such tariff existed. These high duties were, therefore, clearly founded in injustice, by taxing the consumers of the whole country, for the exclusive benefit of the few engaged in manufactures.[30]

For Buckingham then the nullification crisis was rooted in the divergent policy demands of the industrializing North and agricultural South. Nullification therefore represented a clear sectional division, based on socio-economic distinctions, that was being expressed in the political sphere. Buckingham also echoed the views of earlier commentators such as Marryat by speculating on the possible development of a fruitful commercial relationship between Britain and the South, due to the latter's emphasis on agriculture.[31]

Between them, the works of Marryat, Brothers, and Buckingham encapsulate popular British attitudes toward American political life during this period. Although each man had a distinctive political philosophy, there was a remarkable level of coherence in their descriptions of US politics and a widespread recognition of sectional divisions. For the most part, political culture was viewed in national terms. All three portrayed the United States as a rough-and-tumble democracy, dominated by party passion and press bombast. The politics of free trade were, however, presented in exclusively sectional terms. The legacy of nullification ensured a strong connection between the South and free trade, while also fostering a British interest in the relationship between state and national government in America. For these reasons it is imperative that British discourse on US politics in the 1840s is seen in both sectional and national terms. That an overarching US political culture was recognized (and usually criticized) did not mask the existence of sectional strife over specific policies and ideas.

In some cases these discussions about the policy demands of the sections led commentators to examine the merits of states' rights ideas as a constitutional issue. Given the subsequent connection between pro-slavery fire-eaters and the states' rights doctrine, it is perhaps surprising that one of the most compelling British passages on the subject appeared in the abolitionist Joseph Sturge's 1842 text *A Visit to the United States in 1841*. Sturge was a

Birmingham Quaker who played an active role in a number of significant British reform campaigns during the first half of the nineteenth century. Domestically, he was a committed free trader, as well as an advocate for the expansion of the franchise. He also sat at the heart of a major international network of abolitionists that brought together prominent activists from across Europe and the United States. Given his interest in the extension of voting rights in Britain, it is not especially surprising that he decided to visit the United States. His time there, however, forced Sturge to confront the simultaneous existence of slavery and democracy. This experience led him to explore the states' rights doctrine and to claim that it accounted for the continued use of slave labor in America.[32]

In Sturge's analysis, the reputation of American democracy should not have been tarnished by slavery since its continuation was a result of the federal system whereby "neither the free states, nor the general Government, can . . . constitutionally abolish slavery in any one of the existing slave States." He explored the relationship between state and national government as part of his analysis of slavery, then expanded into a broader examination of US politics. Sturge claimed that "each state constitutes within itself a distinct republic, virtually independent of the general Government; so long as its legislation does not conflict with the specific articles of the constitutional compact, all the rights and powers of sovereignty, not specifically designated to the Government in that instrument being retained by the States."[33] Thus, Sturge explicitly emphasized the levels of independence of each state in the Union and in doing so contributed to a British understanding of the politically and legally divided nature of the United States.

The noted phrenologist George Combe echoed these claims, explaining that the national government had no practical power to abolish slavery in individual states, since each was "an independent sovereignty within its own territories." Combe cited a resolution brought by the Democratic senator from New Hampshire, Charles G. Atherton, on the nature of the national government; it contended that "this Government is of limited powers, and that, by the constitution of the United States, Congress has no jurisdiction whatever over the institution of slavery in the several States of the confederacy." Even British diplomats imbibed this understanding of state-nation relations with Lord Lyons, noting that "each separate State is in most respects independent of the Federal Government."[34] The recognition of states' rights ideas by a diplomat is indicative of the extent to which the doctrine became a feature of British debates about American politics in both the public and private spheres. Often this discussion was relatively abstract. The cases of Sturge and Combe, however, demonstrate the specific use of the doctrine among abolitionists to explain the continued use of slave labor in the United States. The final irony, of course, was that this doctrine would later be repackaged by pro-Confederates when they disputed the right of the Union to interfere with secession during the Civil War.

Crucially, however, it was not necessary for commentators to dispense with their critiques of national political culture in order to recognize the existence of state rights' ideas. Despite discussing the complex relationship between nation and state in some depth, Combe still returned to the image of American politics as an incoherent mass of democratic institutions, universal manhood suffrage, and pervasive partisanship in his broader characterizations of political life. The merchant William Rathbone VI would surely have agreed with Combe's views on both party and democracy. After a visit to New York in June 1842, Rathbone reported that "rich & poor, take all their opinions on trust from those who are interested in deceiving them . . . rather let us [in Britain] have a selfish aristocracy than a selfish people." Combe similarly found that the party system resulted in the subordination of "the intrinsic merits of a measure" to the "despotism of party." The implications of this phenomenon were quite obvious to Combe, who contended, after seeing a riot in Harrisburg, Pennsylvania, that "a democracy is a rough instrument of rule . . . and I have not met with a British radical who has had the benefit of five years' experience of it, who has not renounced his creed, and ceased to admire universal suffrage."[35]

This narrative of disillusion with American politics would certainly sum up the experience of one the period's most famous tourists—Charles Dickens. Prior to visiting the United States, Dickens had been both a committed liberal and an enthusiastic supporter of America as a political model. His time in the nation, however, changed his views. He wrote a letter on 22 March 1842 that made his disillusion clear: "This is not the Republic I came to see. This is not the Republic of my imagination." Rather than an ideal polity, the United States was dominated by "despicable trickery at elections; under-handed tampering with public officers; cowardly attacks upon opponents, with scurrilous newspaper of shields and hired pens for daggers." The consequence of this, as Dickens saw it, was to discourage the best people in the nation from becoming involved in politics.[36]

Writing in the same year, the conservative MP and later prime minister, Benjamin Disraeli, offered more specific criticisms of US mob power. Disraeli drew attention to the Alexander McLeod affair, which had brought the burning of the *Caroline* in 1837 back into the public eye. After drunkenly boasting about his involvement in the original dispute, the Canadian McLeod was arrested in November 1840. New York governor William Seward pushed for McLeod to be tried for murder, which led the British government to respond with a threat of war if the captive was not released. McLeod was allowed to go free after a short diplomatic standoff, yet soon afterward reports emerged that a mob had formed to re-imprison him. In the end it transpired that McLeod had nothing to do with the attack on the *Caroline* and that he had simply been playing up his military record in front of his drinking buddies. Despite this, Disraeli pointed to the actions of the US government during the McLeod affair as indicative of the power of the mob in American politics.[37] Furthermore, Seward's role in the affair contributed to his growing reputation in Britain as an Anglophobe and mob agitator. In the short term, this reputation may have helped with Seward's political career, but during the Civil War it made him a popular target for pro-Confederates, whose propaganda frequently connected him to the aspects of US political culture that Britons found most objectionable.

The attempt by later commentators and pro-Confederate propagandists to emphasize the relationship between the North and American democracy was predicated on an understanding that the South was, in some sense, politically distinct from the rest of the United States. Charles Daubeny made this phenomenon of southern political uniqueness especially clear in his 1843 *Journal of a Tour Through the United States and Canada*. One Virginian he had met "spoke of the Union as of little importance to the South, and contemplated its dissolution as neither distant nor greatly to be depreciated," while another group of southerners informed him in unambiguous language that "the Southerners . . . are losers by this national compact." Daubeny also found the issue of the tariff very much alive and concluded that "the South Carolineans [*sic*] seem to even now pay a dear price for their Union with the North."[38] Once again we have evidence that US disharmony was a major point of emphasis in British commentary. In this analysis, rather than being a source of strength, the Union itself was an artificial arrangement that forced unwelcome political policies on the South.

From a British point of view, the debate over free trade was not only the most prominent sectional policy division in the United States but also resonated with an increasingly vocal free-trade lobby. As a result, when the popular association between free trade and the South emerged during the 1840s, something akin to an informal Anglo-southern alliance developed. Probably the most prominent group involved in this transatlantic network was the British Anti-Corn Law League (ACLL). The existence of a relationship between the ACLL and southern free traders is indicative of the significance of the tariff dispute in Britain. The group was dominated by abolitionists, such as Bright, Cobden, and Sturge. Despite this, the ACLL boardroom contained the busts of the southerners John C. Calhoun and George McDuffie, both of whom were involved in free-trade activism. That they were major slaveholders seems to have been something the ACLL members were prepared to overlook. More broadly, it appears that there was enthusiasm among British reformers about the spread of free trade in the United States, even if the cause was spearheaded by southerners. The historian Simon Morgan has noted that ACLL members saw potential for a working relationship with the administration of the Virginia slaveholder John Tyler because of this apparent antipathy to protectionism. Cobden viewed the apparent success of slaveholding free traders in reducing import rates with the Walker Tariff of 1846 as such a significant milestone that he personally congratulated Calhoun. The tariff's importance in British perceptions of American politics in the antebellum period should not be underestimated. At one level the differences between North and South on the issue implied disunity over economic policy among the states, which in turn helped to familiarize the British with the divisions in the United States. Understanding the importance of free trade to many Britons, and the long-standing association between free trade and the South, helps to explain the stance of a number of British liberal abolitionists who refused to support the Union during the Civil War.[39]

The issue of free trade was undoubtedly significant for the British liberals who rejected the Union during the Civil War. A more general disillusion with American democracy and an increasing association between the worst features of the system and the North may, however, also have played a role in their rejection of the Union. In Dickens's 1844 novel, *The Life and Adventures of Martin Chuzzlewit,* we are able to see the wholesale critiques of American politics that characterized British writing during the period, as well as glimpses of sectional commentary. Before Martin and his servant

Mark Tapley have even set foot on the shore of the United States, news sellers board their ship to hawk their wares. Their papers' titles include the "New York Sewer," "New York Plunderer," "New York Peeper," "New York Stabber," and the "New York Keyhole Reporter." The titles themselves appear to have entered quickly into the public lexicon, with the *Morning Post* directly comparing the *New York Herald* to Dickens's "New York Sewer," in its 21 October 1843 edition. In the case of both the novel and newspaper article, the most obvious target was the American political press. That being said, Dickens's focus on New York highlights a connection between the city and negative characteristics of the US political system which would be reinforced in time.[40]

Dickens also redeployed the image of confused party politics (which had characterized the nation in *American Notes*) in *Martin Chuzzlewit.* His protagonists are exposed to the activities of the fictional Watertoast Association of United Sympathizers (with its obligatory newspaper the *Watertoast Gazette*) and a variety of American political figures, including La Fayette Kettle, Cyrus Choke, and Mr. Hannibal Chollop, who shot a man "for asserting in the Spartan Portico, a tri-weekly journal, that the ancient Athenians went a-head of the present Locofoco Ticket." This mocking attack on American political life was echoed in a short sketch entitled "An Aristocratic Dinner in New York," which was published in *Ainsworth's Magazine* in 1842. It included the character "Mr. Titus Offley Champkin, one of the most patriotic Whig editors of this State; a terror to all locofocoes, soap-locks, loafers, and nullifiers: a friend of internal improvement laws, Texian [*sic*] annexation and all the truly American institutions. Great with the pen, great in Tammany Hall. New York owes him a debt of lasting gratitude."[41] Although New York is specifically mentioned, the overall focus of this article and *Martin Chuzzlewit* was primarily national when it came to political culture. The language of bewildering party politics and an aggressively partisan press was in keeping with earlier portrayals by figures like Buckingham and Combe. Those, in turn, permeated popular discourse, as the writings of Disraeli and Rathbone demonstrate.

The mention of "Texian" annexation in the *Ainsworth's Magazine* sketch indicates the return of the republic to the center ground of Anglo-American diplomacy in the mid-1840s. In many ways, the tensions that characterized Anglo-American relations during this period can be traced back to the failure of the Webster-Ashburton Treaty (1842) to adequately deal with the

Oregon question. That the treaty provided little clarity on the Northwest border resulted in considerable unease on both sides of the Atlantic. In the United States, increasingly vocal calls for expansion and the emergence of the concept of Manifest Destiny (which had not been silenced by the failed annexation of Texas) led many to look at the Northwest and the South as potential sources of new territory. Much to the chagrin of the British government, President Tyler seemed to be paving the way for expansion as early as 1842, and by the 1844 election both Tyler and James K. Polk incorporated into their platforms plans to expand the Union into Texas and Oregon. The tone of the political debate became increasingly Anglophobic after this contest, with many Americans believing that the British were the primary obstacle to the acquisition of both Oregon and Texas, given British control of Canada and the public flirtation between the Texas government and British diplomats. Despite these concerns, the situation in the mid-1840s mirrored that of the later 1830s in the sense that the British government had no interest in becoming involved in a Mexican-American dispute. As a result, the British specifically informed the Mexicans that they would not support a war against the United States, despite popular American concerns that the two nations might cooperate to prevent expansion.[42]

As Sam W. Haynes has noted, there has been a tendency among historians to see pro-annexation sentiment in the United States during this period as being driven by southerners. In truth the situation was more complex, since there was support in the North and South for an expansion of the Union. In the case of Texas, slavery undoubtedly played a major role in expansion. This was something contemporary Britons had noted—although, as the case of Harriet Martineau illustrates, the desire for annexation was not understood solely as a southern phenomenon. The role of slavery in Oregon was considerably more ambiguous. Furthermore, the Anglophobic language that underpinned much of the era's general expansionist rhetoric played especially well with immigrant communities in the North. It goes without saying that this aggressive Anglophobia was a source of annoyance for the British populace and politicians.[43] Seen against this diplomatic and political backdrop, the description of Mr. Titus Offley Champkin offered in *Ainsworth's Magazine* becomes more meaningful. It offers an overarching critique of the US system and connects to territorial expansion the negative features associated with democracy.

The sense that northern life was characterized by the "anarchy and confusion" of democracy would be juxtaposed by some Civil War commentators with the image of a stable and structured South. Such a view of the South, however, predated the war by a considerable period. In 1846, for example, *Blackwood's Edinburgh Magazine* noted the almost aristocratic state institutions of Virginia, a description in stark contrast to the account *Ainsworth's* gave of New York politics. Similarly, British consul Robert Bunch claimed that "South Carolina would scorn to be classed with the venal electors of the North."[44] The *Blackwood's* article deserves particular attention here because it tapped into an extant belief that American democracy did not fit comfortably in Virginia. In *Domestic Manners,* Frances Trollope had highlighted the political conduct of Virginia statesmen who eschewed the rough and tumble of their fellows, while an editorial in the *Essex Standard* during the early 1830s had portrayed Virginians as cynical about American democracy. The division between North and South in terms of political culture was certainly not noted by all British commentators. Significantly, however, when it was highlighted, the distinction invariably involved a contrast between a skeptically democratic South with an avidly democratic North. This distinction would be integral to pro-southern propaganda during the Civil War, as it allowed writers to disassociate the Confederacy from the negative tropes of American democracy, just as a common "British" ethnicity allowed them to dissociate the South from northern ethno-cultural heterogeneity.

This recognition of the divergent political attitudes in the North and South complemented the existing British belief that the United States lacked national political coherence. Usually observations about this lack of coherence focused on political policy, but a number of commentators during the mid-1840s went a step further and mentioned the national government's want of legal or practical control. Despite nominally traveling to survey the geology of North America, Sir Charles Lyell frequently turned his eye to politics in his 1845 *Travels in North America.* He emphasized the lack of national coherence, remarking in one passage that "the territorial extent and political independence of the different States of the Union remind the traveller rather of the distinct nations of Europe than of the different countries of a single kingdom like England." The same year Benjamin Disraeli explained in a letter to the banker and politician Baron Lionel de Rothschild that the national government of the United States had "no more influence over the Western States, than over Devonshire or Dorset."[45]

As many British commentators saw it, the level of independence possessed by the individual states seemed to pose a problem because of the different socioeconomic systems and political attitudes of their populations. In his *Letters from America* (1844), John Robert Godley reported being "more struck than I expected to be with the difference between the northern and the southern people, and . . . surprised at the acrimony with which they appear to speak of the matters upon which their respective opinions or interests clash." These differences manifested (at least partly) through party politics and via the existence of divergent regional attitudes toward democracy. On the latter subject, Godley noted how southerners "predict all sorts of evils to the North from their universal suffrage and the supremacy of the mob," before explaining that "in Virginia there is a limitation of the franchise, even among the whites, a property-qualification being required." Godley made this latter claim despite contending earlier in his text that, regardless of their aristocratic pretensions, southerners had embraced the abstractions of "Jeffersonian democracy."[46]

In policy terms, nullification continued to be the primary point of reference for Britons analyzing the tensions in the Union. Increasingly, however, the events of the early 1830s were seen as indicative of the sort of fundamental divisions Godley had emphasized, rather than an isolated dispute. Broadly speaking, the different economic interests of the sections were presented as an explanation for the nullification crisis and the tensions that had continued to characterize sectional relations. Godley commented briefly on the peculiarly agricultural character of the South, while, in a text published in the same year, George Featherstonhaugh highlighted the policy implications of the division between agricultural and manufacturing areas. Featherstonhaugh recounted a conversation with the secessionist academic Thomas Cooper, during which the southerner pontificated on nullification and the economic interests of North and South to make a broad point about the lack of unity between the states. Featherstonhaugh then went on to say that "if the children of these Nullifiers are brought up in the same opinions, which they are very likely to be, here are fine elements for future disunion; for, imbibing from their infancy the notion that they are born to command, it will be intolerable to them to submit to be, in their own estimation, the drudges of the northern manufacturers."[47]

The idea that North and South had distinct economic interests underpinned a great deal of the prewar British commentary emphasizing sectional divisions in the United States. In many cases, commentators would expand their analysis beyond the economy to consider how this division was manifested in the political sphere as part of a broader southern identity. In the sequel to his 1845 travelogue, Lyell noted that "in many of the Southern and Western States, the commercial policy of Massachusetts was represented to me as eminently selfish, the great capitalists wishing to monopolise the manufacturing trade, and by a high tariff to exclude foreign capitalists, so as to grow rich at the expense of other parts of the Union [*sic*]," a view propounded in print in the same year by the Manchester journalist and free-trade advocate Archibald Prentice. The association between the South and free trade as described by Lyell and Prentice contributed to the development of a positive southern identity based around a popular British cause. In addition, however, Lyell rejected the claims of members of the press and earlier travelers that northerners dominated national politics, quoting a source from the section who told him that the North was held in "political thralldom" by southerners.[48]

Despite possessing more than a modicum of sympathy for the North, Lyell did not treat everything above the Mason-Dixon Line in apologetic terms. He tapped into a rich tradition of anti–New York sentiment in the collective understanding of his readers and recounted the accusations of an acquaintance who maintained that the election of President Polk had only occurred because of "5000 fraudulent votes given in the city of New York." The specific emphasis on New York provides a neat reassertion of the significance of the city to negative characterizations of the prewar North. The popular association of New York with the Irish, mob rule, and American democracy ensured that, as the historian Robert Saunders has put it, "New York embodied all the worst feature of American politics in their most concentrated form."[49]

By the 1850s three key issues had emerged in British commentary on the relationship between American politics and sectionalism. However false the division was in practice, the British identified a major distinction in policy aims between the agricultural South and the manufacturing North. For the most part, this policy division was manifested in the differing attitudes of the sections toward free trade. As a result, the nullification crisis remained a key point of reference for the British long after the 1830s. At the level of political culture, ideas of democracy, Anglophobia, and expansionism were still frequently described as national characteristics of the United States, although some commentators associated them more closely with the North. Finally, on the subject of states' rights, a general recognition existed in Britain that the government in Washington either lacked the legal right or the practical ability to impose legislation on individual states. The prevailing British view was, therefore, that the US political system was seriously fragmented. The idea persisted that the United States retained national policy priorities and a national political culture, yet this view was commonly intertwined with an alternative discourse about sectional political disunity. Taken together, debates over policy, political culture, and political structure provided an invaluable store of ideas for Civil War propagandists, who remolded and deployed these prewar images.

As the midcentury approached, neither the flood of British travelers nor popular interest in US politics showed any signs of ceasing. By this time, free trade had been enshrined as economic gospel in the minds of most Britons. As a result, even conservatives like Disraeli were prepared to concede that ending protectionist economics was one of the primary missions of the nation. In terms of perceptions of the United States, the new economic orthodoxy ensured that the contrasting views of northerners and southerners on protectionism continued to provide a peculiarly pertinent illustration of the divisions between the sections. In her *Travels in the United States* (1850), Emmeline Stuart-Wortley highlighted this difference by explaining to her readers that "the South are for free trade," while protectionist economics continued to dominate in the North.[50]

An article in the *Leeds Mercury* on 24 July 1852 provided readers with an analysis of how these debates over free trade fed into US politics more broadly. Emphasizing the sectional characteristics of the parties, the editorial described the Democrats as a "warlike party, favourable to free trade, but hostile or indifferent to the abolition of slavery: and the Whigs as the conservative and peaceful party, fond of commercial 'protection,' but desirous of limiting and ultimately extinguishing the foul institution of slavery." The same piece went on to make a clear sectional distinction: "the Democrats find their strength among the haughty planters of the South," while "the Whigs have their chief force in the industrious North."[51] For a publication such as the fiercely free-trade and abolitionist *Leeds Mercury*, the stance of the sections on trade policy was a cause of consternation, since it prevented editorial writers from pursuing a consistent line in their sectional commentary. The sense that the British global mission involved both abolition and free trade made it unfeasible to suggest a clear moral division between North and South, since each was representative of one of the major evils the British claimed to be fighting on the international stage.

The continued emphasis on sectionally divisive policy aims needs to be understood against the ongoing British debate over US political culture and the Constitution. In this regard the publications of the British legal scholar Hugh Seymour Tremenheere are particularly significant. In *Notes on Public Subjects* (1852) and *The Constitution of the United States Compared to Our Own* (1854), Tremenheere was particularly critical of the political press, which he claimed fostered arrogance and Anglophobia among the people, while failing to properly educate them in their political duties. In his later study, Tremenheere continued his criticism of American politics, using the election of Franklin Pierce in 1852 as a case study to illustrate the problems he had identified. He determined that the American system always required a compromise candidate for the presidency, and for this reason it was likely that a "nobody" would be nominated by each party. Tremenheere was certainly not alone in making this assertion. Both Stuart-Wortley and Charlotte Houstoun had noted a similar dynamic in earlier elections.[52]

Given Tremenheere's scholarly focus, it is perhaps unsurprising that he attempted to extrapolate the politics of the 1840s and 1850s into a broader analysis of the US political system and its history. Beginning from the premise that the founding fathers had never intended for the republic to develop into a democracy, Tremenheere proceeded to explain how the democratic system had reduced the quality of US statesmen to an unacceptable level. His criticism was not unique. An article printed in the *London Times* during the period provided a similar analysis of US political history. Tremenheere's publication, however, was one of the most coherent discussions of the subject.[53] While his text provides a valuable reminder of the continued importance of national politics to the British understanding of the United States, it also contributed to the vocabulary of American political life which could be sectionalized. We have already seen the extent to which aspects of US political culture were being associated with the North and South by commentators who claimed that the nation was divided not simply by policy priorities but also by attitudes to democracy. Tremenheere's text offered these commentators a scholarly framework in which to place their emerging idea of a sectional democracy.

An illustration of the simultaneous critiques of northern democracy and the national political system is provided by Lucy Bird's *The Englishwoman in America* (1856). In her descriptions of New York politics, Bird evoked Dickens's earlier analysis of the city's political corruption and governing problems. Bird was, however, equally critical of the national political system and claimed that "the President, the Members of Congress, and to a still greater extent the members of the State Legislatures, are the *delegates* of a tyrannical majority rather than the *representatives* of the people."[54] Criticisms of US politics in sectional and national terms were clearly, therefore, not mutually exclusive. In a Civil War context, pro-Confederates and anti-Unionists were keen to use the claims of commentators like Bird regarding American politics. They frequently fused these claims with the idea that southerners generally disdained democracy. Of course, to do this successfully it was necessary for these writers to play down the extent to which the British had recognized the national popularity of democracy before the war. Nevertheless, enough emphasis had been placed on democracy as a northern phenomenon to make the connection viable, even if it was not unanimously accepted.

The diplomatic correspondence of the era demonstrates how much the British mainstream by the 1850s had embraced a vision of the United States as lacking unity in terms of political culture and political policy. Writing in 1853 to the foreign secretary, Lord Clarendon, the British ambassador in Washington, John F. T. Crampton, noted with exasperation that sectional difference "insinuate[s] itself into every part of their proceedings; discussions begun upon subjects apparently most remote, invariably degenerate into Northern and Southern squabbles." Perhaps even more telling was a letter from Clarendon to the Earl of Aberdeen (at that time prime minister), in which he suggested that "the union won't last forever," though he doubted "it being dissolved in our time."[55] There was clearly a broad recognition among prominent British politicians and intellectuals that the US political system was sectionally divided in terms of both policy and culture. When understood in these terms, the attitudes of many Britons toward disunion in the early 1860s is immediately easier to comprehend.

By the 1850s two clear, but often related, strands of thought existed among the British populace on the subject of American politics. One emphasized the existence of a unified polity, usually described in explicitly negative terms. A second maintained that the United States was politically divided into regions or sections and that this division was consistent with the Constitution. Although it might be tempting to see the latter image as being pro-southern (given its Civil War applications), this was not necessarily the case. In a newspaper article discussing the Fugitive Slave Law in 1855, Martineau mused on the right of secession. She did so, however, with reference not to the South but to Massachusetts (toward which she was particularly sympathetic). Martineau explained to readers of the *Daily News* that Massachusetts "cannot obey the contradictory laws of the Union and the State." She then rhetorically asked, "Is Massachusetts ready to withdraw from the Union, or to be declared excluded from it? If so she may, we think, reasonably hope for the companionship of all the best states."[56]

Martineau's main point of reference when discussing the US political system was the Fugitive Slave Law. More broadly, however, the mid-1850s saw the emergence of a number of diplomatic disputes that focused British attention on US politics. Particularly pertinent were the short-term consequences of the Clayton-Bulwer Treaty of 1850. A notoriously ambiguous document, the treaty was drafted to diffuse growing Anglo-American tensions over Central American territory. By the mid-1850s the treaty's flaws were clear to both sides, as US filibusters took an increasingly aggressive stance toward Nicaragua and Cuba. The drive for expansion in the area was a particular bugbear for the British, who believed that the filibusters were supported by the US government. Evidence of this sympathy for expansion was found in the US attempt to purchase Cuba from Spain in 1854 and the decision to recognize the Nicaraguan government of William Walker (a prominent filibuster) in 1856. The result of these developments was antipathy toward the Franklin Pierce administration among the British public and government, which became even more pointed when US electoral politics were brought into the debate.[57]

The British view of the Pierce administration and its relationship to democracy was thrown into sharp relief by the second major Anglo-American tension of the mid-1850s. As the Crimean War (1854–56) dragged on, the British government became concerned about dwindling manpower and by November 1854 was already exploring the possibility of recruiting troops in North America. This decision alone would have sparked controversy, given its questionable legality. That the United States was publically supportive of Russia during the conflict, however, meant that the recruiting issue became a major diplomatic incident. James Buchanan (then US minister to Britain) lodged a complaint with Lord Clarendon about recruitment in the United States, which led to Ambassador Crampton being ordered to dismantle the network he had set up for this purpose. More controversially, the British consul in Cincinnati, Charles Rowcroft, was actually arrested for his involvement in recruiting activities in July 1855.[58]

Expansion, filibustering, and recruitment might have remained discrete diplomatic flashpoints if not for the presidential election of 1856. As Sam Haynes has pointed out, Pierce's campaign for renomination relied partly on ratcheting up Anglo-American tensions. Although the scheme failed Pierce in electoral terms, it resulted in a period of extensive diplomatic posturing and popular criticism among Britons over the use of Anglophobia for party political purposes in the United States. Some Britons saw the decision to expel Crampton in May 1856 for his apparent involvement in the recruiting controversy as an attempt by Pierce to reinforce his Anglophobe reputation to secure renomination. A poem published in *Punch* during the following month is indicative of how filibustering, recruitment, and the expulsion of Crampton were yoked together by commentators. In essence, the short satirical piece implied that these diverse and controversial issues played a role in US electoral politics because of the existence of democracy in the nation.[59]

The overarching critique of American democracy, which reached fever pitch during the Pierce presidency, continued to characterize British responses to US politics under the Buchanan administration, despite a reduction in the diplomatic tensions between the nations. In his 1857 travelogue *Letters from the Slave States,* James Stirling wrote of the increasing power of the mob and ominously suggested that "politics in this country [has] got beyond the control of politicians." In his diary on the US political situation in June 1856, Charles Greville expressed a similar fear of the "ignorant and unreasoning mob."[60] For both men, the system of American democracy had placed political power in the hands of the mob, which in turn forced politicians to pander to their base demands.

Although Stirling seemed to suggest an urban/rural division in US politics by placing the mobs of New Orleans alongside those of New York and Philadelphia, he wholeheartedly endorsed the view that North and South had distinct policy demands—even if their political cultures were similar.

From Stirling's perspective, these demands had eventually coalesced around specific political parties. As the United States marched westward and added territory, discussions about the extension of slavery were inevitably stimulated and different parties developed, representing the interests of North and South. Therefore, "[in] the late Presidential election . . . North and South were arrayed against each other," and "the Democratic party was, in truth, a Southern party, adopting the interests and views of the South." When it came to future prospects, Stirling maintained his sectional line: "The supremacy of the North is assured. Already she excels her sister in every element of power, and the rate of her progress is infinitely greater. Nothing but her oligarchical organization and the prestige of her old associations—now almost extinct—saves the South from political subjection."[61]

Stirling discussed these "old associations" at length in his analysis of the sectional divisions that he believed complemented the divergent policy demands of the North and South. He posited that "it is a gross blunder to speak simply of American democracy," since "the American government is one half democratic, one half aristocratic. There is a bona-fide Democracy in the North, founded on a material equality of condition; but the South is a downright oligarchy." He even linked these differences in political outlook to the mythology of the Puritan North and Cavalier South.

> The North, then, was originally, and is yet, Puritan and Plebeian; the South, on the contrary, was Cavalier and Patrician; Virginia and the Carolinas were settled mainly by English gentry, with a sprinkling even of the nobility. They brought with them not only their aristocratic feelings, but even their aristocratic laws, entails, and the law of primogeniture. And though these laws, as such, have been repealed, the spirit and custom, which are stronger than all laws, and without which all written law is but waste parchment, exist more or less to this day; and in the older Southern States it is the custom for the eldest son to take the family estate where it yet exists, and portion off the younger children. The South, then, is to all intents and purposes an Aristocracy, nay, an Oligarchy; for in addition to aristocratic feeling, there is also an anti-democratic in equality of fortune.[62]

By establishing this division, Stirling explicitly connected ethno-cultural identity to the political differences between the North and South. In doing so, he presented his readers with a multifaceted and relatively coherent version of American sectionalism.

These divisions of ethnicity, culture, and political attitudes were compounded in Stirling's account through a reassertion of the policy priorities of the sections. The tariff remained the vital touchstone here, with Stirling describing "the stupid old system of protection" that helped create "the mobs of New York, Philadelphia, and all the other manufacturing districts." Stirling then emphasized the explicitly sectional nature of the tariff debate by highlighting the strong support for protectionist economics that he believed existed in the North. His overall conclusions, therefore, were couched in the language of sectional difference, and while he appreciated the role of slavery in accounting for sectional divisions, he maintained that "the present antagonism of North and South has really originated in their opposed social idiosyncrasies and habits." For him, slavery "has acquired this pre-eminence [in public discourse] by accidental circumstances, partly by the error and misdeeds of American politicians."[63] Consequently, the tariff and slavery were of similar significance. Both were expressions of deep-seated differences and—crucially in terms of British relations with the American sections—the southern fight against protection had considerable sympathy in Britain.

It is also worth noting that the intersection between politics, culture, and ethnicity, which Stirling discussed at length, resonated with changing ideas about nationalism. As the historian Paul Quigley has argued, nationalism evolved in this period from an inclusive and civic model to one based around ethnicity and culture. Stirling's descriptions of the American South seemed to suggest the existence of a distinctive southern nationalism in both its civic and ethnic form.[64] This preexisting sense of southern identity proved useful for Civil War commentators who wished to emphasize the long-standing claims that they believed the South had to nation status. Of course, that such a connection was never entirely coherent may explain the failure of the Confederacy to secure widespread support in Britain, even if the existence of this same connection also helps to account for the popular antipathy evinced toward the efforts of the Union to reunite America.

The sense of disharmony that Stirling conveyed was not understood in isolation from practical political developments. In fact, debates over state sovereignty peppered the press during the 1850s and provided the backdrop for British discussions of political culture and policy in America. The *Leeds Mercury* noted, with reference to the Fugitive Slave Law, that "the United States are in theory a confederation of independent and sovereign states," while the *Freeman's Journal and Daily Commercial Advertiser* made a more specific observation about the lack of presidential power over the states with reference to the "Bleeding Kansas" controversy. A comment in the *Era* in June 1856 neatly summed up the British perspective on the relationship between individual states and the national government: "Above thirty separate Republics have been formed, which, federally united, recognise in certain cases the authority of a supreme executive at Washington."[65] These texts presented the British public with a version of the United States in which the individual states appeared to have many of the rights of independent nations. In the short term this understanding seemed to validate the state rights' doctrine, while in the longer term it was integrated into the arguments of those who claimed that the Union had no right to prevent Confederate secession.

Although not unanimously accepted, the view that the United States lacked a coherent national political culture permeated all levels of British society and influenced people with a range of political views. Sir William Gregory, who would go on to be one of the most active members of the pro-Confederate lobby in Britain, pointedly identified Baltimore as "one of the most aristocratic towns in the Union" when traveling around the United States in the late 1850s. Naturally, the term "aristocratic" had social and culture connotations, which influenced Gregory's decision to use it, but it also implied a general antipathy to political democracy. More pronounced were the views of the British diplomat Lord Napier, who mused on the existence of different attitudes toward universal suffrage between the sections in a letter to Lord Malmesbury: "I have not met in America more than two persons of thought and political experience who in their hearts believe in the permanent working of the popular sovereignty and universal suffrage machine—but no one dares declare himself, *at least in the North,* and no one knows how the prerogatives abandoned to the mob are to be resumed by the better order of people" (my emphasis).[66] As we have seen throughout this chapter, Napier's views were not unique. While it would be untrue to claim that Britons saw US democracy as an entirely northern phenomenon, it is equally undeniable that Napier was simply one of a number of commentators who implied that democracy had a closer connection to the North.

While the precise relationship between the various facets of American politics and sectionalism remained somewhat ambiguous through to the Civil War, a number of conclusions can be drawn about popular attitudes in Britain. In policy terms, the British were familiar with the idea that the demands of the North and South were not always the same. The nullification crisis was a crucial point of reference in this regard. To British readers the crisis turned upon a fundamental difference in economic priorities; this difference suggested a basic incompatibility between the interests of the sections. Furthermore, the increasing importance of free trade to British policy and national identity over the antebellum period led to expressions of popular sympathy for southerners, as well as the emergence of a fledgling Anglo-southern free trade alliance. Nullification also played a key role in the emergence of a British discourse of states' rights. The stand that South Carolina took in the 1830s sparked a British interest in the relationship between state and national government in the United States that transcended the question of free trade. Over the subsequent thirty years, many Britons explored the states' rights doctrine and often concluded that the federal government lacked the right to enforce legislation against the wishes of a state. British commentators were, however, a lot less coherent when it came to placing political culture in a sectional context. Across the period as a whole, most writers implied that a national political culture existed in the United States. This culture tended to be associated with the power of the mob, the press, and unscrupulous political parties. Despite the usual focus on the United States as a national entity, a sense of sectional division can also be identified in discussions of political culture. Crucially, in terms of the Civil War, some Britons went as far as to suggest that areas of the South actually rejected the democratic political system. Furthermore a number of commentators explicitly tied the negative characteristics of American democracy to the urban North. Given the overall sense of disunity that characterized British discussions of US policy, states' rights, and political culture, it is probably not a surprise that the explicitly sectional result of the 1860 presidential election caused the British consul Lord Lyons to speculate that the end of the Union might be near (even while he rejected the practicability of secession).[67]

While Lyon's observation on the potential consequences of Lincoln's election may have been correct, his claim was hardly unprecedented. For at least thirty years, British commentators had explored publically the divisions in the American Union. While almost every individual added his or her own wrinkle to the fabric of American sectionalism, it was generally accepted that North and South were different. British observers presented the sections as having distinctive economic, social, and cultural complexions (as has been attested to in previous chapters) and noted how the interests these divisions engendered were expressed in the political sphere. As a result, most literate Britons were accustomed to the states' rights doctrine and the argument that the North and South had different policy priorities. Some even believed that the South had developed a distinctive political culture in which the rough-and-tumble democracy (so often associated with the United States) had been rejected. Interestingly, while the sectional nature of US political culture was highly ambiguous, its Civil War legacy was significant. Many of those who had been most critical of the South in the antebellum period had unintentionally made the task of propagandizing for the Union during the Civil War considerably more difficult. Figures such as Stirling, Martineau, Buckingham, and Godley had often focused on the differences between the sections in their critiques of the South. At least until 1863, however, the popular British view of the Civil War centered on the validity—rather than the morality—of the Confederate cause. As a result, the works of earlier writers who had criticized the South contained a range of justifications for Confederate independence and thereby undermined the popularity of the federal cause in Britain.

CHAPTER FOUR

"AN ARROGANT AND INSULTING NORTHERN MAJORITY"

Britain and the American Civil War, 1861

When the Virginia secessionist Edmund Ruffin fired the first shot of the Civil War on the morning of Friday, 12 April 1861, it is unlikely that he had any inkling of the global significance of his actions. The conflict that followed the attack on Fort Sumter was significant beyond the borders of the United States. In practical terms it had major economic, military, and diplomatic consequences. It also forced international observers to confront the possibility that the American Union might permanently end. The complexity and closeness of the Anglo-American relationship naturally resulted in nervous British glances as events unfolded across the Atlantic. Crucially, however, Britons did not react to Civil War developments, such as the attack on Fort Sumter, as isolated events. As the previous three chapters have demonstrated, the British had a sophisticated understanding of US sectional and regional identity long before 1860.[1]

Since at least the 1830s, Britons had commented on the divisions within the American Union. Although their discourse was never entirely coherent, certain characteristics were frequently associated with particular regions or sections. While slavery was often commented upon, it was rarely used as a blunt instrument with which to beat the South. Instead, although most Britons condemned slavery in the abstract, many also suggested that the worst excesses of the system were mitigated by southern paternalism. Commentators also frequently highlighted instances of racial violence in the North and emphasized the role played by the free states in the continued existence of slavery. When it came to ethnic and cultural identity, the United States was commonly divided into three regions. Both the South and New England were understood as being ethnically British but divided by their respective cultural inheritance (Cavalier and Puritan). The mid-Atlantic, however, was usually "othered" and associated with non-Britishness and political Anglophobia. On the subject of politics more broadly, the British were well aware that the North and South had distinct policy priorities. There was also a level of familiarity with the states' rights doctrine, which stemmed from popular debates about the nullification crisis. In terms of political culture, there tended to be an enduring belief that the United States had a number of defining national characteristics. Even here, however, there was scope for sectional differentiation. Some British commentators claimed that the South had developed a distinctive political culture in which the rough and tumble of popular democracy had been rejected.

It is worth briefly pausing here to clarify the overall purpose of the final two chapters of this work. Although concerned with British reactions to the Civil War, neither of these chapters attempts to provide an empirical analysis of the levels of support enjoyed by the belligerents. Works on this subject already exist, and their conclusions are relatively compelling. Most Britons were ambivalent toward the war, although a mild strain of anti-Unionism frequently characterized public discourse. Nevertheless, this anti-Unionism was not enough to lead to the development of a mass movement in favor of the Confederacy. In terms of those who had a pronounced commitment to one side or the other, scholars such as R. J. M. Blackett have done an impressive job of quantifying levels of support across the British Isles.[2] My focus, therefore, is on explaining the general apathy and lukewarm anti-Unionism of the British populace, as well as on accounting for views of the war held by prominent activists on both sides. As a result, these chapters are not designed to offer a comprehensive catalogue of all of the Civil War propaganda produced in Britain. Instead, Chapters 4 and 5 focus on key texts produced by prominent activists, as well as journalists, politicians, and public intellectuals. By analyzing popular texts produced by both partisan and neutral figures, the two chapters demonstrate the extent to which Britons presented and understood the Civil War with reference to antebellum sectional discourse. Through this analysis the chapters explain the general ambivalence of the populace toward the war. They also account for the failure of the Confederate government to secure recognition and of pro-Unionists to establish an effective national movement against the South.

The purpose of Chapter 4 is to explore how the discourse of sectionalism played out during the early stages of the Civil War. The chapter is specifically focused on the period between Jefferson Davis's inaugural address as Confederate president in February 1861 and the *Trent* affair in November of the same year. When it comes to examining the Civil War in an Anglo-American context, it is useful to distinguish the pre-*Trent* era in this way. Prior to the seizure of this ship, the British were able to maintain a sense of distance from the conflict because of their lack of direct involvement in events. Nevertheless, American affairs were a staple of political and journalistic discourse over this nine-month stretch. It was also during this period that many of the major propagandists for the Union and the Confederacy first began their attempts to sway public opinion.

Although journalists, politicians, and propagandists had a range of motivations for commenting on the Civil War, their work was united by an attempt to place the conflict within a preexisting sectional framework. The debate over free trade proved to be vital in this regard because of the long-standing British awareness of the role played by protectionism in sectional relations and the attitudes expressed by the Union and Confederate governments toward free trade. Of particular significance here were Davis's inaugural address on 18 February 1861 and the decision by the Lincoln administration to pass the Morrill Tariff on 2 March. While Davis asserted in his speech that the Confederate States would be committed to "the freest trade," the Morrill Tariff raised import duties to the detriment of British exports.[3] Although the announcement of this tariff upset many in Britain, it surprised few. Since the nullification controversy, British writers had discussed the existence of a North/South division based on the issue of trade policy. The Morrill Tariff was, therefore, seen as evidence of the divergent economic interests of the North and South.

This awareness of the importance of the tariff debate during the early stages of the conflict helps to account for the almost immediate indifference that British commentators expressed toward the Union. Lord Lyons, then Her Majesty's envoy in Washington and a man with little sympathy for secession, wrote to the committed British free trader, and later pro-Confederate activist, William Schaw Lindsay in 1861 to report a conversation with Vice President Hannibal Hamlin. Lyons emphasized to Hamlin the power of free trade in transatlantic diplomacy. He described how he had told the vice president of the "bad impression which the abominable new tariff has . . . produced" and contrasted North and South in explicit terms by recognizing that in "commercial matters in general the southern confederacy [are] of course disposed towards liberality." Similarly, Lyons wrote to the foreign secretary, Earl Russell, in April 1861 to describe the effects of the tariff and criticize the "protectionist bigotry" of those who acquiesced in it. The significance of sentiments of this sort was not lost on southern sympathizers in Britain, such as the MP William Gregory, who made sure to draw the attention of the Commons to the passage of the tariff. Moreover, it is evident that the public did not disconnect the Morrill Tariff from their broader historical understanding of US sectional disputes. Instead, they saw the act as indicative of the long-term tensions between North and South and as an illustration of the unfair treatment that the preindustrial South intermittently experienced.[4]

British reaction to the Morrill Tariff was characterized by dramatic language emphasizing the damage that the policy had done to the prospects for reunion. One liberal London newspaper (the *Daily News*) described the act in particularly stark terms as "a selfish defiance cast by the North at the South," while an American living in Scotland wrote to the *Glasgow Herald* in March 1861, suggesting that "Mr Morrill's new tariff shows plainly to the world what the Southerns [*sic*] had always had to complain of." Given his role in the development of British ideas about the United States before the war, Charles Dickens's views on the subject are of particular interest. Writing in his own magazine, *All the Year Round,* Dickens examined the legislation in some depth. He argued that the new tariff was simply the latest in a long line of attempts by politicians to enrich the North at the expense of the South. Dickens also maintained that widespread antipathy toward protectionist economics had motivated southern secessionists.[5] When the number of prewar texts that had described the sectional relationship in similar terms is taken into account, it becomes easy to see how viable Dickens's claims would have appeared to the public.

Given the output of British journalists on the tariff issue, it is unsurprising that the official pro-Confederate lobby moved quickly to exploit the controversy. To understand how they did this, however, it is necessary to provide some brief background on the aims and operation of Confederate diplomacy. From the outbreak of the war, Confederate politicians were aware of the importance of foreign intervention as part of their effort to gain nation status. The announcement of British neutrality (which Queen Victoria issued on 13 May) brought with it certain advantages in international law that southerners were keen to exploit. In the longer term, the Confederacy hoped to secure recognition of its independent status by major European powers as soon as possible and thereby gain the legal status to form alliances. Because Confederate statesmen placed such an emphasis on international recognition, the Davis government mobilized a network of commissioners well before their northern counterparts. By March 1861, the Confederate government had already appointed the former Mississippi congressman Pierre Rost, former Virginia secretary of state Dudley A. Mann, and fire-eating South Carolinian William L. Yancey to travel to Britain and lobby for recognition.[6]

A letter sent early in the war by the Confederate secretary of state Robert Toombs to the three men is particularly striking as it provides evidence of the significance attached to the tariff question in diplomatic relations by those in the Davis administration. Toombs tellingly advised the commissioners that, as part of their diplomatic efforts in Britain, it would be worth highlighting the 1828 tariff, which had ultimately lead to the nullification crisis. The emphasis on the debate over protectionist economics would have resonated with a British public accustomed to viewing the tariff as a sectional issue and to referring to the nullification crisis in their prewar discussions of US politics.[7] The hope for the Confederate government was that recognition could be secured by highlighting the role of free trade in the South's secession.

Toombs also suggested other issues he thought Yancey, Mann, and Rost should emphasize. These included the apparent economic exploitation of the South by the North and the legal basis for secession. Toombs thought the commissioners should focus on the fact that southern secession represented a struggle for national liberation with parallels to the Italian independence movement. This was a diplomatically savvy move, given the widespread support in Britain for Italian liberation. Framing the war in these terms helped to convince some Britons that the northern states were attempting to subjugate the southern "nation"—a claim powerful enough to discourage a number of abolitionists from endorsing the Union. Through an examination of Toombs's advice, we gain insight into the diplomatic approach of the Confederacy and southern politicians' belief that secession needed to be characterized in a particular way to gain British support. Toombs accentuated the need to present the Confederacy as a nation attempting to liberate itself from a Union it should have been allowed to leave freely.[8]

To justify this stance it was necessary to differentiate the North from the South, yet doing so posed a potential problem. While highlighting southerners' desire to secure the long-term existence of slavery would have helped to establish a fundamental division between the sections, it also would have rendered the Confederate war effort objectionable to most Britons. The task for pro-southerners, therefore, was to justify Confederate nationhood without reference to slavery. Crucially, from a southern point of view, there was no consensus in Britain during the early stages of the conflict regarding the role played by abolition. This ambiguity was vital, as it allowed figures like Toombs to ignore slavery and differentiate the North from the South by referring to elements of sectionalism (such as free trade) that had long been recognized in Britain and that seemed to lend themselves to the sympathetic treatment of the Confederacy.

The importance of prewar British knowledge about the role of the tariff in sectional relations has often been underappreciated. As a result there has been a tendency to underestimate the significance of the debate over protectionist economics when examining British responses to the outbreak of the Civil War. The Morrill Tariff, for example, was significant enough to produce what Martin Crawford has described as an "astonished" reaction among the staff of the *London Times,* who could not believe that Lincoln's government would pursue such an aggressively protectionist economic policy. Such a response should not be a surprise, given the strong hold that free-trade ideas had over British intellectuals, including Dickens, John Stuart Mill, William Makepeace Thackeray, Thomas Carlyle, R. H. Horne, Elizabeth Barrett Browning, and Robert Browning, among others. Considering the liberal politics of some of these figures, it should come as no surprise that even those who would go on to be the fiercest supporters of the Union in Britain (including John Bright and Richard Cobden) were critical of the passage of the tariff. Its significance was such that even the long-time abolitionist Harriet Martineau considered severing her ties with American antislavery activists over the issue of protective duties. While it is true that in the long term Bright, Cobden, and Martineau put aside the tariff issue and took up the Union cause with enthusiasm, it is also worth noting that a number of other doctrinaire free traders, such as Lindsay, remained hostile to the North.[9]

While the commitment to free trade that Jefferson Davis announced as part of his inauguration elicited a positive response from across the British political landscape, Abraham Lincoln's address on 4 March proved to be a disappointment, even for those who had evinced sympathy for the North. Crucially, Lincoln rejected the idea that the Union was fighting the war for abolition. In response, both the *London Times* and the *Economist* concluded that the war must be a fight for territorial domination, given Lincoln's refusal to place the conflict on a moral footing. The situation was not improved by Lincoln's secretary of state, William Seward, who echoed the president's stance during his first foreign-policy address later in the month.[10] The decision of the two most prominent politicians in the Union to distance themselves from abolition was obviously motivated by a range of domestic concerns. To British audiences, however, their speeches seemed to confirm a preexisting belief that the free states were not committed to the abolition of slavery.

Despite this apparently unequivocal rejection of the connection between the Union and abolition, a number of British commentators spent the early months of the conflict publicizing an interpretation of the war in which Lincoln's long-term aim was the abolition of slavery. The pro-Union clergyman, William Arthur, endeavored to reassure his readers that, despite the ambiguous language emanating from Washington, the Union was motivated by a desire to end slavery. He contended that the only reason for the government failing to take action against the peculiar institution was its fidelity to the Constitution. Others turned their gaze on the Confederacy during these early months and emphasized the continued existence of slavery in the South, rather than debating the chances of abolition being undertaken by Lincoln. *Punch,* an organ of mainstream British opinion, noted in its 9 March 1861 issue that "the Southern Secessionists must be admitted to be blest with at least the philosophical virtue of self-knowledge. They term their new league 'The Confederate States of America.' Thus they call themselves by . . . their right name. They are confederates in the crime of upholding Slavery. A correct estimate of their moral position is manifest in that distinctive denomination of theirs, 'Confederate States.' The title is a beautiful antithesis of that of the United States of America. The more doggedly confederate slavemongers combine, the more firmly good republicans should unite." *Punch* further developed this theme the following month by publishing a song entitled "Rule Slaveownia," in a mocking attack on the Confederacy and slavery.[11]

The aforementioned William Arthur made a similar attempt to equate the Confederacy with slavery. Arthur specifically juxtaposed the connection between the North and abolition with the Confederate vice president Alexander Stephens's "cornerstone speech," given in Savannah, Georgia, on 21 March 1861. Stephens's infamous oration included the assertion that the Confederate "government is founded upon exactly the opposite ideas [to those of the Union]; its foundations are laid, its cornerstone rests, upon the great truth that the negro is not equal to the white man; that slavery, subordination to the superior race, is his natural and normal condition." By contrasting the cornerstone speech with his own claims that antislavery sentiment was widespread in the North, Arthur wanted to portray the war as a morally unambiguous battle between freedom and slavery.[12]

Arthurs's attempt to divide the sections on the basis of slavery was echoed in the work of another early federal propagandist, the Quaker social reformer William Tallack. The primary purpose of Tallack's 1861 pamphlet was to show how slavery had become an increasingly significant aspect of the sectional division and to highlight the growth of abolitionism in the northern states. Tallack claimed that over time "Southern insults . . . aroused the North . . . for [every] one anti-slavery man that there was in the North twenty years ago there are now a hundred." The descriptions of North and South given by Arthur and Tallack were intended to construct a northern identity centered on abolition, with a Union war effort built around it. By presenting the war in these terms, they hoped to make the decision of any Briton on the conflict an apparently obvious moral one rather than a complex political conundrum.[13]

Despite ambiguity among Britons regarding the role played by slavery in the war, the first group of Confederate commissioners (Yancey, Mann, and Rost) was aware of the issue's potential importance. In May 1861, Yancey and Mann wrote to Toombs, explaining that "the public mind here [in Britain] is entirely opposed to the Government of the Confederate States of America on the question of slavery." A subsequent letter to Earl Russell, sent on 14 August, saw Yancey, Mann, and Rost reinforce this idea and emphasized "the anti-slavery sentiment so universally prevalent in England." Reading their correspondence, it becomes clear that the commissioners were well aware of the widespread British antipathy toward the slave system. As a result, they made a major effort to disassociate positive endorsements of slavery from the Confederacy and rejected claims that abolition was a significant factor in the war. This approach was typified by the work of Edwin De Leon, another Confederate diplomat, who claimed in a letter to the *London Times* in May 1861 that slavery was a "mere pretext" for the war on the part of the Union.[14] Given the well-known British commitment to end slavery, it is not hugely surprising that the more savvy Confederate propagandists rejected the claim that the South had seceded to preserve the system. What is noteworthy, however, is that even if they were not entirely convinced by this pro-southern argument, many Britons seem to have been cynical about the claims made by writers like Tallack who attempted to connect the Union war effort with abolition. For this reason, support for the Union failed to spread quickly across the country.

In March 1861, in the same month that it criticized slave-holding in the South, *Punch* published a poem that demonstrates that slavery was just one of many factors influencing the British public.

> O Jonathan and Jefferson
> Come listen to my song;
> I can't decide my word upon,
> Which of you is most wrong.
> I do declare I am afraid
> To say which worse behaves,
> the North, imposing bonds on Trade
> Or South that man enslaves.
> And here you are about to fight,
> And wage intestine war,
> Not either of you in the right:
> What simpletons you are.[15]

This verse provides compelling evidence of the comparable significance of slavery and free trade in British engagements with the war. During the summer of 1861, another poem in *Punch* made this connection explicit.

> We for North and South alike
> Entertain affection;
> These for negro Slavery strike;

Those for forced Protection.
Yankee Doodle is the Pot;
Southerner the Kettle:
Equally moral, if not
Men of equal mettle.[16]

In both instances, slavery was presented as a factor in the war but not the sole point of contention between the North and South. That slavery was given similar prominence as the dispute over protectionism is indicative of the extent to which British observers viewed the conflict through a complex framework of sectional relations that went beyond the distinction between the free and slave states. Recognizing this fact helps to explain the widespread antipathy toward the Union within Britain.

Despite the existence of this public discourse in Britain, most northern commentators seem to have entirely disregarded the complex British understanding of sectionalism. As a result, these northerners often did not understand the motivations of the British public and policymakers. Through the diary of Benjamin Moran (who remained a member of the American legation in London after the outbreak of war), we get a glimpse of the extent to which the views of the conflict held by Britons and northerners differed. Moran noted on 7 January 1861 that the Confederacy was motivated to fight by the desire to protect slavery. For this reason he concluded that the lack of British support for the Union was illustrative of a lack of sincerity in British abolitionism. Of course, what Moran failed to grasp was that most British observers did not see a strong connection between the Union war effort and abolition, due to the lack of a historical commitment to end slavery in the North and the federal government's failure to act on the issue when the conflict began. Later in the year, in the December edition of *All the Year Round,* Dickens commented that if the Union was actually committed to abolition, it would allow the South to secede, thereby ridding itself of slavery. The same course of action was suggested by both Walter Bagehot in the liberal *Economist* and Lord Cecil in the conservative *Quarterly Review.* Dickens, Bagehot, and Cecil all advocated this policy for the North on the basis that if the primary aim of the Union was to rid itself of slavery, accepting secession would immediately accomplish it. The failure of the Washington government to allow secession was, therefore, seen as evidence that the war was being fought for control of the Union rather than to abolish slavery.[17] The distinction between the British journalists and Moran in this regard is telling. For the latter, Britain was a nation of insincere abolitionists, while the former saw the Union in exactly the same terms.

One specific event that annoyed Moran—and that he saw as indicative of British attitudes toward abolition—was the reception given to the Confederate commissioners Yancey, Mann, and Rost upon their arrival in London in May 1861. Moran criticized the fact that "the *noble* merchants of the realm see nothing dishonourable in slavery now," and he noted how he had been convinced that "the Anti-Slavery of England is a mere sentiment." He pointed to the reception given to the commissioners at the Fishmonger's Company Hall in London and claimed to have found it telling that Yancey received applause despite being an avowed advocate of the reopening of the slave trade. Moran concluded that "the very journals that 8 years ago could not too loudly condemn slavery, and which lauded *Uncle Tom's Cabin* to the skies, now see no great crime in the infamous system, and applaud the very slave owners."[18] Moran, however, failed to appreciate the complexity that characterized prewar British attitudes toward American slavery in general and *Uncle Tom's Cabin* specifically.

The US minister to Britain at the time—Charles Francis Adams—provided a more considered analysis of British views of slavery and the Union during the early exchanges of the war. Boasting a circle of acquaintances that included such political and intellectual heavyweights as Lords Palmerston, Russell, and Derby, as well as W. E. Gladstone, Benjamin Disraeli, Thackeray, and William Nassau Senior, Adams provides a window on British educated opinion. While some of these figures (specifically Senior) did offer support to the North, Adams noted in a letter to his son that pro-Union feeling was far from universal.[19] While Moran may have overstated the level of sympathy for the Confederacy in Britain, he and Adams seem to have been in agreement about the widespread indifference evinced toward the Union cause.

As Moran's critique of British abolitionism shows, northern commentators often struggled to account for the mixture of antipathy and indifference that they believed characterized the British response to the war. The reasons for these difficulties stemmed from an inability to understand the place of slavery in British perceptions of the conflict. Because the Lincoln government had done nothing to connect itself with abolitionism, Britons had no choice but to draw on prewar models to explain the relationship between the North and slavery. In these models they found slavery presented as a *national* problem that had critics and supporters across the United States. Without explicitly mobilizing the prewar language of New England abolitionism, the Union had little chance of convincing the British public that it was driven by a desire to end slavery. This being the case, it is unsurprising that many Britons showed little or no sympathy for the Union prior to 1863.

Tellingly, even those who were (or subsequently became) key cogs in the British pro-Union machine were not immediately prepared to describe the war as an antislavery crusade. Francis William Newman observed in a letter in June 1861 that slavery was indeed significant to the conflict but that the North retained a "pro-slavery faction." Similarly, John Bright, the heartbeat of the northern cause in Britain, explained in a speech in Lancaster in August that "they say that they are not going to liberate slaves. No; the object of the Washington government is to maintain their own Constitution, and to act legally, as it permits and requires."[20] For the majority of the British population, regardless of their sympathies during the early months of the war, it was generally accepted that the cause of the Lincoln government was not abolition. The British literati had been schooled in American affairs by writers like Frederick Marryat and James Silk Buckingham, who had consistently rejected an association between the free states and abolition during the antebellum period. Most Britons saw no obvious connection between the Union war effort and abolition when the conflict began. Furthermore, despite a number of propagandists claiming otherwise, their preconceptions regarding the relationship between the Union and abolition seemed to be confirmed early in the war with the refusal of the federal government to immediately announce a plan to end slavery.

Since the claim that the war was being conducted to abolish slavery lacked credibility in Britain, a few early Union propagandists mobilized prewar ideas of Anglophobia and ethno-cultural identity in an attempt to secure support for the North. William Arthur, for example, placed great store in the connection between Britain, antislavery, and the Republican Party when he argued in favor of the Union. He claimed that "in all contests, [the] Pro-slavery party was the Anti-English party, and was invariably swelled by the Irish Romanists," and that "the South professes to be well effected to England. This is a 'mere pretence.'" Arthur here attempted to equate the traditional notion of Anglophobe antebellum American politics with a southern, proslavery agenda, despite its usual associations with the

North (specifically New York). Tallack, in his pamphlet, suggested that the feeling toward an Englishman in the South was "most disagreeable." Both Tallack and Arthur were evidently attempting to appropriate certain characteristics of the prewar United States for the purpose of furthering the northern cause. They clearly appreciated the significance of the Anglophobic/Anglophilic rhetoric of the prewar period and were keen to harness it to undermine the South.[21]

However aggressively Tallack and his fellow pro-Unionists attempted to link the Confederacy with anti-British attitudes, they appear to have been unable to alter the minds of the British government. Many ministers saw the position of the two belligerents in precisely the opposite terms. Lyons, for example, wrote to Russell in June 1861 to inform him of the almost irrational desire on the part of some northerners to deal with the secession of the South quickly so that a campaign could be launched against British possessions in North America. Questions over whether the scheme was actually under consideration within the Lincoln administration or whether it was even practical are of little importance here.[22] The concept of an expansive and Anglophobe Union played into preexisting British fears and cemented an association between the North and Anglophobia.

During the early years of the conflict, few commentators made the reasons for British antipathy to the Union war effort clearer than *London Times* correspondent William Howard Russell. After coming to prominence for his reporting during the Crimean conflict, Russell became one of the most respected journalists of the day. Given his reputation as a war correspondent, there was probably little debate within the offices of the *Times* about who should be sent to report on the unfolding crisis in America. While in the United States, Russell spent the majority of his time in the South and, following the publication of his account of the battle of Bull Run, became a household name on both sides of the Atlantic. He was interested in more than military matters, though. Taken together, his published and private materials on the Civil War provide a comprehensive analysis of the causes and progress of the conflict. His *Pictures of Southern Life: Social, Political and Military* reveals southern attitudes toward Britain that are starkly different from those described by Tallack and Arthur. While in Charleston, for example, Russell found "an intense affection for the British connection, a love of British habits and customs, a respect for British sentiment, law, authority, order, civilization and literature." Speaking more broadly, Russell reported that "the Carolinians regard the Northern States as an alien and detested enemy, and entertain, or profess, an immense affection for Great Britain." In Mobile, he met a lieutenant from Louisiana who was "all admiration for English scenery, life and habits."[23]

Historically speaking, American Anglophobia had often been linked explicitly to the northern states through an emphasis on ethnic heterogeneity. It is probably, therefore, unsurprising that ethno-cultural characterizations of the North were connected to the Union in Russell's work. After watching a Federal military parade outside of Cairo, Russell disconnected the North from ideas of Britishness by emphasizing the lack of American-born soldiers in the Union army. He estimated that "two out of twelve of the soldiers were native-born Americans" and noted the number of Irish recruits in each of the different companies as they passed him. Russell's view of ethnic heterogeneity within the northern ranks may well have been accurate, since, according to some estimates, 40 percent of Union forces were foreign born. Yet the contemporary significance of the remarks does not stem from their accuracy. In essence, Russell's description of the Federal army disconnected the North from Britishness and the positive connotations that most of his readers would associate with the term.[24]

Russell's position at the *Times* brought with it the necessary social and political prestige to secure meetings with a number of key Confederate politicians. In one such encounter—with the infamous South Carolina fire-eater Edmund Rhett—Russell was told that "there were few persons in South Carolina who would not sooner ask Great Britain to take back the State than submit to the triumph of the Yankees." Rhett then went on to explain to his new British acquaintance that southerners were "an agricultural people, pursuing our own system, and working out our destiny." Whether sincere or not, the claim echoed one made during the secession crisis by Edmund Rhett's relative Robert Barnwell Rhett. According to the historian Brian Schoen, Barnwell Rhett had suggested, "only half jesting," that South Carolina could become a free-trade protectorate of Britain if no other states joined her in seceding from the Union.[25] The purpose of the Rhetts' comments was probably to demonstrate the antipathy of southerners toward the Union, but that both men emphasized the apparent Anglophilia of the Confederacy is telling. Furthermore, by touching on the related issues of free trade and agriculture versus industry, they tapped into preexisting British ideas regarding sectionalism to present the South in a sympathetic light.

Also telling was Russell's description of Robert Toombs as "something of an Anglo-maniac, and an Anglo-phobist—a combination not unusual in America." Russell went on to clarify that Toombs "is proud of being connected and descended from respectable English families, and admires our mixed constitution, whilst he is an enemy to what is called English policy, and is a strong pro-slavery champion."[26] Toombs presents a neat personification of the different wartime pressures at work between Britain, the North, and the South. His views highlight the ideological differences that each party needed to negotiate if they wished to endorse another. For his part, Russell illustrated his perceptive abilities by latching on to the idea of the ethnically British and culturally Anglophile South, while also recognizing the inherent Anglophobia of American politics and the fundamental disconnect between proslavery and Britishness.

The example of Toombs provides an insight into a broader set of issues relating to British perceptions of American and Confederate nationalism. As late as the 1830s, Alexis de Tocqueville had highlighted the "political" nature of American national identity. In its simplest form this meant that to be an American entailed subscribing to a set of common political values. Over the next thirty years, however, the "enlightenment" model of the nation de Tocqueville evoked was eroded by a version of "Romantic" nationalism built on ideas of language, custom, race, and ethnicity. Many Americans imbibed these ideas from a combination of German Romantic philosophers and British intellectuals, such as Carlyle, Samuel Taylor Coleridge, and Sir Walter Scott. As a result, residents of both the northern and southern states increasingly began to see nationalism through this new lens. Although Romantic nationalism was a confused combination of race, culture, and nation, it took root in America and provided a vital foundation for the construction of Confederate identity during the Civil War. By drawing on existing tropes of southernness, citizens of the Confederacy were able to assert their national identity by highlighting their ethnic and cultural distinctiveness from the North. In doing so, they also asserted their status in terms compatible with prevailing European ideas about what constituted a nation. Thus, the image of an ethno-culturally British South (which Russell highlighted with reference to Toombs) became a way for the Confederacy to assert its nation status as distinct from the Union.[27]

Presenting Confederate identity in this way was significant in an Anglo-American context for a number of related reasons. The idea of a British

South brought with it an obvious ethno-cultural sympathy, while also resonating with British ideas regarding regional identity in the United States. As Russell's description of Toombs suggests, however, even if these developments justified the dissolving of the Union, they did not result in unqualified endorsements of the South. All of the ethno-cultural signifiers that led Russell to describe Toombs as an Anglophile could be offset by slavery. As I have already suggested, the relationship between the South and slavery was rarely seen in the sort of stark moral terms that some have implied. Nevertheless, the majority of Britons would have seen an endorsement of the institution as a positive good (rather than a mitigated evil) as morally unacceptable and antithetical to their national values. Russell's image of Toombs the Anglophobe was, therefore, grounded in the statesman's advocacy of slavery, just as his image of Toombs the Anglophile centered on ideas of ethnicity and culture.

Despite his avowed antislavery position and his lack of sympathy for secession, Russell's discussion of southern slavery illustrates the nuance that characterized British Civil War debates about the system. Russell frequently drew on older British ideas regarding the institution, and he located slavery within a recognizable prewar narrative centered on the paternal connection between slave and master. As if to illustrate this point, Russell highlighted his experiences on the Natchez plantation of former Louisiana governor Andre B. Roman: "Here were abundant evidences that they [the slaves] were well treated, for they had good clothing of its kind, good food, and a master who wittingly could do them no injustice." Such a depiction echoed the work of many antebellum British commentators and is particularly reminiscent of Emmeline Stuart-Wortley's description of Zachary Taylor's plantation a decade earlier.[28]

Russell found that any sense of a clear moral distinction between the Union and the Confederacy was broken down further when he visited the North. He recalled a conversation with a group of politicians in Washington during the buildup to the war. They were confident that in the event of a conflict, the British would reject any diplomatic overtures from the South because the northerners would be fighting "an active war of emancipation." Not only did most Britons fail to see the war in these terms but they also criticized the treatment of freedmen by northerners, which undermined Union claims to moral superiority. During his travels in the North, Russell found plenty of evidence that free blacks were not in an especially enviable position when compared to southern slaves. While traveling up the Mississippi, he noted that he did not "find that the free Negroes, who acted as attendants possessed any advantages over their enslaved brethren a few miles lower down the river." Conversely, although critical of the conditions endured by some slaves, Russell noted the benevolent treatment he saw on a number of plantations, including those of the aforementioned Governor Roman and a planter named Mrs. Trescot. From his experience as a whole, Russell contended that "such kindly acts as [he had seen on these plantations] are more common than we may suppose; and it would be unfair to put a strict or unfair construction on the motives of slave owners in paying so much attention to their property."[29] The emphasis on the paternalistic, reciprocal connection between slave and master in these descriptions was rooted in the prewar tradition of seeing southern slavery as mitigated. Descriptions of this type, combined with an awareness of the high levels of discrimination that blacks suffered in the northern states and the lack of legal action against slavery on the part of the Lincoln government, allowed even Britons who rejected slavery in the abstract to justify remaining distant from the Union cause. Rather than seeing the war as a stark moral choice between freedom and slavery, they identified a complex set of attitudes toward these issues in the sections. These attitudes were, in turn, integrated into a broader understanding of political, economic, and ethnic divisions.

The consistently controversial issue of American politics was among the most significant of these additional factors. As with popular discussions of slavery and ethnicity, the reasons why an understanding of the US political system sat at the heart of the British response to the Civil War can best be understood with reference to the antebellum period. Unlike slavery and ethnicity, however, the antebellum relationship between sectionalism and politics had often been ambiguous. Britons had been familiar with the idea that the North and South might have distinct policy priorities since at least the nullification crisis. Furthermore, British engagement with nullification had fostered an awareness of the importance of states' rights to US politics. At the same time, however, the image of a coherent and national US political culture with an emphasis on the mob, political party, and press bombast had proved to be remarkably durable in Britain. Nevertheless, mainstream British commentators during the later years of the antebellum period were increasingly associating the worst excesses of these aspects of US political culture with the North (specifically New York). Unsurprisingly, when they discussed the conflict, anti-Union Civil War writers often drew on both the long established notion of sectional policy divisions, as well as the more recent idea that the North and South had distinct political cultures.

Commenting on the nation as whole, Russell wrote to his editor at the *Times* (J. T. Delane) that universal suffrage had "frightened moral courage." Interestingly, however, Russell saw evidence of differing sectional attitudes toward democracy and noted in his diary a conversation with a group of men in Charleston who had expressed open admiration for "monarchical institutions on the English model." This idea that prominent citizens of the Confederacy were sympathetic to monarchical government and a landed aristocracy tapped into to a preexisting British vision of the anti-democratic South. This view had been encapsulated by a detailed *Blackwood's Magazine* commentary from April 1846 that examined the institutions and society of Virginia.[30] In a Civil War context, Russell's interlocutors implied that these divisions had increased over time and that southerners were now so disillusioned with the US political system that they were prepared to reject Republicanism entirely to guarantee social stability and undermine the power of the mob.

Although Russell's descriptions of the United States appear anti-northern on the surface, it is worth recalling that, as far as Henry Adams (son of Charles Francis) was concerned, Russell favored the Union during the Civil War. Adams's comments on Russell are indicative of complexities of contemporary sectional debate in Britain. Russell appreciated America's extensive sectional divisions and the various factors that needed to be taken into account for the British to respond to the conflict in an informed manner. Even though he sympathized with the North broadly, he did not reduce the war to simplified categories, which would have allowed him to actively preach the cause of the Union in the manner of John Bright. Furthermore, it is crucial to recognize that neither Russell nor the majority of his readers would have had any sympathy with many of the views expressed by proslavery fire-eaters like Edmund Rhett. Yet prior to 1863 the relatively complex image of sectional relations that Russell conveyed to his readers ensured that the terms on which the war was debated transcended slavery. Interestingly then, and despite the fact that he was not a Union propagandist, Russell's output provided a valuable alternative to the work of the pro-Confederate businessman and political conservative James Spence, whose *The American Union; its effect on National Character and Policy, with an Enquiry into Secession as a Constitutional Right, and the Causes of the Disruption* was published in September 1861.[31]

Before moving on to considering Spence's work in depth, it is worth being explicit about the intellectual climate in which it was produced. As this chapter has demonstrated, there was considerable ambiguity in Britain about what the Union government was actually fighting for. Aware of the almost unanimous British antipathy toward slavery, some contended that northerners were motivated by a desire to abolish the system across the United States. Yet a lack of meaningful action against slavery by the Lincoln government ensured that the British public remained somewhat cynical about such claims. As a result there was something akin to a moral vacuum at the heart of the war from a British point of view. By shying away from endorsing slavery as fundamentally good, southerners were able to exploit the lack of action against the system on the part of the Union to suggest that secession could be explained and justified with reference to prewar British ideas of sectionalism relating to politics and ethno-cultural identity. This approach, however, was entirely reliant on continued Union inaction against slavery and would prove inadequate after the Emancipation Proclamation. Nevertheless, popular pre-1863, pro-Confederate propaganda relied on this formula, and no writer offered a more comprehensive version of it than Spence.

Spence's *American Union* met with considerable success and went through four editions in less than a year. It also caused consternation among pro-Federals, not only as a result of its popularity but also because of the apparent viability of Spence's argument. Crucially for our purposes, the pamphlet provides one of the most comprehensive illustrations of the image that British pro-Confederates wanted to project. Spence's sophisticated analysis combined arguments drawing on his antebellum knowledge of sectionalism in the British mind while sectionalizing many aspects of the United States. In taking this course, Spence echoed Russell by presenting the Union as an extreme democracy, dominated by the mob and a rabid press. Significantly, this view was consistent with the tropes deployed by commentators before the war. Spence did not claim that the Union had been flawed from its inception; rather, he emphasized the instability that had come to dominate the Union as the nation grew. This territorial growth meant that, among the people, "the only connecting link is a common desire for the success of the party," and this imperative for party gain was what underpinned secession. Spence also claimed that the territorial growth of the Union had exacerbated the economic differences between the sections, meaning that "the common view in the Southern States, is, that the South has been used as a tributary, drained for the benefit of the North." For Spence, the consequences of the changes in the United States were that "to the Southern, the Union appears an artificial arrangement, wise at the time of its formation—rendered injurious now by the progress of events." This emphasis on the different interests of the sections, and the political debates stemming from them, built on a basic narrative of American sectional tensions that reached back at least as far as the nullification crisis. In his work Spence focused on these divisions in order to explain and justify the secession of the South.[32]

Spence's pamphlet also raised a number of constitutional points that echoed the commentary of earlier writers who had envisaged the dissolution of the Union. A certain irony exists here, since the arguments Spence deployed to convince his readers of the legality of secession were reminiscent of those utilized by prewar abolitionist travelers, such as Martineau and Sturge, who had emphasized the power of state over national governments. Despite being used for very different purposes, the similarity of the states' rights argument as used by Spence and these abolitionists is indicative of a British familiarity with the doctrine. Spence also liberally sprinkled his pamphlet with examples and quotations drawn from American history in order to illustrate the legitimacy of the southern cause. In a brief history of the nation, he discussed the attempts by the state of Massachusetts to secede, as well as a conversation between James Madison and Patrick Henry during which the former demonstrated that the phrase "we, the people" referred not to one social body but to "the people as composing thirteen sovereignties."[33] For Spence then, the southern cause was not simply defensible because of the significant differences between the sections—it was also constitutional.

This same argument over the legal status of secession featured in the work of the *Quarterly Review* journalist William Forsyth, who posited that, since the states predated the Union, they must possess the right to withdraw from it. The reasons that led Spence, and to some extent Forsyth, to conclude that secession was legal were essentially the same given by Sturge in 1841 when he attempted to explain why the national government could not abolish slavery: "As each of the original States acceded to the Constitution by an act of convention, and this forms the only bond of union, it follows that each of those States, as a sovereign community, has, according to the principles of America, the inherent right to appeal that act."[34] In the view adopted by Sturge, Spence, and Forsyth, the American Union itself was a pragmatic solution to a specific problem, rather than a compact of national foundation. The states held sovereign status and logically, therefore, had the right to withdraw from the Union when it failed to fulfill their needs. By extension, any attempt to prevent secession was unconstitutional.

Spence extended the underlying premise that the Lincoln administration was usurping powers it did not legally possess into a broader analysis of the emerging "despotism" of the Union government. He noted how "the writ of habeas corpus is treated with contempt, whilst the police forbid petitions to the Government, in violation of the express right of the constitution." Spence concluded, "There is ample evidence that, whatever may have been the love of liberty in other days, it has become a thing of the past." He then proceeded to connect the concepts of democracy and despotism by rhetorically asking his readers, "What, indeed, is really the basis of extreme democracy, except brute force?"[35] In his analysis of despotism and democracy, Spence was essentially invoking long-standing British concerns about democratic governance in general and US politics in particular but with a focus on current Union policy. The intention was clear enough—to present the North in as damaging a light as possible.

These critiques of democracy in the context of US sectional relations were not solely the preserve of the pro-Confederate lobby. Rather, they were part of the broader public discourse regarding sectionalism and the Civil War. Given the intermittent public focus on the role of the US political system in the conflict, it is probably unsurprising that Russell characterized the doctrine of states' rights as a reaction to the development of democracy in the North. He suggested that the idea had been part of an attempt by southerners to resist "the blasts of universal suffrage." Much as Spence had done, Russell also cautioned readers that "republics in crisis have always had a recourse to dictators," a warning with reference to the Lincoln administration.[36] Through these examples we see figures from various political positions offering an analysis of American politics and exploring the connections between democratic political culture and secession. The precise relationship that individuals saw between these features was often ambiguous (and in some cases downright illogical); nevertheless, almost all commentators were united by an antipathy to democracy. Furthermore, this antipathy tended to be expressed in terms consistent with the prewar critiques of US politics offered by Marryat, Amelia Murray, and George Combe.

The temptation here is to move toward an interpretation of the British response to the Civil War as dictated by politics or class, with an emphasis on conservative sympathy for the aristocratic South and reformist/radical support for the democratic North. In some sense the distinction has validity. It is certainly true that prior to the conflict many reformers across Europe had looked to the United States as a progressive model. It is equally true that some prominent conservative politicians, including the Earl of Shrewsbury and Sir John Pakington, interpreted the outbreak of the war as evidence that democracy was not a viable political system, while reformers such as Bright tied the success of liberalism on the global stage to the victory of the Union. Yet the situation was more complex than these examples might suggest. Before the Civil War, both mainstream liberals and radical reformers had intermittently identified US democracy with the North, which made the relationship between the northern states and liberalism somewhat viable. At the same time, however, they had not always endorsed US democracy wholeheartedly. As a result, the positive connotations that figures like Bright believed a connection between the Union and democracy would convey were not always in evidence, even for the most committed British reformers.[37]

In a sense, Bright's refusal to temper his unrelentingly positive portrayal of the Union undermined his public appeals for support during the early stages of the war. Spence could certainly not be accused of a similar tactical error and was prepared to concede that the South had made mistakes, if he believed such a stance would increase the appeal of the Confederacy. This willingness to concede was especially clear in his discussion of the Anglophile nature of the South and the ethno-cultural relationship between Britain and the section. Spence was acutely aware of the need to lay claim to the prewar image of the Anglophile South, yet he decided to discuss the historical tensions between the North, the South, and Britain during the Revolutionary era. Spence conceded that "all of them alike—Puritan of Massachusetts, Cavalier of Virginia and Friend of Pennsylvania" had their roots in Britain. Subsequent events had, however, undermined both their shared identity and ability to coexist in the United States. Spence informed his readers that the North, more so than the South, had been the destination for immigrants and that New York was "not really American. Its population is largely composed of foreigners of all nations, whose manners and sentiments are essentially foreign to American soil." Crucially, in the context of the conflict, Spence tied the Union's cause explicitly to that of New York (rather than Boston or New England): "Unfortunately, perhaps, for the liberties of the country, the Union has now a Paris. Whoever had studied [the] progress of the momentous events now occurring, will have seen, that the Washington government simply follows the impulse of the people; indeed, that in obedience to this impulse, it reversed the policy it had wisely adopted. But the people of the North, in their turn, implicitly follow the lead of New York."[38] In this context, New York was an invaluable point of reference for pro-Confederates in Britain. Boston had an undeniable British heritage, but the literature of the prewar period had reinforced the image of New York as an alien city. Consequently, if the cause of the Union was the cause of New York rather than New England, it was less "British."

The tropes of the Cavalier and Puritan, which Spence utilized, also appeared in mainstream media in discussions of the war. Lord Wolseley, for instance, informed readers of *Blackwood's* that southerners were "the descendants of our banished cavaliers," while northerners were "descended from the offscourings of every European nation." Similarly, Thackeray expressed sympathy toward southerners, while criticizing the "Dutch traders of New York and the money-getting Roundheads of Pennsylvania and New England." Given the terminology he had used to describe Virginia and New York in his 1859 novel *The Virginians,* Thackeray's decision to filter the war through the lens of ethno-cultural identity seems natural enough. Yet, as the examples of Spence and Wolseley demonstrate, such a view of the conflict was not uncommon.[39] Furthermore, appeals to Cavalier mythology and ethno-cultural sectionalism credited the South with a distinctive national identity that could accompany claims to political self-determination. By combining the political and ethno-cultural, the case could be made for Confederate nationhood in terms of enlightenment politics and the Romantic nationalism that had proved so effective in mobilizing British public support for Italy, Poland, and Hungary.

When it came to the thorny issue of slavery, Spence drew once more on ideas with well-established historical roots in his attempt to make the Confederate cause as appealing as possible to the British. He maintained a theoretical abhorrence of the system, acknowledging its debasing effects on the slaves themselves and conceding the existence of instances of cruelty by specific masters. For Spence, slavery resulted in "an absolute injury sustained by the whole white community, apparent to any observer." While whites lost out, however, the seriousness with which slaveholders took their paternalistic responsibilities meant that the condition of the slaves was never as bad as might be assumed.[40] Spence's position here echoed that of numerous prewar travelers, such as Buckingham, Stuart-Wortley, Charles Lyell, and Charlotte Houstoun, who had all emphasized the mitigated nature of southern slavery.

Along with affirming the existence of a paternalist connection, Spence integrated a range of arguments rooted in the idea of racially defined labor relations to justify southern slavery. In basic economic terms, he noted that it was in the interests of the planters to treat their slaves well and contended that "the negroes have at all times abundant food; the sufferings of fireless winters are unknown to them; medical attendance is always at command; in old age they fear no workhouse; their children are never a burden or a care; their labour, though long, is neither difficult, nor unhealthy. As a rule, they have their own good ground, and fowls and vegetables, of which they frequently sell their surplus. So far then, as merely animal comforts extend, their lot is more free from suffering than those of many classes of European labour."[41]

The notion of "European labour" would have struck a particular chord among certain members of the British labor movement who had criticized the government's decision to free slaves while white workers existed in a "state of deplorable poverty and degradation." The critique of "wage slavery," which often appeared in the works of these labor activists, had its roots in the debate over West Indian emancipation and was invoked by key figures such as Joseph Rayner Stephens, Bronterre O'Brien, and Robert Owen. For a number of prominent working-class political activists of the Civil War era (including William Aitken and T. J. Dunning), the idea of "wage slavery" intersected with a sense of cynicism about the role of abolition in the war leading to antipathy for the Union.[42] The cogent point here is that even if abolitionist sentiment was strong in Britain, it was for abolition of slavery in an abstract sense, as opposed to a commitment to interfere with slavery on the global stage regardless of the domestic or international context.

The distinction between abstract slavery and southern slavery was vital to the work of British pro-Confederates. The prewar British language of

American ethnic and political division offered a potentially powerful vocabulary for those who favored the Confederacy, yet slavery represented a moral Rubicon. To publically endorse slavery as desirable in the South would have been enough to alienate all but a few British extremists. By consistently distinguishing between a positive endorsement of slavery and a preparedness to accept the system in the short term, it was possible to prevent a massive public movement developing in favor of the Union. Furthermore, it seems that many British pro-Confederates not only publically discussed slavery in these terms but sincerely believed in the distinction between southern and abstract slavery. The MP William Gregory, for example, had corresponded with key secessionists in the years leading up to the war. In 1860, Gregory wrote to the South Carolina politician (and subsequent secessionist) William Porcher Miles that "abstractly, of course, all we Englishmen are opposed to slavery." Gregory, however, recognized a level of disillusion with immediate emancipation in Britain that he believed stemmed from the nation's experience in the West Indies.[43] When the British discourse of mitigated southern slavery is considered in tandem with the limited rejection of the institution in practice, the potential for slavery to be obscured in the public debate before 1863 becomes clear. Pro-Confederates in Britain, such as Spence, attempted to exploit the lack of clarity on abolition by drawing on the prewar period to offer alternative explanations for southern sectionalism. While not wholly successfully, the tactic certainly influenced popular responses to the war and contributed to the widespread anti-Unionism that characterized British reactions—even if pro-southern activists were not always able to translate this into explicit support for the Confederacy.

While Spence provided various excuses to his readers for the continued use of slavery in the southern states, he also attacked the implausibility of abolition as the principal cause of war on the part of the North. In the first place, he rejected the idea that there had been a morally motivated popular campaign in favor of the abolition in the northern states at the turn of the nineteenth century. Instead, he suggested that the decision to end slavery there had been based on economic pragmatism. In the context of the Civil War, Spence drew his readers' attention to an address in which Lincoln stated that the Union would not interfere with slavery, as well as an amendment to the same effect passed by Congress.[44] Spence's intention here was simple. In historical terms he wished to disassociate the northern states from the "moral" abolitionism so significant to British identity. In doing so, his work echoed the criticisms of American abolitionism offered by prewar commentators. Spence then extended his analysis to the Civil War itself in order to undermine claims that the Union government had resisted secession in order to abolish slavery across the United States. In emphasizing the lack of historical and contemporary abolitionist sentiment in the North, Spence attempted to combat the claims of early Union propagandists who presented the war as a contest between slavery and freedom.

Given the intellectual climate of the period, it should come as no surprise that prominent figures echoed Spence's cynicism regarding northerners' commitment to end slavery. Within government itself, Lord Palmerston responded to the American historian John Motley's assertion that the Union was fighting slavery by asking northerners to prove it "by joining us in our operations against the slave trade." Palmerston was evidently as doubtful as Spence about the connection between the Union and abolition. Key to Spence's stance on this issue was a belief that slavery represented a political rather than a moral cause in America. He pointed to the Missouri Compromise of 1820, which he saw as evidence that the South did not wish to extend slavery for the purposes of utilizing it as a labor system (something he believed was not viable in the case of New Mexico) but rather wanted to maintain a balance between slave and free states in national politics. Spence was engaging directly with the slave-power argument that had been broached in Britain before the conflict, but he was attempting to subvert it. In fact, Spence used this politicization of slavery as an explanation for the active defense of the system offered by some southerners. As he saw it, "Originally, slavery was on the defensive, admitted to be an evil, deplored as a sad necessity; but stung by the language of the North, the Southerners have turned round upon them, and have wrought themselves into the monstrous belief, now prevalent throughout the South, that slavery is actually a blessing." Consequently, the politicization of slavery and its integration into southern identity was not based on a genuine belief in its moral acceptability, but was a reaction against the North and its political agenda.[45]

The nuanced analysis of the Civil War that James Spence presented to readers of the *American Union* meant that his work resonated with the editorial material of mainstream newspapers, as well as the speeches of politicians on both sides of the Atlantic. It was precisely this nuance that accounts for the relative success of Spence's work and the consternation it caused among the pro-Union lobby. In essence, by placing an emphasis on the complex nature of sectional relations, Spence offered readers the option to reject the Union without embracing the cause of slavery. The efficacy of this approach, however, rested on the Lincoln government's continued inaction against the slave system. The stark moral choice that emancipation would later offer the British population reduced the power of Spence's argument and compelled pro-Confederates to engage in a propaganda war that would be fought on firm Union ground.

The place of slavery in US politics was a subject of particular interest to Hugo Reid, a Scottish educationalist who published *Sketches in North America, with some Account of Congress and of the Slavery Question* while employed at Dalhousie College in Nova Scotia. Despite reassuring his readers that he personally abhorred slavery, Reid noted that the system was "recognized and supported by the constitution of the United States, and by repeated Acts of Congress." He claimed these acts asserted that "each State is regarded as sovereign in respect of its own domestic institutions." When it came to the political tensions between the sections, Reid maintained, "the States of the North are in great part responsible for the present condition of this unhappy conflict and the bad feeling between the North and South." Their culpability stemmed from a variety of factors, including "Personal Liberty Acts, calculated (though, ostensibly for defence of their own citizens) to impede or prevent the capture of fugitive slaves." According to Reid, these legislative acts were "at variance with the constitutional compact between them and the slave States, as well as with various deliberate acts of Congress."[46] In essence, Reid maintained that the division of the Union was as much the result of the refusal of the northern states to honor the Constitution as it was a moral contest over the future of slavery.

As Reid saw it, the consequence of this legal wrangling was that "when pressed hard by the doctrines of the Abolitionists," proslavery Americans had "boldly advanced to higher ground, and maintained that slavery is right, founded on justice, reason, and humanity, supported by Scripture, and in reality a beneficent institution, advantageous to the Negro." In Reid's account then, the shift to a "positive good" interpretation of slavery in the South was a political reaction to northern pressure. Reid also noted how, as the political balance tilted in favor of the North, the South "drew from the Constitution the doctrine of Popular Sovereignty in the Territories, and used it to overthrow the Missouri Compromise, and bring the whole of the

Territories within their reach." As far as he was concerned, this should have encouraged northern secession: "When the free States came to loathe the odious task assigned to them of delivering up runaway slaves, and desired that the curse of slavery should not be admitted into new regions, which they were able to people with free men, and in which they judged it right that only free institutions should be implanted, their course was clear: they should have given notice of their determination to withdraw from a Union which imposed an odious thralldom upon them." As it was, this course was not followed, and as a result "the slave-owners of the South have been maddened by the wild and incendiary proceedings of the Northern Abolitionists." Given this state of affairs, Reid maintained that Britons should not "be surprised that the South hated the North with a fierce hatred that has never been surpassed, or that the Southern States desire to secede and save themselves from the tyranny of an arrogant and insulting Northern majority."[47] By suggesting that both slavery and abolition were primarily political as opposed to moral issues in the United States, Reid (and Spence before him) attempted to further undermine the image of a moral division between North and South. Both men contended that if abolition motivated the North (something they personally doubted), it was not the selfless form that had driven the British during the 1830s. Instead, abolitionists in the Union were political pragmatists who used antislavery to mask their intentions.

The rejection of a simple moral division between the sections was combined with a discussion of the treatment of free blacks in the North. To make this point, Reid drew his audience's attention to a New York newspaper that had told readers, "So far from believing negro slavery a curse, we regard it as a great blessing in the tropical climates, and in the Southern States of our republic—a blessing to the slave, to the master, and to this Union." In addition, Reid focused on the views of the New York politician John Cochrane, who had apparently claimed, "I sympathize, sir, deeply sympathize with our friends of the South" and had censured "that which has occurred and is occurring all over the North, endangering the peace of the Union, and teaching rebellion to its constitution." Reid offered his own view on the situation, noting that even outside of the slave states, "blacks are despised and shunned" and that "in the cities in the northern United States separate omnibuses are provided for 'coloured persons.'"[48] For Reid, as for many prewar commentators, the position of black Americans varied little between the sections in practice, whatever the legal distinction between slavery and freedom. In essence, Reid believed that the debate over slavery in a sectional context had molded these men and women into pawns on the political chessboard and that the abolition debate during the Civil War was little more than an extension of this phenomenon.

Of additional significance in Reid's case, and following the prewar geography of the nation established by commentators, were the ethnic and cultural differences between areas of the United States. Reid maintained that "the Americans cannot be spoken of now as one race; climate, and institutions are developing at least two sections, nearly as distinct as British and French, or English and Irish—the North and the South." These divisions in turn had a relationship to European ethnicity and culture, since "the Southerners seem, in other respects, to have deviated least from the type of their ancestors, having the quiet and composed bearing of the English."[49] Here Reid invoked a distinctive ethnic geography for the United States that presented the South as an embodiment of a form of Britishness and the North as an ethno-cultural other.

Overall, the opening months of the war can best be seen as a period in which supporters of both sides and neutrals staked out their positions on the causes and likely consequences of the conflict. A particularly striking feature of these early months was the extent to which the terms of the debate seemed to undermine the cause of the Union. This is not to say that a massive groundswell of pro-Confederate activism occurred. Rather, it is simply to recognize that commentators (and the public) were viewing the war through a prewar lens that appeared to lend itself to an anti-Union stance. As previous chapters have highlighted, this lens magnified the political, cultural, social, and ethnic differences between the sections, while simultaneously minimizing the moral division between them. The existence of this complex discourse, in tandem with the failure of the Union government to announce abolition as a war aim, proved enough to lead many Britons to question Lincoln's justification for going to war. It should also be noted that at this early stage of the conflict the debate tended to occur in relatively abstract terms, since Britain had little diplomatic or direct political involvement in the war. This situation changed at the end of 1861, however, as events conspired to alter the nature of British engagements with both belligerents.

CHAPTER FIVE

"DAM YOU BOTH!"

Britain and the American Civil War, 1862

The worst fears of the British public regarding the "aggressive, irrational and rabidly Anglophobic" Union seemed to be confirmed on 8 November 1861 when Captain Charles Wilkes of the USS *San Jacinto* boarded the HMS *Trent* and forcibly removed two Confederate statesmen. Wilkes's decision to board the British vessel and capture the newly appointed Confederate commissioners John Slidell and James M. Mason sparked intense debate on both sides of the Atlantic about the legal rights of seizure and whether British sovereignty had been breached. When news of the *Trent* affair reached London, it caused consternation for many. Benjamin Moran, for example, noted gloomily in his diary that it would "do more for the Southerners than ten victories." Though the British government had no stomach for a war against the Union, it was a genuine possibility at this juncture, and, for only the fourth time in history, the cabinet established a war committee in response to the seizure. In the end, Lincoln's government backed down and released Mason and Slidell, notifying Palmerston's administration of the fact on 8 January 1862 but doing so without a formal apology in an attempt to save face.[1]

This final chapter focuses on the period between the *Trent* affair and the official implementation of emancipation by the Union government on 1 January 1863. It considers the seizure of HMS *Trent,* as well as the aftermath of the event, and examines how this major diplomatic development was understood in Britain. The particular focus here is on the extent to which responses to the *Trent* drew on antebellum British ideas about mob democracy and the urban North. By examining key texts produced by propagandists and popular commentators during the latter half of 1862, the chapter highlights the extent to which figures from across the political spectrum continued to engage with the war through antebellum ideas about US sectionalism. It then concludes with an analysis of the British response to the Emancipation Proclamation, with a focus on how this shift in Union policy not only altered popular opinion on the war but also undermined the ideas of sectionalism that had been developing in Britain since the 1830s.

British popular reaction to the conduct of the Union during the *Trent* affair was overwhelmingly negative, and responses to the event drew heavily on previous British commentary about the Anglophobic United States. The crucial difference was that this rhetoric was now transferred to an explicitly northern context, whereas previously there had been scope for debate about the importance of Anglophobia to each section. The seizure itself "had done incalculable damage to the British public's view of the United States," and the press reacted immediately and with indignation. A piece in the *Birmingham Daily Post,* for example, quoted a report that described Wilkes's actions as "piratical," while the *Morning Post* conjectured that "the British Government will clearly be entitled to reparation and apology." An "indignation" meeting was even held in Liverpool as a response to the seizure, while on 12 December the traditionally abolitionist Adelphi Theatre in London replaced the stars and stripes that usually hung outside with a Confederate flag.[2]

The belief that northerners were publicly praising Wilkes was widespread in Britain, and critiques of the Union in the mainstream press became more aggressive as a result. The *London Times* in particular took a more coherently anti-Union editorial line after the *Trent* incident—a line it continued to pursue through to the end of the war. In a letter printed in the paper on 3 December 1861, William Howard Russell reported the popularity of Wilkes's actions in almost all quarters of the northern states. He then raised the specter of Charles Dickens's unscrupulous newspaperman from *Martin Chuzzlewit* in his observation about "a writer, an officer of the Congress, who this morning invites all the Monarchs of Europe generally to come on if they like and join the South, in the Jefferson Brick style." Even members of the government bristled at the attack on national sovereignty implied by the *Trent* case. Prime Minister Palmerston observed with anger that Britain should "read a lesson to the United States which will not soon be forgotten."[3]

The *Trent* was an unmitigated disaster for the pro-Union cause in Britain. Even so, one of the leading names involved in the campaign, John Bright, took to a stage in Rochdale on 4 December 1861 and attempted to save face for the North. Bright began his oration by outlining the issues at stake in the war from an explicitly pro-Union perspective—something that is just as enlightening about the significance of the prewar period as southern propaganda. On the issue of slavery, he tackled the claim that the North lacked abolitionist credentials and maintained that "the conscience of the North [had never been] satisfied with the institution." It had been unable to take action, however, since "if we look at the government of the United States . . . [since the formation of the Union] we shall find the Southern power has been mostly dominant." Bright similarly attempted to tackle the tariff problem from a pro-Federal position and to downplay the significance of free trade in the war by claiming "that no American, certainly no one I ever met with, attributed the disasters of the Union to that cause [the tariff]." He also noted that "whatever might be the influence of the tariff upon the United States, it is as pernicious to the West as it is to the South." After laying this groundwork, Bright then went on to criticize those defending the South based on its antipathy to protectionist economics, claiming that anyone who "contends that [the cause of the war] is the tariff, or anything whatsoever else than slavery, is either himself deceived or endeavors to deceive others."[4]

On the topic of the *Trent* specifically, Bright essentially rejected the interpretation of the Crown law officers (that Wilkes's actions were illegal), while conceding that, whether legal or not, the seizure "was both impolitic and bad." In some ways, however, the minutia of the case was of limited concern to Bright. Instead, his interests lay in the treatment of the *Trent* in the British press. Bright was particularly critical of the *London Times* and suggested that the newspaper's editorial stance was part of an attempt to persuade "people that this is merely one of a series of acts which denote the determination of the Washington government to pick a quarrel with the people of England." Bright certainly had a legitimate grievance here. Not only did Delane and his writers increasingly attempt to "sectionalize" American Anglophobia during this period, but they also spent time looking back at the history of Anglo-American relations and frequently implied that the tensions between the nations could be traced to northern policies. While the eventual release of Mason and Slidell reduced the levels of vitriol on both sides, the *Trent* affair had demonstrated the combustibility of British involvement with the Civil War.[5] From the perspective of an analysis of sectionalism, the real significance of Bright's rhetoric was the extent to which it demonstrated an engagement with the key tropes of the prewar era as they were integrated into British discourse on the conflict. Bright emphasized the historical abolitionist sentiments of the northern states and the Anglophilia of the Washington government, while rejecting the role of the tariff in the conflict—utilizing language similar to that of his adversaries but with a very different aim.

The press reaction to Bright's Rochdale speech is illustrative of the controversial nature of his interpretation of the war. The *London Times* described him as a "devil's advocate" before dismantling his view of the *Trent* affair and dismissing his ability to influence policy. As part of its critique of Bright, the *Times* trumpeted its own neutrality, even though the newspaper invoked obviously sectional tropes that emphasized the difference between North and South. The stance of the *Times* here is indicative of a more general trend in British reactions to the American Civil War. There is no doubt that Delane and his writers were anti-Union, but to describe the newspaper as pro-southern is not an accurate reflection of its stance. Certainly, many articles focused on the divisions between North and South, but this was as much a reflection of orthodox ideas that had developed during the prewar period as a concerted effort to justify secession. The result of this editorial line was an implied sympathy for the Confederacy, yet the paper was not pro-southern in the sense that someone like James Spence was. In fact, the *Times*'s broad anti-Unionism and acceptance of sectional divisions can probably be taken as indicative of British opinion in the period more broadly.[6]

The *Blackburn Standard* was similarly critical of Bright, stating in its 11 December 1861 edition that "John Bright is against England and in favour of the Federalists of America" before declaring that, "Mr. Bright, in the face of nearly the universal opinion of this country, of perhaps all Europe, and of many of his own friends, contends that the North is fighting against slavery in the South." The same editorial also played up the image of the South as being adversely affected by its connection to the Union, claiming that "England never attempted to tax the United States half so much as the North have taxed the South over and above her due share for the purposes of the Union." Similarly, *Punch* published a satirical poem entitled "John Bright," which mocked his views on the *Trent* and the American conflict generally. It described him as an unhesitant apologist for the actions of the Union, criticized his hypocritical neutrality, and suggested that if he failed to recognize international law, then he might recognize "the two Yankee laws, Mob and Might."[7] The mention of the mob in this *Punch* piece demands particular attention. As Chapter 3 demonstrated, the democratic political culture of the United States was one of the most frequently criticized characteristics of the nation in antebellum British discourse. The use of this phrase in *Punch* suggests an intimate connection between the North and the mob. Taken as a whole, the vehemence and relative coherence of these responses to Bright are indicative of the lack of uncritical support for the Union within Britain, as well as evidence of the sophisticated understanding that many literate Britons had of US sectionalism.

The pro-Confederate MP, businessman, journalist, and Southern Independence Association (SIA) member, A. J. B. Beresford-Hope evinced a similar awareness of these complex sectional issues in his 1862 pamphlet *England, the North and the South.* Beresford-Hope's text drew on prewar tropes in much the same way that Spence's work had and provided a similar assessment of the conflict. When discussing slavery, Beresford-Hope explained that the division between slave and free states had come about as a result of the economic impracticability of slaveholding in the North, thereby rejecting a connection between moral abolitionism and the Union. He also noted that, even after the abolition of slavery, the merchants and bankers of New York and Boston had continued to fund the slave trade and to mortgage plantations worked by slave labor.[8]

The belief that northerners were politically and economically implicated in the slave system provided another useful way for pro-Confederates and anti-Unionists to undermine claims that the Civil War was a moral contest with the ultimate aim of compelling the South to abolish slavery. Crucially, these claims regarding the economic and political involvement of the northerners in the slave system had enough grounding in reality and prewar British discourse to be viable to members of the public. The merchant classes of New York were heavily involved in the international cotton trade, which itself was enmeshed with slave labor in the South. Furthermore, there was a long-standing awareness in Britain that northern voters had frequently acquiesced in measures that had allowed the expansion of slavery. Such themes were significant enough to be taken up in diplomatic discussions, with Lord Lyons criticizing both the profits made by New Yorkers from the slave trade and President James Buchanan's decision to appoint a government official who had previously allowed slave traders to operate out of the same city.[9]

As part of his discussion of slavery, Beresford-Hope attempted to connect the apparent lack of northern abolitionist sentiment before the war with the actions of the Union government. He noted, for example, how President Lincoln had countermanded Gen. John C. Fremont's order for immediate emancipation in Missouri in 1861. Beresford-Hope also drew on an important prewar tradition that contended that whites in the North expressed more active aversion to free blacks than white southerners did toward slaves. He noted that "in the free States the negro is treated with unchristian cruelty, excluded from the same church, from the same table, from the same railway carriage, from the same altar of god." By contrast, he maintained that "in the South, no doubt, the slave is held as a chattel, but he is well treated; in social matters he is regarded as a fellow creature; he kneels at the same altar as the white man, and travels in the same train." These sentiments echoed those found in travel narratives written by figures like Frances Trollope and are particularly reminiscent of Edward Sullivan's remark that "he [the black American] is treated equally as a dog in both [sections] . . . with this difference, that in the south he is sometimes a pet dog, whereas in the north his is always a cur, kicked and hooted on every occasion."[10] Beresford-Hope's pamphlet presented slavery and abolition in a manner consistent with much of the prewar literature examined in Chapter 1. This literature had eschewed strict differentiation between the free and slave states, favoring a more nuanced version of sectionalism that rejected the connection between the North and abolition, while also asserting that the condition of free blacks above the Mason-Dixon Line was worse than that of enslaved southerners. By presenting the system in this way, propagandists such as Beresford-Hope attempted to reinforce the idea that chattel slavery existed in a mitigated form in the South.

The claim that the condition of slaves in the section was relatively congenial and the related belief that southerners did not consider slavery as a "positive good" were both crucial to the efficacy of British pro-southern propaganda. Those who most competently advocated the South in Britain understood that a public endorsement of slavery as an abstract concept would have elicited an immediate backlash against the Confederacy. They realized that the institution needed to be presented as a short-term evil that southerners accepted and attempted to make as palatable as possible until abolition could be safely achieved. A number of southerners, however, failed to register the necessity of using this idea as foundational when interacting with Britons. In one notorious incident, Robert Barnwell Rhett informed the British consul in Charleston, Robert Bunch, that the Confederacy wished to reopen the international slave trade at some point. Lord Lyons noted that such a move would be entirely unacceptable even for those in British society who had little or no sympathy with abolitionism.[11]

Given the levels of British antipathy toward the international slave trade, it is probably unsurprising that the most prominent southern journalist working in Britain, Henry Hotze, was keen to distance the Confederate cause from a desire to reopen the slave trade. The Swiss-Alabamian Hotze had arrived at the beginning of 1862 and had immediately begun to have letters published in the *London Post*, the *Standard*, and the *London Herald* before eventually establishing a pro-Confederate newspaper (the *Index*) in April of that year. Hotze's intention with this weekly publication was to offer readers a "worthy representative in journalism of the highest ideal of the Southern civilization which is as yet only in its infancy." While the *Index* never exceeded sales of 2,250 copies per week, it was not a pointless endeavor. Hotze had not designed the paper to reach a mass readership; instead, he wanted to influence those "by whom public opinion is formed." It was presumably these same opinion makers whom Hotze wanted to reach when he produced an article rejecting the *Daily News* claim that southerners favored reopening the Atlantic slave trade.[12]

The necessity of refuting the accusations that Confederate statesmen such as William Yancey wished to reopen the international slave trade stemmed from Hotze's understanding of the British relationship with American slavery. The idea that a paternalistic connection existed between the southern slaveholder and the slave had been a feature of prewar literature and underpinned pro-Confederate discourse in Britain. Nevertheless, both before and during the war, the majority of Britons still advocated abolition as a long-term goal and identified paternalistic care as nothing more than a short-term method by which slavery could be made more palatable. The reopening of the slave trade appeared to imply a "positive good" view of the institution in the South, since it was interpreted as a way to extend the life of the system. For this reason, and to appeal effectively to their audience, the pro-Confederate lobby in Britain vehemently rejected the existence of such a scheme.

While this nuanced debate over slavery was vital to British engagements with the Civil War, both pro-Confederates and anti-Unionists continued to consider the sectional dispute with reference to other issues, including ethnicity and politics. On the subject of the tariff, Beresford-Hope emphasized how "the Northern States grow a certain amount of grain, but it is a manufacturing rather than a purely agricultural [region] . . . [in the South] the pursuits are almost solely agricultural." According to Beresford-Hope, the interests of each region should have been respected by the federal government, "since . . . each of the colonies retained substantial rights as an independent 'State.'" The government had, however, ignored this fact and jeopardized the economic future of the South by employing a policy of industrial protection. Here Beresford-Hope grounded his argument in the work of earlier writers such as William Cobbett, Harriet Martineau, James Silk Buckingham, and Sir Charles Lyell, who had all emphasized the sovereignty of individual states and highlighted the major sectional divisions over trade policy.[13]

Beresford-Hope also attempted to justify secession by emphasizing in his pamphlet the fundamental differences between the sections with reference to the development of democracy and party. In basic terms he contended that, by rejecting US political culture, the South had asserted its civic national identity. This move strengthened its claim for recognition as a sovereign state. Although his historical accuracy might be questionable, Beresford-Hope told his readers that "the Whigs became more and more identified with the North, and really represented the Democratic principle—the Democrats became more and more identified with the South and represented the Conservative and landed interests." By describing the party system in this way, Beresford-Hope was able to associate the controversial idea of democracy (described so negatively in the works of Dickens and Trollope before the war) with the northern states. In doing so, he suggested that the Union had inherited the democratic system and implied that the Confederacy was forging a new political identity based around its own distinctive sectional characteristics.[14]

Beresford-Hope moved his sectional analysis of US politics beyond democracy itself and associated the negative tropes of American political culture with the Union. His treatment of the political mob is particularly telling in this regard. Just as Russell had done the previous year, Beresford-Hope dissociated the idea of a mobocracy and extreme democracy from the South. He suggested instead that mob rule was resulting in "a perfect reign of terror" in the North in which any anti-government activity was suppressed. Beresford-Hope later went on to place Lincoln in the role of archetypal dictator, telling his readers how the president "ordered the Provost-Marshall at Washington to station a sentry at Judge Merrick's door [not allowing] him to administer the common law of the land!" Beresford-Hope extended this image across the Union and played on the fear of the mob by claiming that "in the North a perfect reign of terror exists. The mobs destroy newspaper offices and silence all free thought." Such claims were echoed in the popular British press, with publications including the *Illustrated London News* and *Reynolds's Newspaper* criticizing the limits placed on political and press freedom in the North. In a letter published in the *Morning Post*, Hotze implied that the situation was very different in the Confederacy, where core ideas such as the freedom of the press were still respected.[15]

These critiques of Union politics tapped into a long-standing British discourse that focused on the negative characteristics of US political culture. Unlike other features of the Civil War debate, however, their connection to prewar sectionalism was somewhat ambiguous. While commentators during the antebellum period had occasionally connected the most negative aspects of US political culture with the northern states, they had primarily used such rhetoric to characterize American politics in national terms. Nevertheless, the terminology associated with US political culture as a whole was often sectionalized and used for propaganda purposes during the conflict. Crucially, in the context of the Civil War North, these criticisms appeared to possess at least a grain of truth. One of the most prominent British pro-Confederates, William Schaw Lindsay, received a letter from an American friend in New York, informing him that "the respectable portion of our citizens, men of property and intelligence are so thoroughly intimidated by the government that they will not publically express their sentiments."[16] That a Liberal MP such as Lindsay would be struck by these apparently flagrant abuses of power is unsurprising. Yet the use of this negative imagery, which balanced ideas of despotism and the mob with democracy, ensured that the most committed, anti-reform conservatives in Britain found the cause of the North equally unappealing.

It was not simply in terms of the machinery of politics that Beresford-Hope aggressively sectionalized tropes about the prewar United States; he also did so with reference to the press. In his description of the newspaper industry as "violent, untruthful, [and] scurrilous to a degree which we cannot imagine in this orderly land" and his specific focus on "the ribald press of New York," Beresford-Hope invoked a specter that had been represented in its most popular form by Dickens's "New York Stabber" and "New York Peeper." Russell also focused on the New York press and made specific reference to the *New York Herald*. *Punch*'s commentary on the topic offered further detail and tied another prewar trope (that of the ethnically heterogeneous North) directly to the press by making reference to the connection between the Irish and the *Herald*. *Punch* remarked that the paper presented the "characteristic effusions of Irish malignity which render the Federal papers ludicrous." Even the Union diplomats in Britain, Charles Francis Adams and Henry Adams, at least partially blamed the press for scuppering their own diplomatic efforts.[17] These various associations between newspapers, the Irish, and the city of New York brought with them a range of negative images that both propagandists and journalists linked to the cause of the Union.

As well as being a key pro-Confederate activist, Beresford-Hope was also a committed advocate of the established church in England. His religious affiliation requires comment here since it points to a connection between British pro-Confederates and Anglicanism. After reviewing the makeup of a number of pro-Confederate and pro-Union organizations, the historian R. J. M. Blackett reasonably concluded that "supporters of the Confederacy were solidly Anglican."[18] Examined in the context of prewar tropes, the potential reasons for the connection between Anglicanism and the Confederacy becomes clear. Most antebellum commentators had noted the strong influence of Irish Catholicism in New York and the history of religious dissent in New England. The "Old South" on the other hand had often been identified with a continued fidelity to Anglicanism long after the American Revolution. For someone like Beresford-Hope, the religious affiliations of the regions that made up the Union and the Confederacy implied a commitment to sociopolitical stability and ethno-cultural Britishness in the South. This was something that the North (and in particular the "Catholic" areas of New York) lacked. In short then, Beresford-Hope repacked prewar ideas about ethno-cultural regionalism into pro-Confederate propaganda.

During a lecture given in Maidstone, Kent, Beresford-Hope further developed the idea of a close ethnic and cultural relationship between Britain and the South. He asked his audience, "Do you believe that those Southern men and women, speaking our own tongue, with our own blood running in their veins would quietly endure the iron yoke?" In terms of the ethnic makeup of each region, his early pamphlet provided a statistical gloss to these claims: "The South has nearly 9,250,000 inhabitants, of which almost 6,000,000 are whites, nearly all of English blood, with the exception of the French stock in Louisiana; while the addition of the Border States would add 2,500,000 of whites to less than 500,000 slaves. The North has rather over 19,000,000 of a very mixed race." Beresford-Hope connected these ethnic profiles to the attitudes of each region toward Britain, contending that "the South is not devoid of political sympathies with England. Formerly the South was as guilty as the North in its swaggering, bunkum and tall talk . . . [it] has become moderate." He directly contrasted this statement with the idea that "the friendship and affection of the North is not very strong at this moment."[19]

In his pamphlet, Beresford-Hope even claimed that the ethnic homogeneity of the South acted as a check on democracy in its most disconcerting forms: "Germany . . . and Ireland, and other countries continue to pour in their streams of discontented, destitute immigrants [to the North]. In the South there is the same universal suffrage among the whites, but there, owing to the large landed proprietors and the conditions of the country, the mob has not the same power." Hotze evoked the same cultural and ethnic distinctions as Beresford-Hope in one of his so-called moderator letters to the *Morning Post* in March 1862. He remarked that "for half a century the North has absorbed the surplus population of all Europe," while the South had "relied on the natural increase of the parent stock."[20] This was an ethnic and cultural division writ large, with the aim of emphasizing the differences between North and South and relating them to the apparent distinctions in political culture between the sections.

The complex characterizations that Beresford-Hope used to describe the North and South are indicative of the influence of antebellum ideas regarding American sectionalism on British engagements with the Civil War. Constructing a version of the Union that centered on ethnic heterogeneity, democratic political culture, and northern political tyranny, while simultaneously rejecting claims that northerners were committed to abolition, undermined the reputation of the section in Britain. By connecting these tropes, observers presented the British populace with an image of the Union that was both negative and consistent with their preexisting ideas. These negative characteristics also provided a point of reference for British pro-Confederates, who frequently claimed that the South represented the rejection of such values. It is vital to recognize that this complex analysis of the Civil War was a fundamental feature of British antipathy toward the Union. The North and South appeared distinctive enough to justify secession, even if passionate support for Confederate nationalism in Britain was limited. When the Emancipation Proclamation was issued later in the year, however, the terms of the debate changed. While emancipation did nothing to undermine popular ideas about the distinct identities of North and South, it added a strong moral issue that resonated with the British people. As a result, it became more difficult to publicly express sympathy with secession, as to do so seemed to imply ambivalence about the abolition of slavery.

By the spring of 1862, the public debate over the Civil War in Britain centered on complex discussions of northern and southern identity. In Parliament, however, a group of pro-Confederate MPs had decided to latch onto a specific legal issue to try to drive the government toward recognition. The chosen issue was the Union blockade of southern ports, and in the spring of 1862, William Gregory (the liberal-conservative MP for County Galway), presented a motion to the House of Commons that the British should break the blockade. Before the outbreak of the war, Gregory had traveled in the American South and could boast of a network of correspondents that included Robert Hunter, James M. Mason, and William Porcher Miles. Given his personal connection with these figures, it is probably unsurprising that he became a vocal advocate of the Confederacy with the outbreak of the war. The motion Gregory presented on 7 March was predicated on the assumption that the Union was operating an illegal paper blockade of the South, which he attempted to prove by highlighting the success of blockade-running operations. In the House, Gregory received support from the Conservatives Sir James Fergusson and Lord Robert Cecil, as well as William Schaw Lindsay. In the end, Gregory's legal position was roundly rejected, with the reforming MP for Bradford, W. E. Forster, leading resistance to what the liberal *Leeds Mercury* described as "the mischievous motion of Mr. Gregory."[21]

Both Gregory and the public were aware that, despite being nominally concerned with a specific legal issue, his motion had resonance for the debate about the position of the Confederacy in Britain more generally. Gregory had made clear "his strong sympathy with the struggle for independence now being carried on by the Confederate States, and declared that the separation of the South from the North, and re-construction of the Union were the only means by which we could hope to see slavery abolished in the United States." Later in the year, Gregory supplemented his argument by contending that it had been the North that had dominated the international slave trade. Gregory's purpose here was to emphasize the culpability of the North in the continued existence of slavery.[22] Taken as a whole, Gregory's discussion of slavery drew on the well-established belief that northerners were implicated in the slave system and the claim that their refusal to accept secession provided evidence of the insincerity of Union abolitionism.

Some of the most complex commentary regarding the Civil War in general, and the role of slavery in the conflict specifically, can be found in a text produced shortly after Gregory's motion. In May 1862 the first edition of Anthony Trollope's seminal travelogue, *North America,* was published. Given the importance of his mother, Frances Trollope, as a prewar British commentator on the United States, and his personal commitment to domestic political reform, it should come as no surprise that Anthony Trollope had long evinced an interest in America. With *North America,* he had intended to produce a text that would act as a popular corrective to his mother's travelogue—a work he believed had contributed to the development of the negative stereotypes of US politics and society which dominated British discourse. For this reason Trollope began the first volume of *North America* by rejecting the idea that he was writing an analysis of the Civil War. Despite this claim, the simple fact that Trollope was traveling around the United States during 1861 compelled him to engage with the issues at stake in the conflict. Trollope's position in popular literary culture and mainstream liberalism makes him an ideal case study for middle-class British opinion, which, as *North America* makes clear, continued to place the conflict in the framework of prewar sectionalism. His interpretation of the war, in its simplest form, was a cocktail of antislavery, anti-Unionism, and explicit rejection of racial equality.[23]

Like many of his predecessors, Trollope was critical of slavery as an institution, while being simultaneously underwhelmed by the abolition movement in the northern states. His experience with this group left him so disillusioned that he decided that "as a rule, the men of New England are not abolitionists." In his discussion of the role of slavery in the Civil War, Trollope informed his readers, "Abolition, in truth, is a political cry. It is the banner of defiance opposed to secession." While disagreeing with the abolitionists' assumption "that the negro is the white man's equal," he attacked the racial hypocrisy of the North, which meant that "an American abolitionist would not sit at table with a negro. He might do so in England at the house of an English duchess; but in his own country the proposal of such a companion would be an insult to him. He will not sit with him in a public carriage if he can avoid it. In New York I have seen special street cars for coloured people." These are exactly the sort of images that Dickens's descriptions of New York abolitionism had conjured up in the 1840s. In fact, Trollope provided one of the best accounts of the complex connections between sectionalism and slavery, as well as the relationship each had to the Civil War: "The South is seceding from the North because the two are not homogenous. They have different morals, and a different culture. It is well for one man to say that slavery has caused the separation; and for another to say that slavery has not caused it. Each in so saying speaks the truth. Slavery has caused it, seeing that slavery is the great point upon which the two have agreed to differ. But slavery has not caused it, seeing that other points of difference are to be found in every circumstance and feature of the two people."[24]

To understand Trollope's apparently contradictory attitude toward slavery and abolition, it is necessary to locate *North America* within its contemporary intellectual context. As Catherine Hall notes in her analysis of his 1859 work *The West Indies and the Spanish Main,* Trollope "reaffirmed white superiority and the inferiority of the African," while criticizing the "self-righteous or self-important . . . Philanthropists and evangelicals."[25] Although the imperial framework of *The West Indies* gave it a different emphasis from *North America,* we can see similar ideas expressed in both texts. Trollope's antipathy to racial equality was a recurring theme, as was his rejection of "extreme" philanthropy. In terms of *North America,* specifically, Trollope's analysis relied on the work of prewar commentators, whose texts provided him with the ammunition to dismiss abolitionism in the North as either politically motivated and hypocritical, or naive and potentially destructive. As a result, Trollope could criticize the North while also claiming a desire to see slavery gradually abolished. This stance was precisely the moral undergirding that characterized almost all mainstream British anti-Unionism. Middle-class Britons were able to justify their simultaneous rejection of slavery and the cause of the Union by invoking prewar British ideas that had consistently questioned the connection between the North and moral abolition.

Trollope took the sectional divisions in the United States a step further than most of his contemporaries and speculated that "the great political Union hitherto called the United States of America may be more properly divided into three rather than into two distinct interests." He explained, "It must also be remembered that on commercial questions, the North and West are divided. The Morrill Tariff is as odious to the West as it is to the South . . . the North is a manufacturing country. A poor manufacturing country as regards excellence of manufacture—and therefore more anxious to foster its own growth by protective laws."[26] The sense of disunity conveyed here is palpable. Trollope saw the regions of the United States as three distinctive economic units, each with a particular set of demands. Regardless of its tangible effects on the South or West, the passage of the Morrill Tariff illustrated that legislation could be passed to benefit one section at the expense of another.

The separate identities and economic interests of the North and South, which Trollope highlighted here, were also noted in a letter printed in the *Index* on 1 May 1862. The letter, signed "a Liverpool Ship-owner," pointedly described the cause of "Free Trade and the Confederate States." Emphasizing this connection was evidently important, and the idea that free trade was an integral part of southern nationalism continued to have considerable public influence during 1862. Dickens, for example, noted in a letter on 16 March that slavery had nothing to do with the war and that the conflict was about the South attempting to reassert its own economic and political independence. As Chapter 3 illustrates, the idea that political and economic antagonism underpinned sectional tensions had a long history in Britain. Speaking more generally, Dickens concluded that there was not "a pin to choose between the two parties."[27] Taken together, Dickens's sentiments are indicative of British attitudes to the Civil War prior to the Emancipation Proclamation. Like so many others, he specifically rejected the role of slavery in the war and asserted a range of economic, social, and political reasons for secession that were rooted in the long history of British engagements with sectionalism. This complex discourse of sectionalism was fundamental to the work of anti-Unionists in Britain and continued to provide a credible line of attack for those attempting to dissuade the public from endorsing the North. This situation, however, relied on continuing moral ambiguity over the war and was therefore only sustainable as long as it remained viable to publicly dissociate the Union from "moral" abolition.

The idea of divergent political cultures existing in the North and South provided another compelling way for commentators to highlight the complexity of sectionalism. Anthony Trollope presented US political culture in a sectional context in *North America* by explaining to his readers that "Massachusetts . . . is democratic in its tendencies, but South Carolina is essentially aristocratic," a view reminiscent of the description given by *Blackwood*'s of Virginia's political system in 1852. By discussing politics in this way, Trollope suggested a sectional division on the subject of democracy, something that Hotze also discussed in the pages of the *Index*. It should be noted here that, unlike Hotze, Trollope was not necessarily endorsing either an aristocratic or democratic government (although he did explain that the aristocratic system of the South was bound up with the slave system). In a sense, his personal views are of limited interest. The significance of his thoughts stems from the fact that they were being read by a public familiar with a corpus of literature highly critical of American democracy. Furthermore, the authors of these earlier accounts had not necessarily been reactionary conservatives. They had included noted liberals and radicals like Dickens, Brothers, and Trollope's own mother, who had turned away from democracy after seeing it in operation in the United States. Even if his intention was not the same as that of pro-Confederate writers in Britain, Trollope's claims were similar to those of Hotze, Spence, and Beresford-Hope in the sense that they emphasized the sectional nature of US political culture and associated the negative aspects of the system with the Union.[28]

Trollope and Beresford-Hope were also in agreement about the role of the despot in northern politics, and both men saw the figure manifested in the US secretary of state William H. Seward. The negative terms in which Trollope described the secretary were grounded in the belief that Seward was an Anglophobe who actively wanted war with Britain and had admitted as much in a conversation with the Duke of Newcastle in 1860. Certainly, Seward was an easy target for any British writer of the era. Well before the

Civil War, he had been intimately associated with Anglophobic politics, and during the early months of the conflict, his name was frequently linked with the "foreign war panacea." In essence, this was a plan to reunite the North and South by provoking a conflict with Britain over Canada in the belief that the majority of Americans would rally behind a war against the United States' traditional enemy. Genuine concern existed in Britain that the Union might make a military move of this sort—a situation not calmed by newspapers such as the *New York Herald* and *New York Times,* which both suggested at various points that Canadian lands could replace the seceded areas of the South. Even Lord Lyons expressed concern that the strategy might turn out to be more than bluster after finding that Seward's close friend, George Ashmun, had been dispatched to Canada.[29]

Seward's Anglophobe reputation was further enhanced when, against the backdrop of the *Trent* affair, a portion of his diplomatic correspondence was published which was permeated with anti-British rhetoric. The generally measured Trollope was unusually insulting toward Seward, and, as Charles Francis Adams noted in a number of letters to his son, criticism of the secretary of state was widespread in Britain at this time. Trollope's comments about Seward need to be placed in the context of the *Trent* affair. This major diplomatic dispute had coincided with the novelist's travels in the United States, and during that time he saw Union politicians (including Seward) at their most belligerently Anglophobic. In the same way that a number of Confederate propagandists portrayed Lincoln as the logical outcome of American democracy, Trollope concluded that Seward was the result of a political system that encouraged "governing by the little men." At other times Trollope accused Seward of being ignorant, arrogant, and guilty of incompetence, and he also claimed that Seward reveled in the "privilege of unrestrained arrests." By suggesting that Seward was a flawed statesman who had been elevated by an ignorant mob and who was now attempting to drive America toward despotism, Trollope fused together the negative tropes that had been connected with US democracy before the war, while during the conflict itself writers such as Trollope associated them explicitly with the North.[30] When considering Seward in this context, it is also worth reasserting his prewar connection to the New York Irish. While his Civil War conduct was not always discussed with reference to this political constituency, the fact that he had a negative reputation in Britain before the war made him a useful point of reference for critiques of Union policy.

Seward was not the only individual highlighted by British critics of the North. Lincoln was similarly associated with the most objectionable aspects of US political culture and portrayed as an aggressively Anglophobe despot whipping up the popular passions of the mob. Specific developments in the United States during the war gave the Confederate lobby in Britain a great deal of ammunition when it came to using the Union despot image. Furthermore, the despot label was not limited in its applications to major national politicians. As much (if not more) of the British ire was directed at the Union general Benjamin Butler, who occupied the city of New Orleans from April 1862. Popular perceptions in Britain were that Butler had enforced an unnecessarily harsh regime on the people of the city. Even though John Bright attempted to defend Butler's conduct as an expedient of war, many other significant British politicians, including Prime Minister Palmerston, expressed no sympathy for the general. In some ways, figures such as Palmerston must have seen Butler (and possibly Lincoln and Seward) as the fulfillment of the warnings issued by *John Bull,* Frederick Marryat, and George Combe about the likely emergence of an American despot.[31]

The actions of Butler in New Orleans fed into a broader British discourse that built on the image of democratic despotism and often led to speculation about the possibility of martial law emerging in the North. This discourse was frequently critical of the tyranny of Lincoln's domestic policies and, at its most extreme, led to comparisons between the federal government and that of Robespierre and Danton during the French revolutionary "terror." One speaker in Todmorden, Yorkshire, pleaded with his audience to recognize the historical inevitability of a republic descending into tyranny and pointed to the current actions of the Washington government as an illustration of this. The decision to sink a stone fleet in Charleston harbor was similarly interpreted as the act of a tyrannical government prepared to devastate the economic prospects of the city in both the short and long term.[32] For many in Britain, the actions of Butler, the rhetoric of Seward, the sinking of the stone fleet, and the suspension of habeas corpus were examples of the despotism and tyranny that were the logical consequence of the political culture that the Union had inherited from the United States. This was a culture that had apparently been taken to its logical conclusion under Lincoln's administration.

Even when they were tied to specific events and personalities, such as Butler or the suspension of habeas corpus, British debates over the war tended to move toward a discussion of relatively abstract ideas, including politics, slavery, and ethnicity. Certain issues, however, offered propagandists the chance to anchor their cause in the contemporary experience of members of the British public. The so-called cotton famine provides the most significant example, and even though debate continues among scholars about whether or not the drop in cotton imports from the South was actually significant for British manufacturing centers, a number of contemporary figures posited a connection. Speaking at the Annual Cutlers Festival in Sheffield in August 1862, John Arthur Roebuck offered his audience an overview of the importance of southern cotton to Britain, along with an analysis of the Civil War. Roebuck had followed Lord Palmerston on stage, and their speeches are indicative of pro-Confederate and mainstream opinion—the former represented by Roebuck and the latter by Palmerston. As he neared the end of the speech, the prime minister "referred to the distress in Lancashire, complementing the operatives on their endurance . . . he thought all would admit that government was wise in not attempting to relieve that distress by an interference in the American War." While Palmerston rejected any diplomatic moves in favor of the South to alleviate cotton famine, Roebuck maintained that it was the responsibility of the British government to act.[33]

Even as the two men debated an apparently specific issue relating to the international cotton trade, they both drew on abstract ideas that had been developed by prewar cultural commentators to make their respective cases. In his response to Palmerston, Roebuck emphasized all of the key prewar tropes that had been used to differentiate between the sections. He described northerners as "people possessed of irresponsible and almost omnipotent power" and "as a people that could not be trusted." He similarly noted that when it came to the causes of war, "slavery was a mere pretence," before describing how in "the North the feeling against the black man was stronger than in the South, and if North and South were re-united to-morrow slavery would be more firmly fixed than ever." Roebuck also sectionalized the Anglophobe credentials of the United States when he noted that "America had been intolerant and overbearing towards England, and we had, on almost every occasion given up to her. The consequence was seen in the affair of the *Trent.*" He concluded in similarly sectional terms that "the Northerners would never be our friends. Of the Southerners we could make friends. They were not the scum and refuse of Europe, but

Englishmen."[34] It is worth dwelling on Roebuck's speech at this point, as it provides an illustration of all the prewar tropes that had been used to differentiate North and South being fused together in order to construct a distinctive identity for the sections during Civil War. It also makes manifest the extent to which Civil War rhetoric operated within an existing framework of both national and sectional ideas about the United States.

Despite the shifting diplomatic backdrop and more active engagement with the conflict on the part of the British government, the work of Roebuck's colleague, James Spence, continued to act as a key reference point in public debates on the Civil War. In 1862, for instance, the Liverpool reformer Charles Edward Rawlins Jr. produced an explicit rebuttal to Spence's *American Union,* which attested to the influence of the text a year after its publication. Rawlins described the pamphlet as "at once the most brilliant and most mischievous work" on the conflict before going on to quote the positive responses given to the book by the *Quarterly Review* and *All the Year Round.* Rawlins then proceeded to dismantle Spence's argument through a refutation of the idea that the South was politically and economically subjugated by the North. First, he claimed that "nearly all the presidents have been Southern men," and "the North, absorbed in commerce, and hitherto exhausting their love for the Union in vapid words, [has] been the passive instrument[s] of Southern slaveholders." For Rawlins, the decision in the *Dred Scott* case of 1857 "had at last fairly awakened Northern Freemen from their culpable indifference." The result of *Dred Scott* was "the election of Mr. Lincoln as the representative of a party not desiring to interfere with slavery in the States, but to prevent its further extension. And herein lies the immediate cause of secession."[35] Even in his rebuttal to Spence, however, Rawlins betrayed the continuing weakness of the Federal cause from a British perspective. In the first place, his contention that *Dred Scott* had "awakened Northern Freeman" implied that the free states had acquiesced to slavery for seventy years. Furthermore, in a Civil War context, Rawlins essentially accepted that the Union was not fighting to abolish slavery across the nation. As a result, his work failed to provide the moral clarity that might have led to more widespread support for the Union.

As Rawlins's critique demonstrates, pro-Unionists were on the defensive during 1862 and needed to fend off attacks from pro-Confederates (most notably Spence) and a much larger number of anti-Unionists. It wasn't until 1862 that a text was produced that provided a compelling analysis of the war from a pro-northern perspective. The work that finally did materialize was not the product of a prominent politician, such as Bright or Cobden, but an economist, John Elliot Cairnes, whose book, *The Slave Power: Its Character and Probable Designs: Being an Attempt to Explain the Real Issues involved in the American Contest,* was an attempt to rebut Spence's *American Union.* Cairnes was a noted political economist and a personal friend and ally of the philosopher John Stuart Mill. In truth, Cairnes's claims were similar to those made by Rawlins and Bright, but his analysis of the war was more coherent and nuanced. His pamphlet was explicitly antislavery and maintained the right of the Lincoln administration to hold the nation together. Cairnes, however, conceded that he was personally unimpressed with the Union government. As a consequence, his text (which went into a second edition and was included in the popular circulating library of Charles Mudie) was no federal hagiography. A central tenet of Cairnes's thesis involved a rejection of the claim that the tariff had been a significant factor in the secession of the South. Cairnes noted that, "with the exception of the Morrill Tariff, Congress has never passed a more highly protective law than the tariff of 1842; and this tariff was supported by a large number of Southern statesmen." He also highlighted how "the interest of the Cotton States in free exchange with foreign countries [was] not more obvious than that of Ohio, Indiana, Illinois and Wisconsin," something Anthony Trollope had recognized in *North America.* Even while attempting to downplay the role of the tariff, however, Cairnes still noted that "the North fancied she had an interest in protection; the South had an obvious interest in free trade. On this and other questions . . . North and South came into collision."[36]

The range of reasons that Cairnes identified as key to secession centered on the tropes of prewar sectionalism. This approach was unusual compared to the majority of pro-Union propaganda, which tended to reject nuanced analysis and preexisting British ideas in favor of simplified moral divisions. Cairnes even went as far as to concede that, "as for slavery, it was little more than a pretext on both sides, employed by the leaders of the South to arouse the fears and hopes of the slaveholders, and by the North in the hope of attracting the sympathies of Europe and hallowing a cause which was essentially destitute of noble aims."[37] Cairnes's analysis of the role played by slavery in the war involved concentrating on the political rather than the moral aspects of the system. Consequently, some of his views were strikingly similar to those expressed by Spence. In a way, this should not be surprising. The lack of action by the Union against slavery made untenable any argument that the North fought for abolition as a result of widespread moral revulsion toward the system. Instead, Cairnes contended that the North would be prepared to embrace the cause for pragmatic political reasons. While this may have disappointed many Britons (who hoped that northerners could be convinced to abolish slavery for the same moral reasons that they claimed had motivated their predecessors), Cairnes's approach did provide the public with an apparently realistic pathway toward American abolition.

Cairnes's recognition of the lack of passionate abolitionist feeling in the North may seem strange, given his advocacy of the Union, yet his text is laden with observations that would seem to undermine his cause. In the context of the conflict itself, Cairnes conceded that "when slaves have escaped to the Federal army, instead of being received by the general with open arms as brothers for whose freedom he is fighting, they have been placed upon the footing of property, and declared to be contraband of war." In addition, Cairnes drew attention to the decision of General Fremont to emancipate slaves in Missouri, describing how "when a Federalist general, transcending his legitimate powers, issues a proclamation declaring that slaves shall be free . . . it is not a proclamation of freedom to slaves as such, but only to the slaves of 'rebels,' while no sooner is this half-hearted act of manumission known at head-quarters than it is disavowed and overruled."[38] This was hardly evidence of an abolitionist Union and appeared to do little to legitimize the war, yet the importance of these issues as topics for popular discussion in Britain forced Cairnes to engage with them.

Cairnes even went so far as to incorporate into his work an analysis of the ethno-cultural characteristics of the North and South. He noted the existence of fundamental divisions between the sections that he grounded in the popular prewar mythology of the Cavalier and Puritan. Cairnes described those from "Massachusetts and the other New England States" as being "from the elite of the middle and lower classes," while explaining that "the early emigration to Virginia, Maryland and the Carolinas was for the most part composed of the sons of the gentry."[39] The subject is worth dwelling on, as Cairnes's analysis here is indicative of the approach he took to the conflict as a whole. Despite being an important way to differentiate regions before the war, the ethno-cultural geography of the United States was rarely a point of focus in the battles of Civil War propagandists. Some pro-southerners, such as Spence and Beresford-Hope, invoked images of the Cavalier and Puritan to differentiate the sections. The reasoning behind this was clear enough—ethno-cultural regional identity provided another division that helped to justify secession. For the same reason, pro-northerners often eschewed the subject. Cairnes was different because he engaged with the multifaceted nature of sectionalism and in doing so attempted to develop a pro-northern position compatible with the prewar sectional lens through which his audience viewed the conflict. By explaining the war with reference to a range of sectional tensions in the manner that he did, Cairnes actually offered a more publicly viable analysis of the conflict than had been provided by the basic good-versus-evil narrative of Bright and Cobden.

Despite apparent concessions to the Confederate cause on a number of points, Cairnes rejected any claim that secession was constitutional. He believed that "it was absurd to suppose that one half of a nation should separate from the other because a first magistrate had been elected in the ordinary constitutional course." Cairnes tied the constitutional argument specifically to the slave power thesis, since "the proximate issue with which the North had to deal was not slavery, but the right of secession. For the constitution [has] recognized slavery within the particular states, so long as the South confined its proceedings within its own limits."[40] Essentially, Cairnes accepted a range of differences between North and South, many of which had clearly discernible prewar roots, and emphasized the illegal nature of secession to justify his position on the war.

It was through a combination of rejecting the legality of secession and focusing on the slave-power narrative that Cairnes hoped to present the war to British readers in a way that was both viable and sympathetic to the Union. He emphasized the territorial and political expansion of the slave states as a major factor in the conflict. At one point he even went so far as to describe the history of the United States as a "record of aggressions by the Slave Power, feebly, and almost always unsuccessfully, resisted by the Northern States, and culminating in the present war." More specifically, he described what had occurred since the Missouri Compromise:

> What has been the career of the Slave Power . . . ? It is to be traced through every questionable transaction in foreign and domestic politics in which the United States has since taken part—through the Seminole war, through the annexation of Texas, through the Mexican war, through the filibustering expeditions under Walker, through attempts upon Cuba, through the Fugitive Slave Law of 1850, through Mr. Clay's compromises, through the repudiation of the Missouri Compromise so soon as the full results of that bargain had been reaped, through the passing of the Nebraska Bill and the legislative establishment of the principle of "Squatter Sovereignty," through the invasion of Kansas, through the repudiation of "Squatter Sovereignty" when that principle had been found unequal to its purposes, and lastly, through the Dred-Scott decision and the demand for the protection of slavery in the Territories.[41]

With this record of abuses noted, Cairnes informed his readers that "the true cause of the American contest is to be found in the character and aims of the Slave Power." Cairnes's attempt to sectionalize US territorial expansion was a politically savvy move through which the long-standing British antipathy toward US expansion might be harnessed against the Confederacy. Furthermore, certain aspects of the slave-power model (in particular, the expansion of the Union into Texas to spread slavery) had been a feature of antebellum British discourse. Crucially, however, even though Cairnes presented the Confederacy as a representative of the slave power, he also conceded that abolition had not motivated the Union to fight. While he noted that the British had been disappointed with the realization that the war was not an "anti-slavery crusade," he suggested that, in the Union states, "the anti-slavery feeling is rapidly gaining on the mere unionist feeling, and bids fair ultimately to supersede it."[42]

Cairnes combined his claims about the growth of abolitionism in the North with an emphasis on the increased use of the "positive good" defense of slavery by southerners. He noted the development of labor ideologies in the South that had taken slavery from being viewed "as a barbarous institution" to "a system admirable for its intrinsic excellence." As evidence of the general acceptance of the "positive good" thesis in the Confederacy, Cairnes pointed to Alexander Stephens's cornerstone speech, in the course of which the Georgia statesman had asserted the centrality of the slave system to the South. Of course, others had discussed Stephens's speech, but Cairnes failed to include the coda (used by those sympathetic to the Confederacy) that the positive defense of slavery undertaken by men like Stephens was a response to northern pressure. In addition, Cairnes also highlighted the desire of some southerners to reopen the international slave trade, informing his readers that "it was proposed in the *True Southern,* a Mississippi paper, to stimulate the zeal of the pulpit by founding a prize for the best sermon in favour of free trade in human flesh." These were apparent illustrations of a change in perspective among southerners who no longer treated slavery as a system to be endured until it could be safely ended and instead saw it as something worth actively supporting. Cairnes here was performing a discursive balancing act. Rather than relying on the immediate explanations and basic morality that characterized Bright's response to the war, Cairnes was prepared to concede a great deal about the conflict to keep his arguments in line with preexisting British assumptions about sectionalism and American abolition. Working from this basis, he constructed a pro-Union argument that centered on the question of slavery but did not resort to the stark freedom/slavery dichotomy that had previously failed to resonate with educated Britons. Furthermore, by focusing on the slave-power concept and the desire of southerners to expand their territory to secure the institution, Cairnes presented his readers with a version of the war in which the Union (despite not being associated with abolition per se) was connected with a desire to stem the expansion of slavery. This was an important point, given the claims of antebellum writers who had suggested that the survival of the slave system rested on its continued expansion.[43]

Although Cairnes's analysis of the Civil War provided a sophisticated (and popular) corrective to Spence's *American Union,* the military situation during the summer of 1862 meant that calls for the recognition of the Confederacy became increasingly vocal. Even Palmerston raised his voice in the cabinet in favor of recognition in some form, despite his antipathy to slavery. Speaking in the House of Commons on 18 July 1862, the pro-Confederate MP, Lindsay, reminded his fellow politicians that Lincoln's inaugural address had specifically rejected abolition as a motivation for the war. In a manner reminiscent of a number of popular commentators, Lindsay asserted that "the great majority of the people of the North had no desire to see slavery abolished, and considered with the South, that it was, if not wise, then at least a necessary institution." This attitude was typical of the pro-Confederate British outlook in its acceptance of slavery as a temporary and justifiable evil as opposed to a "positive good." Still, the stance of Lindsay and those like him naturally lead to accusations on the part of some pro-Union American politicians that the British were offering tacit support for slavery. Certainly, Benjamin Moran believed this was the case, noting in his diary on 21 June 1862 that "the entire British people with but few exceptions are heart and soul in favor of slavery and rebellion."[44]

Southerners working in Britain would likely have scoffed at Moran's claims, given their own continued belief that the British populace was almost unanimous in its condemnation of slavery as a social and labor system. Despite this belief, there was still a level of confidence among southern partisans regarding the southern cause in Britain with James Mason claiming that "the educated and enlightened classes [were] in full sympathy" with the Confederacy. John Slidell wrote to Judah P. Benjamin on 29 September reporting a discussion with the Earl of Shaftesbury in which the peer had informed him that levels of support with the South were increasing in Britain. He also told Slidell that the public "were now satisfied that the chances of negro emancipation were much better" if the Confederacy were established as an independent nation. Crucially, however, Shaftesbury encouraged Slidell to pressure the Confederate government to promise future emancipation.[45]

Shaftesbury's involvement with the pro-Confederate movement means that his claims regarding the number of southern supporters in Britain must be viewed with a degree of cynicism. In truth, what Moran and Shaftesbury interpreted as sympathy for the Confederacy can be more accurately described as antipathy toward the Union. Shaftesbury's reading of public opinion rested on the assumption that the Civil War was not viewed as a contest between freedom and slavery. Because of this he believed that it might be possible to increase levels of support for the Confederate cause. He also, however, recognized that the continued existence of slavery in the South was an impediment to this process. Although he saw public support for the claim that emancipation would be secured through the secession of the South, he evidently believed that a concrete promise to this effect would erode northern claims to moral superiority and increase support for the Confederacy.

The Earl of Shaftesbury's hope that the Confederate government might be open to abolition is indicative of the complexity that characterized British perceptions of the Civil War belligerents. Slavery sat at the heart of this understanding, but its precise role was considerably more complex than has previously been recognized. As this analysis has demonstrated, the British public tended to view the US Civil War through the lens of prewar sectionalism that had been created by public intellectuals and that had posited the existence of regional and sectional differences in the United States. In basic terms, the British saw the Union and Confederacy as divided by a range of issues that tended to reduce sympathy for the attempts of northerners to forcibly reconstruct the Union. Britons also frequently eschewed the idea of a moral division between the sections over slavery. This final point was vital. Following the abolition of slavery in the British Empire in 1833, a commitment to ending the institution came to be seen as fundamental to national identity and public morality. However, it did not mean that the British endorsed immediate and unstructured abolition across the globe. Instead, it simply means that the majority of Britons rejected an association with ideologies that described slavery as a positive good. This position, in turn, had implications for the way they understood American sectionalism and, consequently, the Civil War. By suggesting that southerners were ambivalent about slavery in the short term and prepared to abolish it gradually, Britons could reject a moral division between the sections. The viability of this argument, however, rested, on the fact that the Union had failed to act against slavery. The announcement of meaningful legislation that could challenge this belief would ultimate force Britons to confront the possibility of justifying the existence of a government committed to the perpetuation of the slave system. Few Britons were prepared to take this step. Furthermore, the significance of slavery to the British was such that shifting the war onto an abolitionist footing provided commentators with a northern cause that possessed the moral weight to overcome the justifications for secession rooted in ideas of politics, ethnicity, and culture. The announcement of the preliminary Emancipation Proclamation by Abraham Lincoln on 22 September 1862 had such an effect on British perceptions of the Civil War and ultimately began a process by which British ideas of sectionalism were fundamentally revised.[46]

News of Lincoln's momentous decision could only be transmitted by ship across the Atlantic. Thus there was a delay before the British public became aware that emancipation was now an explicit war aim. The first newspaper reports of the proclamation emerged on the 7 October—the very same day on which William Gladstone gave a speech in Newcastle implying that the British government was considering recognizing the Confederacy.

It is difficult to know if the chancellor was actually aware of the change in Union policy before giving his address. Gladstone's diary (which, it must be said, rarely provides much in the way of detail) makes no mention of him having read reports of the Emancipation Proclamation, yet it seems unlikely he would have been ignorant of such a significant development in the conflict, given that he would be speaking about the subject later in the day.[47]

The chancellor approached the war from a practical standpoint during the Newcastle speech. He began by discussing the effect of US events on the cotton industry before engaging more broadly with the issues at stake in the conflict. When he moved on to this more general discussion, Gladstone's language was remarkably similar to that used by pro-Confederates, even though he had no affiliation with any southern lobbying groups. In the first place, he implied that it would be easier to abolish slavery gradually after the international community had accepted the Confederacy as a nation. He then told his audience, "We may have our own opinions about slavery—we may be for the South or against the South, but there is no doubt, I think, about this—Jefferson Davis and the other leaders of the South have made an army—they are making, it appears, a navy—and they have made what is more than either—they have made a nation." According to the *Morning Post,* this final remark was received with "enthusiastic cheering which was prolonged for some time." In his work on Lord Lyons, the scholar Brian Jenkins has suggested that Gladstone may well have been influenced by Hotze's view of the war as a struggle for national self-determination, and certainly the conclusion of the chancellor's Newcastle speech suggests such an understanding of the conflict.[48]

Despite the apparent similarities between Gladstone's views and those held by pro-Confederates, such as Hotze, Lindsay, Spence, and Roebuck, a significant difference existed between them and the chancellor. The deep-seated commitment to the Confederacy evinced by these men was rare. Gladstone (and much of the British public) can best be characterized as anti-Unionists who had little love for either belligerent but who had imbibed an understanding of the United States that had emphasized the existence of long-standing differences between the sections. As a result, they would accept secession as justifiable, even if they were not prepared to support the South in any meaningful way. Crucially, however, the vocabulary of both groups was grounded in the tropes of prewar sectionalism. Pro-

Confederates like Spence and anti-Unionists such as Gladstone understood the war in a relatively coherent way. Recognizing this fact helps us to account for the lack of a genuinely powerful pro-northern movement in Britain.

Reactions to Gladstone's 7 October oration were varied but often predictable. Moran expressed concern that the speech in Newcastle might reflect the views of the cabinet as a whole and could be the precursor to official Confederate recognition. Interestingly, however, Moran was equally disheartened by the British response to the Emancipation Proclamation itself. He described the laughter and jeers that had greeted the announcement and contended that "the London newspapers try to argue away Mr. Lincoln's emancipation project." This reaction confirmed Moran's existing belief that the British, despite their protestations, had little commitment to ending southern slavery. His view on this point was further reinforced when he met Jefferson Davis's former slave and coach driver, Andrew Jackson, who criticized the levels of southern sympathy he found when touring Britain. On Gladstone's speech specifically, Moran found it particularly galling that the chancellor had failed even to note the Emancipation Proclamation: "Mr. Gladstone has been making a speech at Newcastle at which he stated, amid loud cheers, that Jeff. Davis had made a nation of the South, but said not a word about Mr. Lincoln's Emancipation Proclamation."[49]

Regardless of Moran's claims, and despite the fact that the Newcastle speech was given on the same day that news of the proclamation reached Britain, it would be wrong to interpret the speech as an endorsement of slavery. Instead, it is best seen as the beginning of the end for a particular British understanding of US sectionalism which had gradually developed over the previous thirty years. While Gladstone would later regret his speech because he believed he had misinterpreted the role of slavery in the conflict, his mistake seems almost understandable when we consider it in the context of the long-standing British discourse of sectionalism. In a sense, the Newcastle speech was not a direct response to the Emancipation Proclamation or even a commentary on the Civil War. It was rooted as much in Gladstone's reading of *Domestic Manners of the Americans* (and similar texts) as it was in consular dispatches written in the 1860s.[50] Essentially, the Newcastle speech was an instance of Gladstone vocalizing the British understanding of sectionalism that I have attempted to reconstruct. At this stage of the conflict, however, the validity of the antebellum discourse on which he relied began to be seriously disrupted.

Before dealing with the consequences of this disruption, it is worth noting that British views of sectionalism did not change immediately. Reaction to the preliminary Emancipation Proclamation varied, and the responses given to the announcement are indicative of the issues that needed to be worked out before the British populace could begin to accept that the Union was justified in resisting secession. The *London Times* journalist George Wingrove Cooke raised questions about the viability of emancipation. He suggested that it might lead to a violent uprising, and even if this did not occur, a lack of discipline among former slaves would mean that they were not able to operate in a free-labor system, just as Carlyle had claimed in 1849. The proclamation was also frequently characterized as a cynical and hypocritical war move intended to undermine the Confederacy; from the perspective of the British, it smacked of desperation. Crucially, people with a variety of perspectives on slavery reacted negatively to the act. For example, the eminent Leeds industrialist and abolitionist Wilson Armistead described the measure as a "hostile movement against the insurgent," rather than a "declaration against slavery."[51]

Unsurprisingly, these criticisms were embraced wholeheartedly by the *Index,* which added its own embellishments to the specter of a servile uprising. Potentially more interesting is that the image of revolt haunted the imaginations of mainstream thinkers, with both Earl Russell and Richard Cobden expressing reservations about emancipation for this reason. The *Times* was critical of the final emancipation act, coming as it did on the heels of the Union's military defeat at Fredericksburg (11–15 December 1862), while the *Economist* presented the measure as an attempt to encourage Confederate soldiers to return home and defend their property. As James Mason noted, "Even the Emancipation Proclamation, which it is believed was issued under the promptings of their Minister Adams, as the means of warding off recognition, had little other effect than to disappoint the Anti-slavery party here, and met with general contempt and derision." Such a reaction was likely to have surprised Abraham Lincoln, who had expected a positive response to the proclamation across Europe after having being assured by Carl Schurz early in 1862 that he could not "imagine that any European power would dare to recognize and aid the Southern Confederacy if it became clear that the Confederacy stands for slavery and the Union for freedom."[52]

In the longer term, Schurz's analysis of emancipation proved to be correct. The 1862 decision to abolish slavery fundamentally altered how the British engaged with the war. The pro-Confederate lobby in Britain was clearly aware of the potential that emancipation had to undermine the multifaceted justification for secession that it had relied on. Figures such as Henry Hotze, therefore, combined warnings about the possibility of a servile uprising or race war with an emphasis on the hypocrisy they claimed had motivated Lincoln. In an editorial published in the *Index* in January 1863, Hotze explained to his readers that the act only offered abolition in the rebel states, excluding from its provisions the slave states loyal to the Union. The same article also attacked what was termed the extremism of New Englanders. He concluded his analysis by contending that "if the South were to emancipate the slaves to-morrow the thirst of the clergy of New England for Southern blood would not be assuaged." Through this editorial, Hotze was attempting to provide an analysis of the Emancipation Proclamation that would emphasize the continued distance between British abolitionism and the scheme announced by the Union government by focusing on the apparently different motivations for each.[53]

Hotze's article is invaluable, as it offers an insight into the major division between southerners in Britain and the native pro-southern lobby—a division that became increasingly important in the wake of emancipation. For the Alabamian Hotze, the cause of abolitionism and the values associated with New England were distinctly negative aspects of the American Union. For the British, however, it was the cynical politics and racial hypocrisy of New York that underpinned the anti-northern cause. New England and abolitionism tended to have positive connotations in Britain for everyone from mainstream conservatives to the early Marxist George Julian Harney. In fact, the latter sent a letter to Charles Sumner in which he waxed lyrical about New England, noting how "from my boyhood Boston has been to me as the Mecca or Jerusalem . . . happily glorious Massachusetts has been true to herself, happily the Old Bay State has passed through the crisis without affording 'aid and comfort' to the enemies of Freedom and free America."[54] Once abolition became an avowed war aim, American pro-Confederates became more explicitly critical of antislavery and New England. In doing so, they essentially redefined the terms upon which the war was debated in Britain. The result of this shift was that the pro-Confederate message lost its resonance with a British populace that had been responsive to criticisms of New York mob politics and ethnic heterogeneity.

While emancipation led to a reformulation of British ideas about sectionalism, the change was not immediate. In fact, there continued to be widespread confusion regarding the role played by slavery in the war. Two letters sent by James Mason to Judah P. Benjamin during the final months of 1862 allow us the opportunity to glimpse public feeling at this time. On 4 November, Mason reported a dinner with Lord Donoughmore during which he was told the importance of the Confederacy taking some sort of action toward abolition to secure the support of the British public and politicians. Only three days later, however, another letter from Mason to Benjamin discussed the British public's cool reaction to Lincoln's proclamation.[55] These letters suggest that while the British were steadfast in their antipathy toward slavery, they were unimpressed with Lincoln's plan for emancipation.

If Mason and Donoughmore had been correct in their analysis, it might still have been possible to stoke a popular reaction in favor of the South in Britain by announcing some sort of long-term emancipation plan. The Confederate government was, however, loath to take such a step. Eventually, the Davis administration did realize that changing the public stance of the South on slavery was a necessary precursor to recognition in Europe. This led the Confederate president to task Duncan F. Kenner with traveling across the Atlantic to offer Lord Palmerston a deal in which the South would abolish slavery in exchange for British recognition. Davis, however, did not appoint Kenner until December 1864, and the latter did not secure a meeting with the prime minster until 14 March 1865. By that point in the conflict, the offer smacked of desperation. Had it been floated in the immediate aftermath of the Emancipation Proclamation, the result might have been different.[56]

Emancipation was undoubtedly crucial in redefining the British relationship with the American Civil War, yet, as noted above, the effect was neither instant nor absolute. A memorandum penned by Gladstone for a cabinet meeting on 25 October 1862 highlights the continuing ambiguity on the subject at the highest levels of government. The chancellor expressed concern that "the people of England are being rapidly drawn into Southern sympathies," despite the Confederate cause being "seriously tainted by its connection with slavery." In accounting for the continued antipathy of the British toward the Union, he focused on the conduct of Benjamin Butler in New Orleans. When considering the role of slavery in the conflict at this time, Gladstone continued to speculate on the possibility that an independent Confederacy might abolish the system under pressure from

Britain—just as William Gregory had claimed in his motion earlier in the conflict.[57] Both Mason's letters and Gladstone's memorandum show the ambiguity that characterized British ideas in this period. Many of the images that had dominated perceptions of the sections in the antebellum period and early Civil War were in the process of being revised to reflect the reality of emancipation. Clearly, however, the process was only just beginning. The continued use of older ideas demonstrates that the announcement of emancipation as a Union war aim did not completely redefine the British understanding of US sectionalism overnight. Instead, it began the process by which perceptions of northern and southern identity were replaced by a simple moral division based on slavery. This division was crucial, as slavery possessed the ideological power to overshadow other factors that had been used to justify secession.

With hindsight it seems obvious that by 1863 any chance of Confederate recognition by the British government had evaporated. Even though historians such as Phillip Myers, Duncan Andrew Campbell, and R. J. M. Blackett have offered their own particular explanations for this, all agree that slavery was at the heart of the shift. Few in British political life could continue to push the cause of the South in a conflict that had taken on the aspect of a war against slavery. Now that it was explicit, the role of abolition in the northern war effort could viably be used to undermine any positive assessments of Confederate nationalism. The change in popular perceptions was attested to, at least in part, by the change in the editorial stance of the working-class *Bee-Hive* newspaper, which performed an about-face and came out publically in favor of the Union cause, despite two years of publishing pro-Confederate articles. The correspondence of key figures during the early months of 1863 further demonstrates the shift. In the United States, Charles Sumner confirmed to Secretary of the Navy Gideon Welles that "any alliance with slavery will be so unpopular with the English people as to restrain the Government," while from Britain Charles Francis Adams and Henry Adams reported the positive consequences of the Emancipation Proclamation. On 30 January 1863, Henry Adams described how "the anti-slavery feeling of the country is coming out stronger," and "every allusion to the South was followed by groaning, hisses and howls." He also remarked, "The Emancipation Proclamation has done more for us here than all our former victories and all our diplomacy. It is creating an almost convulsive reaction in our favor." Charles Francis Adams echoed these sentiments, noting that "the President's proclamation is doing much for us on this side . . . the middle classes generally see and comprehend the existence of a moral question apart from all political disquisitions." William Seward was similarly positive about the effect of the proclamation overseas, while even the usually cynical Moran noted in his diary on 22 January that "the President's Proclamation continues to be productive of much good here. People now see that slavery is at the bottom of this war, and that the Government is fighting for freedom."[58] Abolition played such a significant role in the British sense of self that no amount of writing that emphasized the ethnic, religious, political, and economic divisions in the nation could persuade the British population to endorse the South.

Some of the more committed British pro-Confederates, such as Lindsay and Roebuck, continued to advocate the cause of the section; however, their faith had been shaken and the relationship they had with American pro-Confederates became increasingly strained. The case of James Spence is particularly informative. His most effective work (including *The American Union*) had relied on the popular British belief that the division between the sections on the issue of slavery was not particularly stark and the related belief that southerners would abolish slavery when it was practical to do so. By drawing on this discourse, Spence had attempted to undermine claims that the North was fighting a principled war and replace this view with a version in which secession was justified because the of major ethnic, cultural, and political divisions between the sections. Spence never relied on claims that slavery was a positive good for southern society. This was a significant problem after 1863, when southerners became increasingly reliant on pro-slavery ideas to justify their cause. For instance, Hotze's newspaper, the *Index,* began an editorial offensive against the Union by emphasizing ideas of racial science to undermine the positive reaction to emancipation.[59] Spence rejected this approach, believing that it would not appeal to British sensibilities. His refusal to shift his argument onto a pro-slavery footing led American Confederate propagandists to ease Spence out of the pro-southern movement.

James Mason similarly lost his place in the movement in the wake of the Emancipation Proclamation, although for different reasons. After Roebuck had humiliated the Confederate cause in Britain with a botched motion for joint Anglo-French recognition on 30 June 1863, Jefferson Davis instructed Mason to abandon his efforts in London. Perhaps Davis accepted that there was not enough popular or political support in Britain to compel the government to recognize the Confederacy. Instead of returning to America, however, Mason decamped to Paris to meet up with John Slidell in August 1863. The decision to move to Paris was not made at random. Even before Roebuck's motion, it seemed that the French government of Napoleon III was more likely to offer support to the Confederacy than Palmerston's administration. While the reasons for this are complex, they primarily relate to Napoleon himself. The French were almost as vociferous in their condemnation of slavery as the British, and, despite widespread discontent stemming from the French cotton famine, there was not enough domestic support for Napoleon to publically side with the Confederacy. Nevertheless, he was sympathetic to the southern cause and took the lead in a number of pan-European efforts in favor of the South. In fact, it had been a meeting with the emperor and Lindsay that had convinced Roebuck to present his June 1863 motion. Napoleon also had political priorities that he believed could be furthered by supporting the Confederacy. Particularly significant here was his desire to gain control over Mexican affairs. Given the wide-ranging nature of Napoleon's southern sympathy, it is unsurprising that when Mason abandoned his efforts in Britain he opted to focus his attentions on France.[60]

Perhaps the most telling moment of all for the Confederate cause in Britain, and the southern identity as the British had formerly understood it, came in January 1863, when Hotze finally conceded that "a changing wind was becoming apparent in public feeling." It was a change that neither Hotze nor anyone else had the power to resist. Even if it did not necessarily mean a change in outcome for the Civil War, it effectively rewrote thirty years' worth of Anglo-American discourse that had given the British public a particular understanding of sectional and national identity in the United States.[61] The majority of the population no longer understood the war primarily through the prewar lens created by commentators who had presented the United States as a nation defined by a complex set of sectional and national characteristics. This level of complexity had been integral to the widespread antipathy evinced toward the Union but had ultimately rested on the assumption that the conflict could not be characterized as a moral abolitionist crusade. With the Emancipation Proclamation, this claim (which undergirded both pro-Confederate and anti-Union thought) was revised. Although it was still possible to advocate the South through prewar notions of politics and ethnicity, once the American Civil War had become a battle for active abolition, these attempts came up against a manifestation of what R. J. M. Blackett described as an "anti-slavery wall." Thus the complexities of the prewar South were eroded, to be replaced with a simple slavery-versus-freedom dichotomy—a choice that, for most of the British population, was no choice at all.

EPILOGUE

The Emancipation Proclamation marked the beginning of a transitional phase in Anglo-American history during which popular ideas about sectional and national identity were reformulated. Since at least the 1830s, British perceptions of the United States had been grounded in a belief that the nation was characterized by interactions between sectional and national forces. By removing slavery from the equation, the Emancipation Proclamation had irrevocably altered the balance of these forces. The post-1863 period, therefore, saw the British populace readjust their understanding of American life to reflect this change. This era was also, however, one in which the groundwork was laid for the Anglo-American rapprochement of the late nineteenth century. Between the Emancipation Proclamation of 1863 and the Treaty of Washington in 1871, many of the issues that had blighted Anglo-American relations across the previous century were resolved.

The process by which Britons redefined their relationship with the United States and their memory of the American Civil War did not occur in isolation from continued developments in both nations. In many cases, the tensions of the Civil War era were deliberately glossed over. Despite this, sectional divisions that seemed to evoke much earlier ideas of northern and southern identity were also highlighted during the Reconstruction era. In its 13 August 1867 edition, the *Morning Post* provided an extensive analysis of the challenges facing Americans in reconstructing the Union. The correspondent maintained that the Constitution needed to be fundamentally rewritten or abandoned completely before reunion could be achieved. The author's reasoning here was that the primacy of the individual state over the nation was enshrined in the document. Similarly, there was recognition that the northerners were considerably more committed to the process of Congressional Reconstruction than former Confederates were. This being said, British discussions of Reconstruction as a whole tended to focus on relatively general reports of political confusion and social upheaval. Commentary on the progress of Reconstruction under the presidencies of Andrew Johnson and Ulysses S. Grant frequently centered on clashes in Congress. Furthermore, old ideas regarding race relations and the US constitution peppered British reports of the period. For example, on 3 April 1868, the *Morning Post* focused on the fact that black suffrage in the North was based on a property qualification. The paper also suggested that the Freedman's Bureau was primarily a political body.[1] In these comments it is still possible to see many of the concepts that characterized antebellum British ideas of both the United States and sectional identity.

When it came to Anglo-American diplomatic relations in the postbellum period, the ongoing controversy surrounding the activities of the Confederate raider CSS *Alabama* were a consistent point of contention. The *Alabama* had been built in Birkenhead, Merseyside, at the Laird Brothers shipyard and, thanks to the careful management of the Confederate agent James D. Bulloch, had left the port and escaped British waters by July 1862. The US consul in Liverpool, Thomas Haines Dudley, cried foul, believing that the British government was complicit in the building of the ship. While it is true that the administration had not been especially proactive in preventing the escape of the *Alabama,* it is also highly doubtful that it were active in the sort of pro-Confederate plot that Dudley implied. Nevertheless, the successful operations of the ship during the Civil War left a bitter taste in the mouths of US statesmen who demanded compensation from the British following the conclusion of the conflict.[2]

Diplomatic wrangling over the *Alabama* claims was essentially ongoing from the surrender of Gen. Robert E. Lee at Appomattox in 1865 through to the Geneva arbitration of 1872. At particular points, however, the negotiations became the subject of considerable public interest—especially when the progress of the claims intersected with attempts by the reunified nation to pursue territorial growth. While plans for expansion transcended Anglo-American relations, Britons still frequently associated schemes to enlarge the United States with Anglophobia. William Seward's purchase of Alaska from Russia in 1867 provides an illustration of this phenomenon.

While the purchase was commented upon in Britain, it was only when it was presented as part of an American plan to expand into Canada that the acquisition of Alaska sparked controversy. British politicians evinced considerable concern that the United States was looking to encircle the British North American territories with a view to potentially invading. Such concerns were not calmed when Seward focused on Alaska as the first step to Canadian annexation as part of his attempt to increase the domestic popularity of the purchase. These concerns over Canada were, in turn, connected to the *Alabama* dispute. Some commentators believed that the United States might try to seize Canada as payment for the claims. While considered fanciful by policy makers like Lord Palmerston, speeches such as Charles Sumner's 1869 address on the results of the Johnson-Clarendon Commission Report seemed to confirm that the United States had designs on Canada that it hoped to achieve through the claims process.[3]

A final factor needs to be taken into account when considering the nature of postbellum Anglo-American relations—the rise of the Fenian movement. The Fenian Brotherhood held its first national convention in Ireland in 1863 and soon developed into a major Irish-American group advocating the cause of Irish nationalism. While the movement was beset with internal divisions between leaders, as well as ongoing tensions relating to the differing policy priorities of Irish and Irish-American members, Fenianism was seen as a substantial enough threat to elicit a British response. Of particular concern for Britons were the reports of armed bands forming in the United States during 1865 who planned to travel over to Ireland and fight for independence. In many ways Britons framed the Fenian threat of the 1860s and 1870s much as they had antebellum Irish-American threats. Reporting on the formation of armed groups echoed the concerns expressed about organizations such as the Friends of Ireland in the 1840s. Furthermore, there was a tendency among British commentators to connect the Fenian movement to popular American Anglophobia and (at least in some instances) to New York.[4]

To understand the significance of Fenianism, annexation, and the *Alabama* claims to this transitional phase in the Anglo-American connection, it is vital to recognize their interrelatedness. From 1865, American Fenians were fixated on the possibility of an Anglo-American conflict. They believed such a conflict would distract the British government and provide the opportunity for an uprising in Ireland. The intermittent tensions over the ongoing *Alabama* claims offered the Fenians some hope that the two nations might go to war of their own accord. At the same time, however, the members of the brotherhood were not prepared to simply sit back and pray that a breakdown in diplomatic relations over the *Alabama* claims might lead to bloodshed. American Fenians took a more proactive stance, believing that they could spark off a conflict by exploiting US pro-annexation sentiment and the continued reliance of key US politicians on the "Irish vote." In more specific terms, the Fenians hoped that by conducting raids on Canadian soil from US bases—with the tacit endorsement of American statesmen—they could bring about an Anglo-American war.[5]

Members of the brotherhood seem to have genuinely believed that they might be able to secure the endorsement of the US government for their endeavors in Canada. They approached the Johnson administration with this aim in mind following a special Congress held in Philadelphia in October 1865. President Johnson was unreceptive to their advances and even issued a proclamation against the Fenian movement. His proclamation pleased the British foreign secretary Lord Clarendon to such an extent that he offered his thanks to both the president and the secretary of state, William Seward. While the national government offered no support for the 1866 Fenian forays into Canada, prominent New York politicians of the era, such as Fernando Wood, continued to court the Irish vote by exploiting the issues of Fenianism and annexation. The political rhetoric of figures like Wood may well help to account for the persistence of American Fenianism between 1865 and 1871. Such rhetoric would certainly seem to explain the claim of the consistently anti-American newspaper *John Bull* that US politicians were exploiting the activities of the Fenians to gain leverage in the *Alabama* dispute. While interesting for its expression of concerns about the connection between the US government and Fenianism, *John Bull*'s analysis implies a level of Machiavellian thinking in relation to the *Alabama* claims which is difficult to credit. A more realistic assessment of the relationship between the US government and the brotherhood was offered by a *Morning Post* article focusing on the role played by the administration in preventing Fenian raiders.[6]

Even the Fenians' most successful attacks (on Campobello Island and Niagara in 1866) were of little tactical or political value, and by the 1870s their activities descended into farce. Yet the failure of these missions cannot be explained simply with reference to the British in Canada or the Fenians themselves. The US government played an active role in undermining the activities of the brotherhood. In doing so they were able to reassure the British that Washington had no interest in working with the Fenians as part of an attempt to expand the Union into Canada. In fact, according to the scholar Adrian Cook, the continued failure of the brotherhood, and the efforts made by US leaders to prevent their activities, helped smooth over the fraught *Alabama* negotiations. In this sense, then, the activities of the Fenians had the unintended effect of bringing Britain and the United States closer together.[7]

Personnel changes also contributed to this process. Although President Johnson and Secretary of State Seward had acted effectively against the Fenians, their replacements Ulysses S. Grant and Hamilton Fish proved even more zealous in this regard. Fish's foreign policy as a whole tended to be more favorable to the British than Seward's. This should not be seen as particularly surprising. Fish was a devotee of British liberalism and Gladstonian foreign policy who wished to pivot the United States toward an alliance with the British. As a result he became an incredibly valuable partner for London in its dealings with the Grant administration. In fact, it was Fish who laid the groundwork for the Treaty of Washington, which would ultimately lead to the Geneva arbitration and the settling of a number of grievances between Britain and the United States—including the *Alabama* claims.[8]

While the resolution of the *Alabama* claims and the change of administration were important factors, they can only partly explain the Anglo-American rapprochement that occurred over the 1870s. Shifting intellectual currents were also vital to the emergence of transatlantic cooperation in the period. Although they had gained a popular following during the 1840s, ideas of a shared Anglo-Saxon identity came to play a prominent role in Anglo-American relations during the 1870s and 1880s. In the case of Anglophiles like Hamilton Fish, the influence of such ideas is hardly surprising. The concept of Anglo-Saxon identity, however, became so pervasive that it also molded the views of Anglophobes such as Seward and James G. Blaine. In terms of broader perceptions, a number of British commentators suggested a growing sense of kinship between the populations of Britain and the United States, while highlighting a reduction in the levels of popular Anglophobia in American society. In the longer term, this tendency toward rapprochement gained from increasing British disillusion with free-trade orthodoxy as the 1870s progressed.[9]

The change in Anglo-American relations that occurred from the 1870s went well beyond the realm of high politics. The end of the war provided the impetus for a new generation of transatlantic travelers and intellectuals who reformulated relations between the two nations. The rise of Anglo-Saxonism led British thinkers like James Bryce, Joseph Chamberlain, and Charles Dilke to see themselves as part of a global diaspora. Even prominent figures from the previous generation repackaged their views of the United States in this period. As early as January 1869, Gladstone publically confessed that his support for the Confederacy had been wrong—he had been misled by the belief that "the abolition of slavery would surely be effected by the independent legislation of the Southern States." In November 1872, he went even further and issued an explanation of his Civil War conduct to the American minister in London, Robert Schenck. Gladstone's penance was essentially completed in 1878 with the publication of his article "Kin Beyond the Sea" in the *North American Review*. As Duncan Andrew Campbell notes, this piece saw Gladstone focus on the shared values of Britons and Americans and represents an "important milestone in the changing Anglo-American relationship."[10]

For all of the undoubted significance of rapprochement, the question remains—how did earlier ideas of sectionalism resonate after the Civil War? As the Anglo-American controversies surrounding Fenianism, annexation, and the *Alabama* claims show, echoes of northern and southern identity could still be founded in British discourse. Even as late as 1878, Gladstone made reference to ideas of Puritan and Cavalier mythology in "Kin Beyond the Sea." Yet there was a fundamental difference in ideas of national and sectional identity by this point in the century. The changing British perceptions of the South following the Emancipation Proclamation had two major consequences. In the short term they made it less publically acceptable to be pro-Confederate or even aggressively anti-Union during the Civil War. In the longer term, they marked the beginning of a transitional period between 1863 and 1872 during which ideas regarding US sectional identity were revised. What we see during this era are continued references to the differences between North and South but very little sense of a coherent and multifaceted sectional division. As a result, the South no longer appeared to threaten the existence of the Union. Instead, Britons saw the section as an unruly area that was, nevertheless, firmly part of the United States.[11]

NOTES

INTRODUCTION

1. *Morning Post,* 9 Oct. 1862. Although Gladstone had a family connection to the slave trade, Roland Quinault makes it clear that by the 1840s he was an advocate of gradual abolition; see Roland Quinault, "Gladstone and Slavery," *Historical Journal* 52.2 (2009): 363–383.

2. The terms *section, sectionalism, sectional identity,* etc., relate here to the divisions between the northern and southern states of the United States. *Region,* however, is employed less strictly and refers to differences within the sections or differences in the nation as a whole.

3. Martin Crawford, *The Anglo-American Crisis of the Mid-Nineteenth Century: The Times and America, 1850–1862* (Athens: University of Georgia Press, 1987); Jay Sexton, *Debtor Diplomacy: Finance and American Foreign Relations in the Civil War Era, 1837–1873* (Oxford: Clarendon, 2005); Phillip E. Myers, *Caution and Cooperation: The American Civil War in British-American Relations* (Kent, OH: Kent State University Press, 2008); Dean B. Mahin, *One War at a Time: The International Dimensions of the American Civil War* (Washington, DC: Brassey's, 1999); Joseph Eaton, *The Anglo-American Paper War: Debates about the New Republic, 1800–1825* (Houndsmill: Palgrave Macmillan, 2012); David Brown and David Waller, "The South in the British Political Mind: Diplomacy and the Sectional Crisis," in Catherine Armstrong, Roger Fagge, and Tim Lockley, eds., *America in the British Imagination* (Newcastle: Cambridge Scholars, 2007), 102–131; Martin P. Claussen, "Peace Factors in Anglo-American Relations, 1861–1865," *Mississippi Valley Historical Review* 26.4 (Mar. 1940): 511–522; Kenneth Bourne, "British Preparations for War with the North, 1861–1862," *English Historical Review* 76.301 (Oct. 1961): 600–632; Stanley Lebergott, "Through the Blockade: The Profitability and Extent of Cotton Smuggling, 1861–1865," *Journal of Economic History* 41.4 (Dec. 1961): 867–888; Judith Fenner Gentry, "A Confederate Success in Europe: The Erlanger Loan," *Journal of Southern History* 36.2 (May 1970): 157–188; Mary Ellison, *Support for Secession: Lancashire and the American Civil War* (Chicago: University of Chicago Press, 1972); Frank Lawrence Owsley, *King Cotton Diplomacy: Foreign Relations of the Confederate States of America* (Chicago: University of Chicago Press, 1931); E. D. Adams, *Great Britain and*

the American Civil War, 2 vols. (New York: Longmans, Greens, 1925); Joseph H. Park, "The English Workingmen and the America Civil War," *Political Science Quarterly* 39.3 (Sept. 1924): 432–457; Philip S. Foner, *British Labor and the American Civil War* (New York: Holmes and Meier, 1981); Joseph M. Hernon, "British Sympathies in the American Civil War: A Reconsideration," *Journal of Southern History* 33.3 (Aug. 1967): 356–367; R. J. M. Blackett, *Divided Hearts: Britain and the American Civil War* (Baton Rouge: Louisiana State University Press, 2001); Don H. Doyle, *The Cause of All Nations: An International History of the American Civil War* (New York: Basic Books, 2015); Duncan Andrew Campbell, *English Public Opinion and the American Civil War* (Woodbridge: Boydell, 2003); Donald Bellows, "A Study of British Conservative Reaction to the American Civil War," *Journal of Southern History* 51.4 (Nov. 1985); Sheldon Vanauken, *The Glittering Illusion: English Sympathy for the Southern Confederacy* (Worthing: Churchman, 1988); Charles E. Shain, "The English Novelists and the American Civil War," *American Quarterly* 14.3 (Oct. 1962): 399–421; Bill Cash, *John Bright: Statesman, Orator, Agitator* (London: I. B. Tauris, 2012), 150.

4. William W. Freehling, *The South Vs. the South: How Anti-Confederate Southerners Shaped the Course of the Civil War* (Oxford: Oxford University Press, 2001); Edward Pessen, "How Different from Each Other Were the Antebellum North and South?," *American Historical Review* 85.5 (Dec. 1980): 1119–1149; Susan-Mary Grant, *North over South: Northern Nationalism and American Identity in the Antebellum Era* (Lawrence: University of Kansas Press, 2000); Maurice G. Baxter, *One and Inseparable, Daniel Webster and the Union* (Cambridge, MA: University of Harvard Press, 1984); W. J. Cash, *The Mind of the South* (New York: A. A. Knopf, 1941); Avery O. Craven, *The Growth of Southern Nationalism, 1848–1861* (Baton Rouge: Louisiana State University Press, 1953); Drew Gilpin Faust, *The Creation of Confederate Nationalism: Ideology and Identity in the Civil War South* (Baton Rouge: Louisiana State University Press, 1988); H. R. Floan, *The South in Northern Eyes, 1831 to 1861* (Austin: University of Texas Press, 1958); George M. Frederickson, *The Inner Civil War: Northern Intellectuals and the Crisis of the Union* (1993; repr., Urbana: University of Illinois Press, 1965); Eugene D. Genovese, *The Southern Front: History and Politics in the Cultural War* (Columbia: University of Missouri Press, 1995); Elizabeth Fox-Genovese and Eugene D. Genovese, *The Mind of the Master Class: History and Faith in the Southern Slaveholders' Worldview* (Cambridge: Cambridge University Press, 2005); Earl J. Hess, *Liberty, Virtue, and Progress: Northerners and Their War for the Union* (New York: Fordham University Press, 1997); Clayton D. James, *Antebellum Natchez* (Baton Rouge: Louisiana State University Press, 1968); John McCardell, *The Idea of a Southern Nation: Southern Nationalists and Southern Nationalism, 1830–1860* (New York: W. W. Norton, 1979); Michael O'Brien, *Conjectures of Order: Intellectual Life and the American South, 1810–1860,* 2 vols. (Chapel Hill: University of North Carolina Press, 2004); Rollin G. Osterweis, *Romanticism and Nationalism in the Old South* (New Haven: Yale University Press, 1949); Lewis O. Saum, *The Popular Mood of Pre-Civil War America* (Westport, CT: Greenwood, 1980); Lewis P. Simpson, *The Man of Letters in New England and the South: Essays on the History of the Literary Vocation in America* (Baton Rouge: Louisiana State University Press, 1973); William R. Taylor, *Cavalier and Yankee: The Old South and American National Character* (New York: George Braziller, 1961); Karen L. Cox, *Dreaming of Dixie: How the South Was Created in American Popular Culture* (Chapel Hill: University of North Carolina

Press, 2011); Jennifer Rae Greeson, *Our South: Geographic Fantasy and the Rise of National Literature* (Cambridge, MA: Harvard University Press, 2010); Eric H. Walther, *The Fire-Eaters* (Baton Rouge: Louisiana State University Press, 1992); Bertram Wyatt-Brown, *Southern Honor: Ethics and Behavior in the Old South* (New York: Oxford University Press, 1982).

5. Charles Knight, quoted in Richard D. Altick, *The English Common Reader: A Social History of the Mass Reading Public, 1800–1900* (Chicago: University of Chicago Press, 1957), 286. For information on the price shifts of the period, see Simon Eliot, "Some Trends in British Production, 1800–1919," in John O. Jordan and Robert L. Patten, eds., *Literature in the Marketplace: Nineteenth-Century British Publishing and Reading Practices* (Cambridge: Cambridge University Press, 1995), 39–41; David Vincent, *The Rise of Mass Literacy: Reading and Writing in Modern Europe* (Cambridge: Polity, 2000); Robert K. Webb, "Working Class Readers in Early Victorian England," *English Historical Review* 65.256 (July 1950): 333–351; George H. Fleming, *George Alfred Lawrence and the Victorian Sensation Novel* (Tucson: University of Arizona, 1952), 34–38; John Sutherland, *Victorian Novelists and Publishers* (London: Athlone, 1976); Robert A. Colby, "'Rational Amusement': Fiction Vs. Useful Knowledge in the Nineteenth Century," in James R. Kincaid and Robert J. Kuhn, eds., *Victorian Literature and Society: Essays Presented to Richard D. Altick* (Columbus: Ohio State University Press, 1984), 59; Brent E. Kinser, *The American Civil War in the Shaping of British Democracy* (Farnham, UK: Ashgate, 2011), 10, 14; William Thomas, "Religion and Politics in the *Quarterly Review*, 1809–1853," in Stefan Collini, Richard Whatmore, and B. W. Young, eds., *History, Religion, and Culture: British Intellectual History, 1750–1950* (Cambridge: Cambridge University Press, 2000).

6. Raymond Williams has described the term *culture* as "one of the two or three most complicated words in the English language." Williams identified it as "(i) the independent and abstract noun which describes a general process of intellectual, spiritual and aesthetic development from the 18 Century; (ii) the independent noun, whether used generally and specifically, which indicates a particular way of life, whether of a people, a period, a group, or humanity in general, from Herder and Klemm [and] (iii) the independent and abstract noun which describes the works and practices of intellectual and especially artistic activity." For the debate and difficulties over the notion of culture, see Raymond Williams, *Keywords: A Vocabulary of Science and Culture* (London: Fontana, 1976); Christopher Mulvey, *Transatlantic Manners: Social Patterns in Nineteenth-Century Anglo-American Travel Literature* (Cambridge: University of Cambridge Press, 1990), 7.

7. Crawford, *The Anglo-American Crisis*; Blackett, *Divided Hearts*; Campbell, *English Public Opinion*; Howard Jones, *Blue and Gray Diplomacy: A History of Union and Confederate Foreign Relations* (Chapel Hill: University of North Carolina Press, 2010); Michael J. Turner, *Liberty and Liberticide: The Role of America in Nineteenth-Century British Radicalism* (Lanham, MD: Lexington, 2014); Jamie L. Bronstein, *Land Reform and Working-Class Experience in Britain and the United States, 1800–1862* (Stanford: Stanford University Press, 1999); Frank Prochaska, *Eminent Victorians on American Democracy: The View from Albion* (Oxford: Oxford University Press, 2012); Jon Roper, *Democracy and Its Critics: Anglo-American Democratic Thought in the Nineteenth Century* (London: Unwin Hyman, 1989); Paul Giles, *Virtual Americas: Transnational Fictions and the Transatlantic Imaginary* (Durham: Duke

University Press, 2002); Sarah Meer, *Uncle Tom Mania: Slavery, Minstrelsy, and Transatlantic Culture in the 1850s* (Athens: University of Georgia Press, 2005).

8. Adams, *Great Britain and the American Civil War*; Park, "The English Workingmen and the American Civil War"; Owsley, *King Cotton Diplomacy*; Foner, *British Labor and the American Civil War*; Ellison, *Support for Secession*; Hernon, "British Sympathies in the American Civil War"; Blackett, *Divided Hearts*; Campbell, *English Public Opinion*; Doyle, *The Cause of All Nations*, 18, 110.

9. Duncan Andrew Campbell warns against an overreliance on Bright as a source for British opinion in *English Public Opinion*. Leslie Butler, *Critical Americans: Victorian Intellectuals and Transatlantic Liberal Reform* (Chapel Hill: University of North Carolina Press, 2007); W. Caleb McDaniel, *The Problem of Democracy in the Age of Slavery: Garrisonian Abolitionists and Transatlantic Reform* (Baton Rouge: Louisiana State University Press, 2013); Robert Saunders, "'Let America Be the Test': Democracy and Reform in Britain, 1832–1867," in Ella Dzelzainis and Ruth Livesey, eds., *The American Experiment and the Idea of Democracy in British Culture, 1776–1914* (Farnham, UK: Ashgate, 2013).

10. Michael de Nie, *The Eternal Paddy: Irish Identity and the British Press, 1798–1882* (Madison: University of Wisconsin Press, 2004), 267–270; Linda Colley, *Britons: Forging the Nation, 1707–1837* (New Haven: Yale University Press, 1992).

11. M. R. D. Foot, ed., *The Gladstone Diaries*, vol. 1 (Oxford: Clarendon, 1974), 581. Gladstone's diary entry for 19 October 1832 specifically mentions him reading Trollope's book.

CHAPTER ONE

1. Title quotation taken from William Rathbone VI to Sam Rathbone, 13 May 1854, RPVX .3.57A, Rathbone Papers, University of Liverpool Library; William L. Yancey, Pierre Rost, and Dudley Mann to Robert Toombs, 14 Aug. 1861, in James D. Richardson, ed., *The Messages and Papers of Jefferson Davis and the Confederacy Including Diplomatic Correspondence, 1861–1865*, vol. 2 (New York: Robert Hector, 1966); Frances Trollope, *Domestic Manners of the Americans* (1839; repr., London: Century, 1984), 7–11.

2. Richard Huzzey, *Freedom Burning: Anti-Slavery and Empire in Victorian Britain* (Ithaca: Cornell University Press, 2012); R. J. M. Blackett, *Building an Anti-Slavery Wall: Black Americans and the Atlantic Abolitionist Movement, 1830–1860* (Baton Rouge: Louisiana State University Press, 1983); Marcus Cunliffe, *Chattel Slavery and Wage Slavery: The Anglo American Context, 1830–1860* (Athens: University of Georgia Press, 1979); James Walvin, *Questioning Slavery* (London: Routledge, 1996); Alan J. Rice and Martin Crawford, eds., *Liberating Sojourn: Frederick Douglass and Transatlantic Reform* (Athens: University of Georgia Press, 1999).

3. Frances Trollope, *Domestic Manners*, 6–7, 208–212. To give an indication of the dissemination of the published texts that are central to this study, I list a sample of reviews, advertisements, editorial material, and letters drawn from newspapers. The newspapers listed in the footnote for each text do not constitute an exhaustive list and are intended to demonstrate the geographical and chronological influence of the text indicated. For *Domestic Manners* (1st ed.), see *Examiner*, 4 Mar. 1832; *Morning Chronicle*, 6 Mar. 1832; *Caledonian Mercury*, 10 June 1833; *Essex Standard, and Colchester and County Advertiser*, 31 Mar. 1832; *Hampshire Tele-*

graph and Sussex Chronicle etc, 9 Apr. 1832; *Derby Mercury,* 2 May 1832; *Poor Man's Guardian,* 16 June 1832. For Trollope's later changes, see "Preface to the Fifth Edition, 27 Apr. 1837."

4. Frances Trollope, *Domestic Manners,* 10–11, 207–212.

5. Ibid., 154. For the myth of paternalism in southern slaveholding, see Genovese and Fox-Genovese, *Mind of the Master Class*; Eugene D. Genovese and Elizabeth Fox-Genovese, *Fatal Self-Deception: Slaveholding Paternalism in the Old South* (Cambridge: Cambridge University Press, 2011); James Oakes, *The Ruling Race: A History of American Slaveholders* (New York: Knopf, 1982). For a contemporary discussion of the racial capacities and hierarchy debate, see *Leeds Mercury,* 23 Feb. 1833. On the development of ethnographical and anthropological racialist theories in the 1840s and the early development of biological racialism, see Philip D. Curtin, *The Image of Africa: British Ideas and Action, 1750–1850* (Madison: University of Wisconsin Press, 1964); J. S. Bratton, "English Ethiopians: British Audiences and Black-Face Acts, 1835–1865," *Yearbook of English Studies* 11, special number, "Literature and Its Audience" 2 (1981): 127–142; Catherine Hall, *Civilising Subjects: Metropole and Colony in the English Imagination, 1830–1867* (Oxford: Polity, 2002), 102, 110.

6. For examples of her abolitionist literature, see Frances Trollope, *The Refugee in America, A Novel* (London: Whittaker, Treacher, 1832). For reviews, see *Morning Post,* 24 Aug. and 16 Dec. 1832; *Examiner,* 2 Sept. 1832, *Bury and Norwich Post, and East Anglian: Or Suffolk, Norfolk, Essex, Cambridge, and Ely Intelligencer,* 27 Nov. 1833; Frances Trollope, *The Life and Adventures of Jonathan Jefferson Whitlaw, or Scenes on the Mississippi* (Paris: Baudry's European Library, 1836). Kathleen Burk has claimed that Trollope's text was the first abolitionist novel; see Kathleen Burk, *Old World, New World: Great Britain and America from the Beginning* (New York: Atlantic Monthly Press, 2007), 293. For a sample of the reviews and advertisements of *Jonathan Jefferson Whitlaw,* see *Standard,* 30 Apr. 1846; *Morning Post,* 3 May and 6 Sept. 1836; *Caledonian Mercury,* 30 May 1836, 26 Jan. 1837; *Morning Chronicle,* 10 Jan. 1837; *London Dispatch and People's Political and Social Reformer,* 8 Oct. 1836. For a biography of Trollope, see Johanna Johnston, *The Life, Manners, and Travels of Fanny Trollope: A Biography* (New York: Hawthorn, 1978). For her American experiences, see Jesper Gulddal, "The Most Hateful Land: Romanticism and the Birth of Modern Anti-Americanism," *Journal of European Studies* 39.4 (2009): 419–454; Elsie B. Michie, "Morbidity in Fairyland: Frances Trollope, Charles Dickens, and the Rhetoric of Abolition," *Partial Answers* 9.2 (2011): 233–251; Tim Worth, "'An Extraordinary Species of Tyranny': Fanny Trollope and the Domestic Manners of the Americans," *Symbiosis* 5.1 (2001): 17–32. *Morning Chronicle,* 29 Apr. 1833; *Hull Packet and Humber Mercury,* 27 Nov. 1832; *Sheffield Independent and Yorkshire and Derbyshire Advertiser,* 18 May 1833, 8 Dec. 1832; *Berrow's Worcester Journal,* 28 Feb. 1833; *Examiner,* 2 June 1833.

7. *Leicester Chronicle or Commercial and Agricultural Advertiser,* 31 Mar. 1832; *Morning Chronicle,* 24 Aug. 1832; *Freeman's Journal and Daily Commercial Advertiser,* 31 Mar. 1833; *Morning Chronicle,* 1 Aug. 1833; *John Bull,* 23 Sept. 1833. For an overview of the British political press in this period see Stephen Koss, *The Rise and Fall of the Political Press,* vol. 1 (London: Hamish Hamilton, 1981).

8. William L. Mackenzie, *Sketches of Canada and the United States* (London: Effingham Wilson, 1833), 24, 209. For popular coverage of the work, see *Freeman's Journal and Daily Commercial Advertiser,* 4 June 1833; *Morning Chronicle,* 20 June 1833; *Examiner,* 23 June

1833. Seymour Drescher, *Abolition: A History of Slavery and Antislavery* (Cambridge: Cambridge University Press: 2009); Seymour Drescher, *From Slavery to Freedom: Comparative Studies in the Rise and Fall of Atlantic Slavery* (New York: New York University Press, 1999); Seymour Drescher, *The Mighty Experiment: Free Labor Versus Slavery in British Emancipation* (New York: New York University Press, 1999); Seymour Drescher, *Capitalism and Antislavery: British Mobilization in Comparative Perspective* (London: Macmillan, 1986); Blackett, *Building an Anti-Slavery Wall*; David Brion Davis, *The Problem of Slavery in Western Culture* (Ithaca: Cornell University Press, 1966); Thomas C. Holt, *The Problem of Freedom: Race, Labor, and Politics in Jamaica and Britain, 1832–1938* (Baltimore: Johns Hopkins University Press, 1992); Catherine Hall, "Troubling Memories: Nineteenth-Century Histories of the Slave Trade and Slavery," *Transactions of the Royal Historical Society* 21 (Dec. 2011): 147–169; Christopher Petley, "New Perspectives on Slavery and Emancipation in the British Caribbean," *Historical Journal* 54.3 (Sept. 2011): 855–880; Howard Temperley, "Capitalism, Slavery and Ideology," *Past and Present* 75.1 (May 1977): 94–118.

9. Harriet Martineau, *Society in America*, 3 vols. (London: Saunders and Otley, 1837), 1:53–54, 2:309. For biographical details on Martineau, see R. K. Webb, *Harriet Martineau: A Radical Victorian* (New York: Columbia University Press, 1960); Deborah A. Logan, "The Redemption of a Heretic: Harriet Martineau and Anglo-American Abolitionism," in Kathryn Kish Sklar and James Brewer Stewart, eds., *Women's Rights and Transatlantic Antislavery in the Era of Emancipation* (New Haven: Yale University Press, 2007), 242–265; see also *Standard*, 14 Dec. 1836, 3 Nov. 1837, 9 Feb. 1838; *Essex Standard, and Colchester, Chelmsford, Maldon, Harwich, and General County Advertiser*, 16 Dec. 1836; *Sheffield Independent, and Yorkshire and Derbyshire Advertiser*, 17 Dec. 1836; *Brighton Patriot and South of England Free Press*, 23 May 1837; *Cheshire Observer and General Advertiser for Cheshire and North Wales*, 19 June 1858. Martineau's work was even reviewed in the American South, with the novelist William Gilmore Simms roundly criticizing it in an 1837 article in the *Southern Literary Messenger* and drawing his readers' attention to the fact that Martineau had been highly critical of South Carolina slavery without ever having visited the state; see McCardell, *The Idea of a Southern Nation*, 150–151.

10. Martineau, *Society in America*, 1:302; Max Berger, "American Slavery as Seen by British Visitors, 1836–1860," *Journal of Negro History* 30.2 (April 1945): 181–202, 192.

11. Martineau, *Society in America*, 2:313–317, 3:192; *Spectator*, 21 Oct. 1837.

12. Martineau, *Society in America*, 1:107; *Leeds Mercury*, 29 Mar. 1845. For Texan independence, see David M. Pletcher, *The Diplomacy of Annexation: Texas, Oregon, and the Mexican War* (Columbia: University of Missouri Press, 1973), 64–88. For the subsequent annexation of Texas, see Frederick Merk, *Slavery and the Annexation of Texas* (New York: Knopf, 1972); Frederick Merk, *Manifest Destiny and Mission in American History: A Reinterpretation* (New York: Knopf, 1963); Steven E. Woodworth, *Manifest Destinies: America's Westward Expansion and the Road to the Civil War* (New York: Alfred A. Knopf, 2010); Sam W. Haynes, "Anglophobia and the Annexation of Texas: The Quest for National Security," in Sam W. Haynes and Christopher Morris, eds., *Manifest Destiny and Empire: American Antebellum Expansionism* (College Station: Texas A&M University Press, 1997); Kinley J. Brauer, "The United States and British Imperial Expansion, 1815–1860," *Diplomatic History* 12.1 (Jan. 1988): 19–37.

13. Duncan Andrew Campbell, *Unlikely Allies: Britain, America, and the Victorian Origins of the Special Relationship* (London: Hambledon Continuum, 2007): 125–129; Sam W. Haynes, *Unfinished Revolution: The Early American Republic in a British World* (Charlottesville: University of Virginia Press, 2010), 219.

14. Martineau, *Society in America,* 2:238–240.

15. Ibid., 1:53–54, 61, 165–177; 2:79–80; 1:163–164. Martineau mentioned anti-abolition mobs as part of a broader discussion of US lawbreaking. For the Gag Rule controversy in the United States, see Leonard L. Richards, *The Slave Power: The Free North and Southern Domination, 1780–1860* (Baton Rouge: Louisiana State University Press, 2000); Robert P. Ludlum, "The Antislavery 'Gag-Rule': History and Argument," *Journal of Negro History* 26.2 (Apr. 1941): 203–243; Daniel Wirls, "'The Only Mode of Avoiding Everlasting Debate': The Overlooked Senate Gag Rule for Antislavery Petitions," *Journal of the Early Republic* 27.1 (Spring 2007): 115–138; Scott R. Meinke, "Slavery, Partisanship, and Procedure in the U.S. House: The Gag Rule, 1836–1845," *Legislative Studies Quarterly* 32.1 (Feb. 2007): 33–57. For a more general discussion of the treatment of free blacks in the North, see James Oliver Horton and Lois E. Horton, *In Hope of Liberty: Culture, Community, and Protest Among Northern Free Blacks, 1700–1860* (New York: Oxford University Press, 1997); Leonard P. Curry, *The Free Black in Urban America, 1800–1850: The Shadow of a Dream* (Chicago: University of Chicago Press, 1981); Joel H. Silbey, *The Partisan Imperative: The Dynamics of American Politics Before the Civil War* (New York: Oxford University Press, 1985), 9; Leon F. Litwack, *North of Slavery: The Negro in the Free States, 1790–1860* (Chicago: University of Chicago Press, 1961); Lorman Ratner, *Powder Keg: Northern Opposition to the Antislavery Movement, 1831–1840* (New York: Basic Books, 1968). Although the incident was not highlighted by Martineau, one of the most prominent British abolitionists, George Thompson, was physically attacked by northern whites during the early 1830s in Augusta, Maine; Concord, New Hampshire; and Lynn and Boston, Massachusetts; see Leonard L. Richards, *"Gentlemen of Property and Standing": Anti-Abolition Mobs in Jacksonian America* (New York: Oxford University Press, 1970), 63–64; Edward Bartlett Rugemer, *The Problem of Emancipation: The Caribbean Roots of the American Civil War* (Baton Rouge: Louisiana State University Press, 2008), 182.

16. Martineau, *Society in America,* 1:198, 2:127.

17. Charles Augustus Murray, *Travels in North America During the Years 1834, 1835, and 1836 Including a Summer Residence with the Pawnee tribe of Indians, in the Remote Prairies of the Missouri and a Visit to Cuba and the Azore Islands,* 2 vols. (New York: Harper and Brothers, 1839), 2:203. For reviews, etc., see *Morning Post,* 10 July 1839, 16 Apr. and 5 Nov. 1840, 25 Mar. 1841; *Preston Chronicle,* 3 Aug. 1839; *Champion and Weekly Herald,* 1 Sept. 1839; *Hampshire Advertiser and Salisbury Guardian,* 12 Oct. 1839; *Blackburn Standard,* 16 Oct. 1839. Frederick Marryat, *Diary in America with Remarks on its Institutions* (Paris: Baudry's European Library, 1839), 106. For reviews, etc., see *Standard,* 21 June 1839, 6 Nov. 1840; *Essex Standard, and General Advertiser for the Eastern Counties,* 19 July 1839; *Manchester Times and Gazette,* 20 July 1839; *Blackburn Standard,* 24 July 1839; *Bristol Mercury,* 3 Aug. 1839; *Charter,* 28 July 1839. For a biography of Marryat, see David Hannay, *Life of Frederick Marryat* (London: Walter Scott, 1889).

18. Some Americans in the North saw slavery in national as opposed to sectional terms. For example, the *New York Tribune* noted that "the Whole country is chargeable with the guilt of American slavery" (quote in Grant, *North Over South,* 48). Howard C. Perkins, "The Defense of Slavery in the Northern Press on the Eve of the Civil War," *Journal of Southern History* 9.4 (Nov. 1943): 501–531.

19. Murray, *Travels in North America,* 1:120.

20. Thomas Brothers, *The United States of North America as they are, Not as they are generally Described: Being a Cure for Radicalism* (London: Longman, Orme, Brown, Green, and Longmans, 1840), 196–198. For a sample of the review, adverts, etc., of this work, see *Morning Post,* 27, 29, and 31 Jan. 1840; *Standard,* 29 and 31 Jan. 1840. Hall, *Civilising Subjects,* 175–176.

21. Brothers, *The United States of North America as they are,* 196–198. For anti-abolition mobs and racially motivated violence in the United States, see Michael Feldberg, *The Turbulent Era: Riot and Disorder in Jacksonian America* (New York: Oxford University, 1980); Richards, *"Gentlemen of Property and Standing"*; David Grimsted, *American Mobbing, 1828–1861: Toward Civil War* (New York: Oxford University Press, 1998).

22. George Combe, *Notes on the United States of North America: During a Phrenological Visit in 1838–9–40,* 3 vols. (Edinburgh: Maclachlan, Stewart, 1841), 3:337. For reviews, etc., see *Examiner,* 6 Dec. 1840, 17 Jan. 1841. In its obituary for Combe, the *Manchester Times* described his text as "one of the most just and faithful estimates ever furnished by the British traveler"; see *Manchester Times,* 21 Aug. 1858.

23. Combe, *Notes on the United States of North America,* 1:52, 298.

24. Draft Petition for Abolition, 1826, RPV3.2; for mentions of John Bright, see Mary Thomas to William Rathbone, 31 May 1847, RPV3.32; William Rathbone V to William Rathbone VI, 22 Aug. 1848, RPV3.35; William Rathbone VI to Sam Rathbone, 13 May 1841, RPVIX.3.54A, Rathbone Papers. For more on the Rathbone family, see Betty Fladeland, *Abolitionists and Working-Class Problems in the Age of Industrialization* (Baton Rouge: Louisiana State University Press, 1984), 17–48. For the so-called Manchester School liberals (of which John Bright and Richard Cobden were leading lights) and for a discussion of the political thought of both, see Miles Taylor, *The Decline of British Radicalism, 1847–1860* (Oxford: Clarendon, 1995), 47–60. For a biography of Bright, see Keith Robbins, *John Bright* (London: Routledge and Kegan Paul, 1979). Curtin, *The Image of Africa.*

25. William Rathbone VI to Elizabeth Rathbone, 1 June 1842, RPVIX.3.67, Rathbone Papers.

26. James Silk Buckingham, *America, Historical, Statistic and Descriptive,* 3 vols. (London: Fisher and Son, 1841), 1:279–280, 2:461–462, 3:291–292, 415–417. For reviews, etc., see *Northern Star and Leeds General Advertiser,* 14 and 24 Apr. 1841; *Morning Post,* 27 Apr. 1841; *Examiner,* 23 May 1841; *Manchester Times and Gazette,* 20 Oct. and 6 Nov. 1841; *York Herald, and General Advertiser,* 18 Dec. 1841, *Newcastle Courant,* 13 Jan. 1843; *Daily News,* 21 May 1846; *Sheffield and Rotherham Independent,* 21 May 1842. For a biography of Buckingham, see Ralph E. Turner, *James Silk Buckingham, 1786–1855: A Social Biography* (New York: McGraw-Hill, 1934). Sven Beckert, *The Monied Metropolis: New York City and the Consolidation of the American Bourgeoisie, 1850–1896* (Cambridge: Cambridge University Press, 2001), 85–88; Sven Beckert, *Empire of Cotton: A Global History* (New York: Alfred A. Knopf, 2014), 240–241.

27. Buckingham, *America,* 1:78–81, 88–89, 149. For more on Elijah Lovejoy, see Merton L. Dillon, *Elijah P. Lovejoy: Abolitionist Editor* (Urbana: University of Illinois Press, 1961); Feldberg, *The Turbulent Era,* 47–49; Richards, *"Gentlemen of Property and Standing"*; Michael Kent Curtis, "The 1837 Killing of Elijah Lovejoy by an Anti-Abolition Mob: Free Speech, Mobs, Republican Government, and the Privileges of American Citizens," *UCLA Law Review* 44.4 (Apr. 1997): 1109–1184. For Daniel O'Connell's relationship with slavery, see Christine Kinealy, *Daniel O'Connell and the Anti-Slavery Movement* (London: Pickering and Chatto, 2010).

28. Maurice Bric, "Debating Slavery and Empire: The United States, Britain and the World's Anti-slavery Convention of 1840," in William Mulligan and Maurice Bric, eds., *A Global History of Anti-slavery Politics in the Nineteenth Century* (Houndsmill: Palgrave Macmillan, 2013), 61–72.

29. Buckingham, *America,* 1:83–84, 87; 2:92–94, 208; 3:55–56; Iain Whyte, *"Send Back the Money!": The Free Church of Scotland and American Slavery* (Cambridge: James Clarke, 2012). For the "positive good" argument and the southern defense of slavery, see Adam L. Tate, *Conservatism and Southern Intellectuals, 1789–1861: Liberty, Tradition, and the Good Society* (Columbia: University of Missouri Press, 2005), 136–245; Michael Perman, *The Southern Political Tradition* (Baton Rouge: Louisiana State University Press, 2012), 29–36; O'Brien, *Conjectures of Order.*

30. Buckingham, *America,* 1:438–439.

31. James Silk Buckingham, *The Slave States of America,* 2 vols. (London: Fisher, Son and Co, 1842), dedication and preface of vol. 1.

32. Ibid., 1:64–65, 355–357, 199–200, 376; 2:427.

33. Ibid., *The Slave States,* 2:7–8, 280; 1:58, 61, 570–571, 553–554. For Thomas Cooper, see O'Brien, *Conjectures of Order.*

34. Charles Dickens, *The Life and Adventures of Martin Chuzzlewit* (1844; repr., London: Wordsworth Classics, 1997), 276–279, 281. Many biographies of Dickens exist; however, two of the more detailed and valuable are Michael Slater, *Charles Dickens* (New Haven: Yale University Press, 2009), and Peter Ackroyd, *Dickens* (New York: Harper Collins, 1990). See also Joseph Gold, *Charles Dickens: Radical Moralist* (Minneapolis: University of Minnesota Press, 1972). For a study of Dickens's relationship with the United States, see Jerome Meckier, *Innocent Abroad: Charles Dickens's American Engagements* (Lexington: University Press of Kentucky, 1990); Sylvere Monod, *Martin Chuzzlewit (London: George Unwin, 1985).* Dickens was already well read in Anglo-American travel literature prior to leaving for the United States; see Amanda Claybaugh, "Toward a New Transatlanticism: Dickens in the United States," *Victorian Studies* 48.3 (Spring 2006): 439–460; Adrian, "Dickens on American Slavery"; Harry Stone, "Dickens' Use of His American Experiences in Martin Chuzzlewit," *PMLA* 72.3 (June 1957): 464–478. For reviews, etc., see *Examiner,* 3 Dec. 1842; *Derby Mercury,* 14 Dec. 1842, 31 Mar. 1847; *Bury and Norwich Post and East Anglian,* 21 Dec. 1842; *Caledonian Mercury,* 29 Dec. 1842, 21 Aug. 1843, 12 June 1851; *Trewman's Exeter Flying Post or Plymouth and Cornish Advertiser,* 29 Dec. 1842; *Leeds Mercury,* 28 Jan. 1843; *Hull Packet and East Riding Times,* 7 Apr. 1843, 23 Mar. 1849; *Newcastle Courant,* 9 June 1843; *Daily News,* 3 Nov. 1852, 7 Feb. 1862; *Royal Cornwall Gazette, Falmouth Packet, and General Advertiser,* 12 Nov. 1852; *Birmingham Daily Post,* 3 May 1858, 12 July 1864; *Glasgow Herald,* 27 Oct. 1862. Dickens's novel was even adapted into a stage play; see *Morning Post,* 8, 9, and 30 July, 2 Aug. 1844; *Morning Chronicle,* 31 July and

3 Aug. 1844; *Era,* 14 July 1844; *Ipswich Journal,* 13 Apr. 1844. Dickens's decision to emphasize that Mr. Bevan was a New Englander was not incidental. He found the New England states to be the most to his taste while in the United States; see Arnold Whitridge, "Dickens and Thackeray in America," *New York Historical Society Quarterly* 52 (1978): 219–237, 223–224.

35. John Robert Godley, *Letters from America,* 2 vols. (London: John Murray, 1844), 2:70, 67–68, 72–75. Godley emphasized the significance of the travelogue genre in the preface. For a sample of the reviews, adverts, etc., of Godley, see *Glasgow Herald,* 1 Apr. 1844; *Bradford Observer; and Halifax, Huddersfield, and Keighley Reporter,* 11 Apr. 1844; *Leeds Mercury,* 13 Apr. 1844; *Hampshire Advertiser and Salisbury Guardian,* 27 Apr. 1844; *Leicester Chronicle: or Commercial and Agricultural Advertiser,* 4 May 1833; *Morning Post,* 17 May and 1 July 1844; *Northern Star and Leeds General Advertiser,* 13 July 1844; *Dundee Courier,* 3 Sept. 1844. For more on the Irish in the North, see Chapter 2.

36. Godley, *Letters from America,* 2:211–212, 216.

37. G. W. Featherstonhaugh, *Excursion Through the Slaves States, from Washington on the Potomac to the Frontier of Mexico; With Sketches of Popular Manners and Geological Notices,* 2 vols. (London: John Murray, 1844), 1:123, 2:342–344. For a sample of the reviews, adverts, etc., of Featherstonhaugh's account, see *Examiner,* 25 May, 1 June, and 16 Nov. 1844; *Standard,* 3 June 1844; *Berrow's Worcester Journal,* 18 July 1844; *Blackburn Standard,* 5 Mar. 1845.

38. Featherstonhaugh, *Excursions Through the Slave States,* 1:126–128. For the development of pro-slavery thought in the South and the relationship it had with these ideas, see Terry A. Barnhart, *Albert Taylor Bledsoe: Defender of the Old South* (Baton Rouge: Louisiana State University Press, 2011); Cash, *The Mind of the South*; Lacy K. Ford, *Deliver Us From Evil: The Slavery Question in the Old South* (Oxford: Oxford University Press, 2009); Fox-Genovese and Genovese, *The Mind of the Master Class*; Genovese and Fox-Genovese, *Fatal Self-Deception*; Oakes, *The Ruling Race*; O'Brien, *Conjectures of Order*; Edward B. Rugemer "The Southern Response to British Abolitionism: The Maturation of Proslavery Apologetics," *Journal of Southern History* 70.2 (May 2004): 221–248; Jeffrey Robert Young, *Domesticating Slavery: The Master Class in Georgia and South Carolina, 1670–1837* (Chapel Hill: University of North Carolina Press, 1999).

39. Sir Charles Lyell, *Travels in North America; with Geological Observations on the United States, Canada and Nova Scotia,* 2 vols. (London: John Murray, 1845), 1:208–213. For more on Lyell discussing American slavery, see Huzzey, *Freedom Burning,* 25–26. For reviews, etc., see *Examiner,* 12 Apr. 1845; *Morning Chronicle,* 19 June and 30 Aug. 1845; *Bradford Observer; and Halifax, Huddersfield, and Keighley Reporter,* 31 July 1845; *Blackburn Standard,* 6 Aug. 1845; *Cornwall Royal Gazette, Falmouth Packet and Plymouth Journal,* 5 Sept. 1845; *Daily News,* 7 Feb. 1846, 12 Oct. 1853; *Manchester Times,* 8 Feb. 1851.

40. Lyell, *Travels in North America,* 1:208–213; Hall, *Civilising Subjects,* 173, 202.

41. Lyell, *Travels in North America,* 1:169, 181–183. Lyell's experiences are noted in James, *Antebellum Natchez,* 124, 154. For an account of the significance of paternalism in British political discourse and its history, see A. P. Thornton, *The Habit of Authority: Paternalism in British History* (Toronto: University of Toronto Press, 1966); David Roberts, *Paternalism in Early Victorian England* (New Brunswick: Rutgers University Press, 1979). For an introduction to the slave narrative, see introduction to *Slavery, Abolition, and Emancipation: Writings in the British Romantic Period,* vol. 6, *Fiction* (London: Pickering and Chatto, 1999); Brycchan

Carey, Markman Ellis, and Sara Salih, eds., *Discourses of Slavery and Abolition: Britain and Its Colonies, 1760–1838* (Houndsmill: Palgrave, 2004). The slave-narrative genre gained considerable popularity in Britain in this period and tended to emphasize the brutality of the slave system. For a concise and informative discussion of the genre in Britain, see Blackett, *Building an Antislavery Wall*; Betty Fladeland, *Men and Brothers: Anglo-American Anti-Slavery Cooperation* (Urbana: University of Illinois Press, 1972); Audrey Fisch, ed., *The African American Slave Narrative* (New York: Cambridge University Press, 2007).

42. Michael Pickering, "White Skin, Black Masks: 'Nigger' Minstrelsy in Victorian England," in J. S. Bratton, ed., *Music Hall: Performance and Style* (Milton Keynes: Open University Press, 1986), 70–85; Sarah Meer, "Competing Representations: Douglass, the Ethiopian Serenaders and Ethnic Exhibition in London," in Rice and Crawford, *Liberating Sojourn*, 141–143; George F. Rehin, "Blackface Street Minstrels in Victorian London and Its Resorts: Popular Culture and Its Racial Connotations as Revealed in Polite Opinion," *Journal of Popular Culture* 15.1 (Summer 1981): 19–38.

43. Charlotte Matilda Houstoun, *Texas and the Gulf of Mexico; or, Yachting in the New World* (London: John Murray, 1844), 236–238, 163–164. For a sample of the reviews, advertisements, etc., for Houstoun's work, see *Morning Post*, 28 Sept. 1844; *Examiner*, 11 Jan., 12 Apr., and 22 July 1845.

44. Houstoun, *Texas and the Gulf of Mexico*, 237–238.

45. Sir Charles Lyell, *A Second Visit to the United States of America*, 2 vols. (London: John Murray, 1849), 1:297, 277–278; 2:40, 61. For reviews, etc., see *Examiner*, 16 and 30 June 1849, 9 Mar. 1850, 11 Aug. 1849; *Standard*, 19 June 1849; *Bristol Mercury*, 7 July 1849; *Daily News*, 19 July 1849; *Morning Chronicle*, 12 Sept. 1849; *Aberdeen Journal*, 7 Nov. 1849; *Derby Mercury*, 24 Apr. 1850.

46. Lyell, *A Second Visit*, 2:93; 1:352.

47. Ibid., 2:99; Richard Huzzey, "The Moral Geography of British Anti-Slavery Responsibilities," *Transactions of the Royal Historical Society* 22 (Dec. 2012): 111–139.

48. Simon Heffer, *Moral Desperado: A Life of Thomas Carlyle* (London: Weidenfeld and Nicholson, 1995), 1.

49. Thomas Carlyle, *Occasional Discourse on the Nigger Question*, in Eugene R. August, ed., *The Nigger Question: The Negro Question* (New York: Appleton, 1971), 4, 24–25; Patrick Brantlinger, *The Spirit of Reform: British Literature and Politics, 1832–1867* (Cambridge, MA: Harvard University Press, 1977), 1–33; John O. Waller, "Charles Kingsley and the American Civil War," *Studies in Philology* 60.3 (July 1963): 554–568; Henry Adams to Charles Francis Adams Jr., 14 Feb. 1862, in Worthington Chauncey Ford, ed., *A Cycle of Adams Letters*, vol. 1 (London: Constable, 1921). For Carlyle's politics and his emphasis on a natural hierarchy based on a feudal model of social relations, see Heffer, *Moral Desperado*; K. J. Fielding, "Carlyle and the Americans: 'Eighteen Million Bores,'" *Carlyle Studies Annual* (1997): 55–64; N. John Hall, "Trollope and Carlyle," *Nineteenth Century Fiction* 27.2 (Sept. 1972): 197–205; Iva G. Jones "Trollope, Carlyle, and Mill on the Negro: An Episode in the History of Ideas," *Journal of Negro History* 52.3 (July 1967): 185–199. Carlyle had originally used the title *Occasional Discourse on the Negro Question*, which he changed to *Occasional Discourse on the Nigger Question* when he revised the work; see Julie M. Dugger, "Black Ireland's Race: Thomas Carlyle and

the Young Ireland Movement," *Victorian Studies* 48.3 (Spring 2006): 461–485, 465; Kinser, *The American Civil War,* 14.

50. John Stuart Mill, *The Negro Question,* in August, *The Nigger Question*; Prochaska, *Eminent Victorians on American Democracy,* 31–47; John Arthur Roebuck, *Autobiography,* in Robert Eadon Leader, ed., *Life and Letters of John Arthur Roebuck with Chapters of Autobiography* (London: Edward Arnold, 1897); Roebuck, *Debate on the Bill Regulating Bleaching and Dye Works,* in Leader, *Life and Letters,* 283–284; O. F. Christie, *The Transition from Aristocracy, 1832-1867: An Account of the Passing of the Reform Bill, The Cause Which Led Up to It, and its Far Reaching Consequences on the Life and Manners of All Grades of Society* (London: Seeley, Service, 1927), 21–22; A. F. Cruikshank, "J A Roebuck M.P.: A Re-Appraisal of Liberalism in Sheffield, 1849–1879," *Northern History* 16.1 (Jan. 1980): 196–214; Taylor, *Decline of British Radicalism.*

51. Holt, *The Problem of Freedom,* 280–283, 73–76, 145–147, 160–165; Hall, *Civilising Subjects,* 349, 352–353; Thomas C. Holt, "The Essence of the Contract: The Articulation of Race, Gender, and Political Economy in British Emancipation Policy, 1838–1866," in Frederick Cooper, Thomas C. Holt, and Rebecca J. Scott, eds., *Beyond Slavery: Exploration of Race, Labor, and Citizenship in Postemancipation Societies* (Chapel Hill: University of North Carolina Press, 2000), 33–36.

52. Charlotte Matilda Houstoun, *Hesperos: Or, Travels in the West,* 2 vols. (London: John W. Parker, 1850), 2:199–201, 205–208. For reviews, etc., see *Morning Post,* 12 Jan. 1850; *Examiner,* 19 Jan. 1850; *Bradford Observer,* 31 Jan. 1850; *Standard,* 4 Feb. 1850; *Aberdeen Journal,* 13 Feb. 1850; *Morning Chronicle,* 19 Mar. 1850; *Nottinghamshire Guardian and Midland Advertiser,* 2 May 1850; *Glasgow Herald,* 6 Dec. 1850; *Newcastle Courant,* 21 May 1852.

53. Houstoun, *Hesperos,* 1:290–291.

54. Ibid., 2:52, 91–92, 137, 157–161, 195–196, 202–204.

55. Lady Emmeline Stuart-Wortley, *Travels in the United States Etc, during 1849 and 1850* (Paris: Baudry's European Library, 1851), 22, 55–56; Muireann O'Cinneide, *Aristocratic Women and the Literary Nation, 1832–1867* (Basingstoke: Palgrave, 2008), 8–9, 66–67. For reviews, etc., see *Morning Post,* 17 Mar. 1851; *Daily News,* 18 Mar. 1851; *Examiner,* 22 Mar. 1851; *Lancaster Gazette, and General Advertiser for Lancashire, Westmorland, Yorkshire andc.,* 19 July 1851; *Blackburn Standard,* 30 July 1851; *Standard,* 13 Dec. 1851; *Huddersfield Chronicle and West Yorkshire Advertiser,* 1 Jan. 1853, 5 Mar. 1853.

56. James F. W. Johnston, *Notes on North America: Agricultural, Economical and Social,* vol. 2 (Edinburgh: William Blackwood and Sons, 1851), 314. For reviews, etc., see *Examiner,* 26 Oct. 1850; *Dundee Courier,* 26 Mar. 1851; *Morning Post,* 10 July 1851; *Preston Guardian etc.,* 31 May 1851; *Leicester Chronicle: or, Commercial and Agricultural Advertiser,* 7 June 1851; *Blackburn Standard,* 25 June 1851; *Belfast News-Letter,* 28 Nov. and 12 Dec. 1851; *Morning Chronicle,* 28 Nov. 1851, 22 Oct. 1855; *Trewman's Exeter Flying Post or Plymouth and Cornish Advertiser,* 11 Dec. 1851; *Berrow's Worcester Journal,* 29 Sept. 1855. Crampton quoted in Crawford, "British Travelers," 218. For the Negro Seaman Laws, see Philip M. Hamer, "British Consuls and the Negro Seamen Acts, 1850–1860," *Journal of Southern History* 1.2 (May 1935): 138–168; Philip M. Hamer, "Great Britain, the United States, and the Negro Seamen Acts, 1822–1848," *Journal of Southern History* 1.1 (Feb. 1935): 3–28; Leon F. Litwack, "The Federal

Government and the Free Negro, 1790–1860," *Journal of Negro History* 43.4 (Oct. 1958): 261–278; Michael Alan Schoeppmer, "Navigating the Dangerous Atlantic: Racial Quarantines, Black Sailors and United States Constitutionalism," PhD diss., University of Florida, 2010.

57. Edward Sullivan, *Rambles and Scrambles in North and South America* (London: Richard Bentley, 1852), 194–196, 199, 202–203. For reviews, etc., see *Examiner,* 14 Aug. and 2 Oct. 1852; *Daily News,* 4 Sept., 20 Oct., and 13 Nov. 1852; *Standard,* 6 and 8 Sept. 1852; *Morning Post,* 8 Sept. and 6 Dec. 1852, 21 Oct. 1857; *Lancaster Gazette, and General Advertiser for Lancashire, Westmorland, Yorkshire, andc.,* 9 Oct. 1852.

58. Sullivan, *Rambles and Scrambles,* 208–210. For Charles Kingsley's reaction, see Waller, "Charles Kingsley and the American Civil War," 563. For more on the Fugitive Slave Law of 1850, see Stanley W. Campbell, *The Slave Catchers: Enforcement of the Fugitive Slave Law, 1850–1860* (Chapel Hill: University of North Carolina Press, 1968); Homan Hamilton, *Prologue to Conflict: The Crisis and Compromise of 1850* (Lexington: University of Kentucky Press, 1964); David M. Potter, *The Impending Crisis, 1848–1861* (New York: Harper and Row, 1976); Linck C. Johnson, "'Liberty Is Never Cheap': Emerson, 'The Fugitive Slave Law,' and the Antislavery Lecture Series at the Broadway Tabernacle," *New England Quarterly* 76.4 (Dec. 2003): 550–592; James Oliver Horton and Lois E. Horton, "A Federal Assault: African Americans and the Impact of the Fugitive Slave Law of 1850," *Chicago-Kent Law Review* 68.3 (Summer 1993): 1179–1197.

59. *Blackwood's Edinburgh Magazine* 72.446 (Dec. 1852): 689–690.

60. William Makepeace Thackeray to Mrs. Carmichael-Smyth, 13 Feb. 1853, in Gordon N. Ray, ed., *The Letters and Private Papers of William Makepeace Thackeray in Four Volumes,* vol. 3 (London: Oxford University Press, 1945), 199–200; John Sutherland, "Thackeray as Victorian Racialist," *Essays in Criticism* 20.4 (Oct. 1970): 441–445, 444; Thomas, *Thackeray and Slavery.* For the growth of racialist ideas, see Lorimer, "The Role of Anti-Slavery Sentiment."

61. John F. T. Crampton to Lord Clarendon, 21 Feb. 1853, in James J. Barnes and Patience P. Barnes, eds., *Private and Confidential: Letters from British Ministers in Washington to the Foreign Secretaries in London, 1844–67* (London: Associated University Presses, 1993).

62. Marshall Hall, *The Two-Fold Slavery of the United States; With a Project for Self-Emancipation* (London: Adam Scott, 1854), 18, 137, 144, 93, 20, 22, 91. For reviews and advertisements of Hall's text, see *Standard,* 11 and 15 Sept. 1856.

63. Hall, *The Two-Fold Slavery,* 122.

64. Sarah Meer, *Uncle Tom Mania,* 168; Amanda Foreman, *World on Fire: An Epic History of Two Nations Divided* (London: Penguin, 2011), 26–27; Nassau William Senior, *American Slavery: A Reprint of an Article on "Uncle Tom's Cabin," of which a Portion was inserted in the 206th Number of the "Edinburgh Review"; and of Mr. Sumner's Speech on the 19th and 20th of May 1856, with a Notice of Events Which Followed that Speech* (London: Longman, Brown, Green, Longmans, and Roberts, 1856), 28–29. For more on Senior, see Marian Bowley, *Nassau Senior and Classical Economics* (London: George Allen and Unwin, 1967).

65. Fisch, *American Slaves in Victorian England.* In terms of popular antislavery during the early 1850s, Fisch notes that, while slave speakers and dioramas that emphasized the brutality of slavery tended to be received well in Britain, positive responses were not unanimous. *London Times,* 3 Sept 1852. For examples of the criticism directed toward slave speakers and

dioramas, see the *Wolverhampton and Staffordshire Herald,* which described an exhibition by the escaped slave Henry "Box" Brown on 17 Mar. 1852 as a "representation of slavery [which was] a gross and palpable exaggeration." Harry Stone, "Charles Dickens and Harriet Beecher Stowe," *Nineteenth Century Fiction* 12.3 (Dec. 1957): 188–202. For more on *Uncle Tom's Cabin* in Britain, see Wendy F. Hamand, "'No Voice from England': Mrs. Stowe, Mr. Lincoln, and the British in the Civil War," *New England Quarterly* 61.1 (Mar. 1988): 3–24.

66. Hall, *The Two-Fold Slavery,* 2, 17, 91, 147.

67. Ibid., 33–34, 118, 153, 52; Crawford, *The Anglo-American Crisis,* 56.

68. Amelia M. Murray, *Letters from the United States, Cuba and Canada* (New York: G. P. Putnam, 1856), 206, 38–39, 162, 164, 193–194, 283, 219; *Morning Post,* 25 Jan. 1856; *Bradford Observer,* 31 Jan. 1856; *Bristol Mercury,* 2 Feb. 1856; *Glasgow Herald,* 6 Feb. 1856; *Daily News,* 7 Feb. 1856; *Belfast News-Letter,* 9 May 1856; *Standard,* 30 May 1856; *Derby Mercury,* 25 June 1856; *Examiner,* 18 Mar. 1865.

69. Murray, *Letters from the United States,* 327, 148, 198, 180–182. For the complexities in British antislavery thought that allowed Murray to subscribe to a gradualist emancipation doctrine, see Huzzey, *Freedom Burning.* For the debate about gradualism in the United States, see Joanna Pope Melish, *Disowning Slavery: Gradual Emancipation and "Race" in New England, 1780–1860* (Ithaca: Cornell University Press, 1998); Anne C. Loveland, "Evangelicalism and 'Immediate Emancipation' in American Antislavery Thought," *Journal of Southern History* 32.2 (May 1966): 172–188; Bruce Levine, *Half Slave and Half Free: The Roots of Civil War* (1992; repr., New York: Hill and Wang, 2005).

70. Murray, *Letters from the United States,* 197–198.

71. James Stirling, *Letters from the Slave States* (London: John W. Parker and Son, 1857), 46–48, 285, 294. For reviews, etc., see *Glasgow Herald,* 31 July and 5 Aug. 1857; *Examiner,* 1 and 15 Aug. 1857; *Standard,* 24 Aug. and 8 Sept. 1857; *Blackburn Standard,* 23 Sept. and 17 Feb. 1857; *Morning Post,* 23 Sept. 1857, 15 Nov. 1862, 17 Sept. 1863; *Royal Cornwall Gazette, Falmouth Packet, and General Advertiser,* 25 Sept. 1857; *Lloyd's Weekly Newspaper,* 25 Oct. 1857; *Bradford Observer,* 12 Nov. 1857; *Aberdeen Journal,* 13 Jan. 1858; *Daily News,* 11 Dec. 1861, 18 Dec. 1862.

72. James Stirling, *Letters from the Slave States,* 53.

73. Ibid., 76, 88, 315–316, 343–344.

74. William Chambers, *American Slavery and Colour* (London: W. and R. Chambers, 1857), 119–120, 126–128. For an account of Chambers's publishing activities, see Aileen Fyfe, *Steam-Powered Knowledge: William Chambers and the Business of Publishing, 1820–1860* (Chicago: University of Chicago Press, 2012). Chambers made specific mention of having read Joseph Sturge's earlier travelogue (138). For reviews, etc., see *Examiner,* 28 Mar. and 4 Apr. 1857; *Aberdeen Journal,* 17 July 1857.

75. Chambers, *American Slavery and Colour,* 131–134, 171–180. These concerns about the importance of the Union to American abolitionists seem to have been given validity by the actions of prominent figures such as Wendell Philips and William Lloyd Garrison during the Civil War; see McDaniel, *The Problem of Democracy,* 213–216. For disunion in a transatlantic context, see W. Caleb McDaniel, "Repealing Unions: American Abolitionists, Irish Repeal, and

the Origins of Garrisonian Disunionism," *Journal of the Early Republic* 28.2 (Summer 2008): 243–269.

76. Chambers, *American Slavery and Colour,* 44, 140, 89, 92–94, 87. For the Missouri Compromise, see Daniel Walker Howe, *What Hath God Wrought: The Transformation of America, 1815–1848* (New York: Oxford University Press, 2007), 147–160; William W. Freehling, *The Road to Disunion,* vol. 1, *Secessionists at Bay, 1776–1854* (New York: Oxford University Press, 1990), 144–161; Robert Pierce Forbes, *The Missouri Compromise and Its Aftermath: Slavery and the Meaning of America* (Chapel Hill: University of North Carolina Press, 2007); Matthew H. Crocker, "The Missouri Compromise, the Monroe Doctrine, and the Southern Strategy," *Journal of the West* 43.3 (Summer 2004): 45–52.

77. Henry Ashworth, *A Tour of the United States, Cuba, and Canada: A Course of Lectures Delivered Before the Members of the Bolton Mechanics' Institution* (London: A. W. Bennett, 1861), 124, 40, 92 (the lectures were given in 1860); Genovese and Fox-Genovese, *Fatal Self-Deception,* 113.

78. Blackett, *Divided Hearts,* 54–57.

79. *Huddersfield Chronicle and West Yorkshire Advertiser,* 7 Dec. 1861.

CHAPTER TWO

1. Title quotation from Marryat, *Diary in America,* 32; D. W. Mitchell, *Ten Years Residence in the United States* (London: Smith, Elder, 1862), 72, 60–61, 147. The actual levels of immigration to the city of New York (as well as other areas of the nation) are explored in Leo Hershkowitz, "Overview: The Irish and the Emerging City: Settlement to 1844," in Ronald H. Bayor and Timothy J. Meagher, eds., *The New York Irish* (Baltimore: Johns Hopkins University Press, 1996); Paul A. Gilje, "The Development of an Irish American Community in New York before the Great Migration," and Hasia R. Diner, "Overview: 'The Most Irish City in the Union': The Era of Great Migration, 1844–1877," in Bayor and Meagher, *The New York Irish*; Kerby A. Miller, *Emigrants and Exiles: Ireland and the Irish Exodus to North America* (New York: Oxford University Press, 1985). While popular perceptions held that Irish immigrants flocked to the North, they did also have a presence in the South; see David T. Gleeson, *The Irish in the South, 1815–1877* (Chapel Hill: University of North Carolina Press, 2001).

2. Roberto Romani, "British Views on Irish National Character, 1800–1846: An Intellectual History," *History of European Ideas* 23.5/6 (1998): 193–219; de Nie, *The Eternal Paddy*; R. F. Foster, *Paddy and Mr. Punch: Connections in Irish and English History* (London: Penguin, 1993); L. Perry Curtis, *Apes and Angels: The Irishman in Victorian Caricature* (Washington: Smithsonian Institute Press, 1971); Donald M. MacRaild, *Irish Migrants in Modern Britain, 1750–1922* (New York: St. Martin's, 1999), 5–6; Miller, *Emigrants and Exiles,* 311; Diner, "The Most Irish City in the Union," 104; Scott Boltwood, "'The Ineffaceable Curse of Cain': Race, Miscegenation, and the Victorian Staging of Irishness," *Victorian Literature and Culture* 29.2 (2001): 383–396; Colley, *Britons,* 19–23, 331–335.

3. Romani, "British Views on Irish National Character"; Oliver MacDonagh, *The Emancipist: Daniel O'Connell, 1830–47* (London: Weidenfeld and Nicholson, 1989); Donal A. Kerr,

"A Nation of Beggars?": Priests, People, and Politics in Famine Ireland, 1846–1852 (Oxford: Clarendon, 1994), 2; Hilary Larkin, *A History of Ireland, 1800–1922: Theatres of Disorder* (New York: Anthem, 2014), 29–57; Alvin Jackson, *Ireland, 1798–1998: War, Peace and Beyond* (1999; repr., Chichester: Wiley-Blackwell, 2010), 6–68.

4. Martineau, *Society in America,* 1:217, 3:23; Kevin Phillips, *The Cousins War: Religion, Politics, and the Triumph of Anglo-America* (New York: Basic Books, 1999), 395; Paul Goodman, "Ethics and Enterprise: The Values of a Boston Elite, 1800–1860," *American Quarterly* 18.3 (Autumn 1966): 437–451; Numan V. Bartley, "The South and Sectionalism in American Politics," *Journal of Politics* 38.3 (Aug. 1976): 239–257.

5. Martineau, *Society in America,* 2:96–97; Martin Crawford, "British Travelers and the Anglo-American Relationship in the 1850s," *Journal of American Studies* 12.2 (Aug. 1978): 203–219, 213.

6. *Morning Post,* 28 Jan. 1835, article reprinted from the *Cork Constitution.* For more on the perceived influence of the Irish in American politics, see Gilbert Osofsky, "Abolitionists, Irish Immigrants, and the Dilemmas of Romantic Nationalism," *American Historical Review* 80.4 (Oct. 1975): 889–912; Angela F. Murphy, *American Slavery, Irish Freedom: Abolition, Immigrant Citizenship, and the Transatlantic Movement for Irish Repeal* (Baton Rouge: Louisiana State University Press, 2010). James H. Murphy, *Abject Loyalty: Nationalism and Monarchy in Ireland During the Reign of Queen Victoria* (Cork: Cork University Press, 2001), 13; MacDonagh, *The Emancipist,* 125, 153, 161; Larkin, *A History of Ireland,* 57–61; Jackson, *Ireland, 1798–1998,* 37–46.

7. Murray, *Travels in North America,* 1:136, 152.

8. Ibid., 2:208, 186–187.

9. The mythology of the Cavalier and Puritan in the context of the United States itself has been discussed in depth by historians. See Cash, *The Mind of the South*; Fox-Genovese and Genovese, *The Mind of the Master Class*; O'Brien, *Conjectures of Order*; Taylor, *Cavalier and Yankee*; Jan. C. Dawson, "The Puritan and the Cavalier: The South's Perception of Contrasting Traditions," *Journal of Southern History* 44.4 (Nov. 1978): 597–614; Robert B. Bonner, "Roundheaded Cavaliers?: The Context and Limits of a Confederate Racial Project," *Civil War History* 48.1 (Mar. 2002): 34–59.

10. Marryat, *Diary in America,* 2, 87, 92–93.

11. Ibid., 30–32.

12. Ibid., 41, 168, 306; Frederick Marryat, *Diary in America with Remarks on its Institutions Part Second* (Paris: Baudry's European Library, 1840), 52–53. For the Irish and American politics in the urban North, see Miller, *Emigrants and Exiles,* 328–341; Gilje, "The Development of an Irish American Community," 80; Diner, "The Most Irish City in the Union," 88, 100–104, in Bayor and Meagher, *The New York Irish*; Dale T. Knobel, *Paddy and the Republic: Ethnicity and Nationality in Antebellum America* (Middletown, CT: Wesleyan University Press, 1986).

13. Matthew Frye Jacobson, *Whiteness of a Different Color: European Immigrants and the Alchemy of Race* (Cambridge, MA: Harvard University Press, 1998), 40–43, 69–70; Knobel, *Paddy and the Republic,* 16, 45 56, 64; Murray, *American Slavery, Irish Freedom,* 11, 69.

14. Buckingham, *America,* 2:71–72; Kerr, *A Nation of Beggars,* 2; Jackson, *Ireland, 1798–1998,* 46–50.

15. Buckingham, *America,* 2:23; 3:13, 38; 2:417–418. Buckingham was by no means unanimously critical of the Irish; for example, in his subsequent work, *The Slave States of America,* 2 vols. (London: Fisher, Son, 1842), he noted how in Natchez, Mississippi, "the Irish emigrants in America preserve most of the generous virtues of their native island" (1:458). Even here however the stereotyping of the Irish was still in play, see Romani, "British Views on Irish National Character," 193.

16. Buckingham, *America,* 2:439.

17. Ibid., 3:238, 428; Charles Daubeny, *Journal of a Tour Through the United States and Canada, made During the Years 1837–1838* (Oxford: T. Combe, 1843), 66 and 69.

18. Buckingham, *America,* 3:421–422.

19. Buckingham, *The Slave States,* 1:20, 32; Buckingham, *America,* 1:455–471.

20. Buckingham, *The Slave States,* 1:565–566. Buckingham notes that this was the second time the British national anthem had been played in his honor. Unfortunately, he does not specify the location or circumstances in which the anthem was first played.

21. Buckingham, *America,* 2:439.

22. Buckingham, *The Slave States,* 2:487–488, 539–540. In terms of the different ethnic complexions of these regions, 1 percent of South Carolina's population was foreign born by 1850, and 2 percent of Virginia's was, while 21 percent of New Yorkers were foreign born. See Richards, *The Slave Power.* For a discussion of the apparent Anglophobia present in southern politics as a response to British abolitionism, see Rugemer, "The Southern Response to British Abolitionism," and Charles S. Sydnor, *The Development of Southern Sectionalism, 1819–1848* (Baton Rouge: Louisiana State University Press, 1948), 224. For the existence of both Anglophobia and Anglophilia in the South, see O'Brien, *Conjectures of Order.*

23. Charles Dickens, *American Notes for General Circulation* (1842; repr., London: Oxford University Press, 1966), 73. For a sample of the reviews, advertisements, etc., of *American Notes,* see *Morning Post,* 30 Aug. 1842; *Ipswich Journal,* 1 Oct., 3 Dec., and 22 Oct. 1842; *Sheffield and Rotherham Independent,* 1 Oct. 1842; *Berrow's Worcester Journal,* 6 Oct. and 8 Dec. 1842; *Examiner,* 15 Oct. 1842; *Lloyd's Weekly Newspaper,* 19 Feb. 1843, 11 Jan. 1852; *Reynolds Newspaper,* 14 June 1857. Claybaugh, "Towards a New Transatlanticism," 446.

24. Daubeny, *Journal of a Tour Through the United States and Canada,* 122, 109, 146.

25. Godley, *Letters from America,* 1:40, 140, 45; 2:167.

26. Ibid., 2:55–58, 197.

27. Featherstonhaugh, *Excursion through the Slave States,* 2:375.

28. Ibid., 2:376.

29. Lyell, *Travels in North America,* 1:135, 181.

30. Ibid., 1:234–235.

31. Ibid.

32. Lyell, *Travels in North America,* 1:229–234. The oft-quoted French traveler Alexis de Tocqueville had reservations about the compatibility of immigrants and American democracy; see Johann M. Neem, "Taking Modernity's Wager: Tocqueville, Social Capital and the American Civil War," *Journal of Interdisciplinary History* 41.4 (Spring 2011): 591–618, 604.

33. *Freeman's Journal and Daily Commercial Advertiser,* 7 Aug. 1844; Murphy, *American Slavery, Irish Freedom*; Berger, *The British Traveler in America, 1836–1860,* 101–102.

34. Murphy, *American Slavery, Irish Freedom,* 43–45, 179–181; Larkin, *A History of Ireland,* 63–67.

35. Murphy, *American Slavery, Irish Freedom,* 46, 181; Larkin, *A History of Ireland,* 67–69, 75–77; Jackson, *Ireland, 1798–1998,* 46–55.

36. Campbell, *Unlikely Allies,* 132–134; Wilbur D. Jones, *The American Problem in British Diplomacy, 1841–1861* (Athens: University of Georgia Press, 1974), 42.

37. The ability of Anglophobia to mobilize the Irish specifically is indicated in the reports given of recruiting officers working in New York during the Mexican-American War who promised those joining the army that they would be fighting against Britain as well as Mexico. See Haynes, *Unfinished Revolution,* 267. Lyell, *A Second Visit,* 1:180–181, 298; Pletcher, *The Diplomacy of Annexation,* 229–392; Scott Kaufman, *The Pig War: The United States, Britain, and the Balance of Power in the Pacific Northwest, 1846–72* (Lanham, MD: Lexington Books, 2004); Richard S. Cramer, "British Magazines and the Oregon." According to Sam W. Haynes, it was the perceived Anglophilia of Daniel Webster that prevented him from being a credible presidential candidate; see Haynes, *Unfinished Revolution,* 121–122,

38. Lyell, *A Second Visit,* 1:249–250, 256, 187–188. For a full discussion of mass politics, see Chapter 3.

39. Ibid., 1:249–250, 2:291.

40. Ibid., 1:159, 182, 208, 299, 322; Onuf, "Antebellum Southerners and the National Idea." For details on American Anglophobia as a phenomenon derived from abolitionism, see Rugemer, *The Problem of Emancipation,* 181; Peter S. Onuf, "Antebellum Southerners and the National Idea," in L. Diane Barnes, Brian Schoen, and Frank Towers, eds., *The Old South's Modern Worlds: Slavery, Region, and the Nation in the Age of Progress* (Oxford: Oxford University Press, 2011), 36–37; Haynes, *Unfinished Revolution,* 290–291.

41. Bourne, *Britain and the Balance,* in particular, 170–206; Archibald Prentice, *A Tour of the United States with Two Lectures on Emigration, Delivered in the Mechanics' Institution Manchester* (London: John Johnson, 1849), 104, 160–161.

42. *Daily News,* 13 June 1848; Kerr, *A Nation of Beggars,* 75–76.

43. *Morning Chronicle,* 30 July 1848; Robert Sloan, *William Smith O'Brien and the Young Ireland Rebellion of 1848* (Dublin: Four Courts, 2000); Richard P. Davis, *The Young Ireland Movement* (Dublin: Gill and Macmillan, 1987); Cian McMahon, "Ireland and the Birth of the Irish-American Press, 1842–61," *American Periodicals: A Journal of History and Criticism* 19.1 (2009): 5–20; Miles Taylor, "The 1848 Revolutions and the British Empire," *Past and Present* 166.1 (Feb. 2000): 146–180. For connections to the United States, see Murphy, *American Slavery, American Freedom,* and McMahon, "Ireland and the Birth of the Irish-American Press." It would be misleading to suggest that Boston was wholly exempt from these perceived connections with Ireland; after all, the *Boston Pilot* was an extremely successful Irish-American newspaper. See Taylor, "The 1848 Revolutions." Despite an Irish population existing in Boston, New York tended to loom large as an Irish haven from a British point of view, particularly as 1848 exiles, including John Mitchel, Thomas Francis Meagher, Richard O'Gorman, and John Blake Dillon, emigrated to the city. Crucially, in sectional terms, newspaper reports did not really highlight Repeal meetings or Young Irelander sympathy in the South. For Irish Brigades

in the United States, see John Belchem, "Republican Spirit and Military Science: The Irish Brigade and Irish-American Nationalism in 1848," *Irish Historical Studies* 29 (1994): 44–65.

44. *Hampshire Advertiser and Salisbury Guardian,* 9 Sept. 1848.

45. John Arthur Roebuck, *The Colonies of England: A Plan for the Government of Some Portion of our Colonial Possessions* (London: John W. Parker, 1849), 60–75.

46. *Northern Star and National Trades' Journal,* 15 Sept. 1849; Thomas Wheeler, *Sunshine and Shadow,* in Ian Haywood, ed., *Chartist Fiction* (Aldershot: Ashgate, 1999); Roebuck, *Colonies of England,* 84.

47. Sam Rathbone to William Rathbone VI, 21 Feb. 1849, RPVIX.3.50, Rathbone Papers; Stuart-Wortley, *Travels in the United States Etc.,* 39. Kevin Phillips notes that by the early 1850s, Cincinnati was "teutonized to the point of having six German-language newspapers"; see Phillips, *The Cousins War,* 433.

48. Houstoun, *Hesperos,* 1:80, 201–202, 281, 179–180; *Belfast News-Letter,* 26 May 1851.

49. John F. T. Crampton to Lord Malmesbury, 12 Sept. 1852, in Barnes and Barnes, *Private and Confidential;* Laura A. White, "The United States in the 1850s as Seen by British Consuls," *Mississippi Valley Historical Review* 19.4 (Mar. 1933): 509–536, 519.

50. Although there is no copy of Whitney's letter in Lindsay's papers, he did transcribe it in full into his diary. See William Schaw Lindsay Diary, William Schaw Lindsay Collection, National Maritime Museum, Greenwich, London (hereinafter WSLC), LND.5.3.

51. *Belfast News-Letter,* 25 Aug. 1852. For details on John Mitchel, see Bryan P. McGovern, *John Mitchel: Irish Nationalist, Southern Secessionist* (Knoxville: University of Tennessee Press, 2009); Aidan Hegarty, *John Mitchel: A Cause Too Many* (Belfast: Camlane, 2005).

52. *Reynolds's Newspaper,* 13 Nov. 1853; *Bradford Observer,* 12 Jan. 1854; *Era,* 30 Apr. 1854; *Lloyd's Weekly Newspaper,* 16 Apr. 1854. For more on the *Citizen,* see McMahon, "Ireland and the Birth of the Irish-American Press." For an examination of the place of slavery in relation to the Irish in America, see Murphy, *American Freedom, American Slavery;* Ian Delahanty, "'A Noble Empire in the West': Young Ireland, the United States and Slavery," *Britain and the World* 6.2 (Sept. 2013): 171–191.

53. *Belfast News-Letter,* 4 Aug. 1855; Jones, *The American Problem,* 150.

54. Murphy, *Abject Loyalty,* 109, 121; Jackson, *Ireland, 1798–1998,* 86–91; MacRaild, *Irish Migrants in Modern Britain,* 169–174.

55. Isabella Lucy Bird, *The Englishwoman in America* (1856; repr., Madison: University of Wisconsin, 1966), 338, 384–385, 120. For reviews, etc., see *Examiner,* 1 Dec. 1855, 22 Mar. 1856; *Lloyd's Weekly Newspaper,* 13 Jan. 1856; *Bradford Observer,* 24 Jan. 1856; *Bristol Mercury,* 26 Jan. 1856; *Trewman's Exeter Flying Post or Plymouth and Cornish Advertiser,* 31 Jan. 1856; *Manchester Times,* 2 Feb. 1856; *Caledonian Mercury,* 9 May 1856.

56. Bird, *The Englishwoman in America,* 120, 393, 447.

57. Stirling, *Letters from the Slave States,* 230, 28, 31.

58. Ibid., 60, 63; Henry A. Murray, *Lands of the Slave and the Free: or, Cuba, The United States and Canada First Volume* (London: John W. Parker, 1855), 403–404. For a sample of the reviews, advertisements, etc., of this text, see *Examiner,* 19 May and 4 Aug. 1855; *Morning Chronicle,* 16 Aug. 1855; *Morning Post,* 22 Aug. 1855; *Derby Mercury,* 12 Sept. 1855; *Daily*

News, 25 June 1856; *Glasgow Herald,* 2 July 1856. For more on the political consequences of this, particularly with regard to democracy, see Chapter 3.

59. William Makepeace Thackeray, *The Virginians* (1859; repr., London: Smith, Elder, 1892), 24–25, 42, 370; Peter L. Shillingsburg, *Pegasus in Harness: Victorian Publishing and W. M. Thackeray* (Charlottesville: University Press of Virginia, 1992); John Sutherland, *Victorian Fiction: Writers, Publishers, Readers* (New York: St. Martin's, 1995). For reviews, etc., see *Nottinghamshire Guardian,* 3 and 24 Sept. 1857; *Berrow's Worcester Journal,* 5 Sept. 1857, 15 Oct. 1859; *Wrexham and Denbighshire Advertiser, and Cheshire, Shropshire, Flintshire and North Wales Register,* 12 Sept. 1857, 12 June 1858; *Examiner,* 10 Oct. 1857, 3 Dec. 1859; *Aberdeen Journal,* 14 Oct. and 11 Nov. 1857; *Morning Chronicle,* 3 Nov. 1857; *Lloyd's Weekly Newspaper,* 8 Nov. 1857; *Standard,* 5 Dec. 1857; *Manchester Times,* 15 Jan. 1859. Blackett, *Divided Hearts,* 84.

60. Entry for 7 Aug. 1858, S. A. Wallace and F. E. Gillespie, eds., *The Journal of Benjamin Moran, 1857–1865,* 2 vols. (Chicago: University of Chicago Press, 1948), vol. 1; Reginald Horsman, *Race and Manifest Destiny: The Origins of American Racial Anglo-Saxonism* (Cambridge, MA: Harvard University Press, 1981); Brian Jenkins, *Lord Lyons: A Diplomat in an Age of Nationalism and War* (Montreal: McGill-Queens University Press, 2014), 98.

61. Entries for 3 Sept. 1858 and 24 Sept. 1859, Wallace and Gillespie, *The Journal of Benjamin Moran,* vol. 1.

62. John Gardner D. Englehart, *Journal of the Progress of H.R.H. Prince of Wales through British North America; and his Visit to the United States, 10 July to 15 November 1860* (London: Privately Printed, 1860); 95, 98–99; Frank Prochaska, *The Eagle and the Crown: Americans and the British Monarchy* (New Haven: Yale University Press, 2008).

CHAPTER THREE

1. For title quotation, see Featherstonhaugh, *Excursion Through the Slave States,* 341–342. *Punch,* 27 Sept. 1856.

2. Marcus Wood, "The American South and English Print Satire, 1760–1865," in Franklin T. Lambert and Joseph P. Ward, eds., *Britain and the American South from Colonialism to Rock and Roll* (Jackson: University of Mississippi Press, 2003). For Anglo-American politics in the period, see D. P. Crook, *American Democracy in English Politics, 1815–1850* (Oxford: Clarendon, 1965); Haynes, *Unfinished Revolution*; G. D. Lillibridge, *Beacon of Freedom: The Impact of American Democracy Upon Great Britain, 1830–1870* (Philadelphia: University of Pennsylvania Press, 1965); Robert Kelley, *The Transatlantic Persuasion: The Liberal Democratic Mind in the Age of Gladstone* (New York: Alfred J. Knopf, 1969).

3. Frances Trollope, *Domestic Manners,* 359; Johnston, *The Life, Manners, and Travels of Fanny Trollope,* 126. The amount of literature on the 1832 Reform Act is vast; however, useful introductions to the subject are provided in J. C. D. Clark, *English Society, 1660–1832: Religion, Ideology, and Political Practice During the Ancien Regime* (1985; repr., Cambridge: Cambridge University Press, 2000), 527–564; Michael Brock, *The Great Reform Act* (London: Hutchinson, 1973); John A. Phillips and Charles Wetherell, "The Great Reform Act of 1832 and the Political Modernization of England," *American Historical Review* 100.2 (Apr. 1995): 411–436; Howe, *What Hath God Wrought,* 275–284.

4. Frances Trollope, *Domestic Manners*, 217–219; *Examiner*, 19 Aug. 1832; Frances Trollope, *The Refugee in America*, 3 vols. (London: Whittaker, Treacher, 1832), 3:117–118. For more on British views of the American party system, see Crook, *American Democracy in English Politics*. In the United States itself, the mob could be given a sectional distinction. Paul C. Nagel, for instance, noted how the southerner James Hammond described "the licentious Sodom of Northern Mobocracy"; see Nagel, *One Nation Indivisible: The Union in American Thought, 1776–1861* (New York: Oxford University Press, 1964), 255.

5. Frances Trollope, *Domestic Manners*, 190.

6. Ibid., 191.

7. For the Nullification Crisis, see William W. Freehling, *Prelude to Civil War: The Nullification Controversy in South Carolina, 1816–1836* (1965; repr., New York: Oxford University Press, 1992); Robert V. Remini, *Andrew Jackson and the Course of American Democracy, 1833–1845*, vol. 3 (New York: Harper and Row, 1984), 12–44; Richard E. Ellis, *The Union at Risk: Jacksonian Democracy, States' Rights, and the Nullification Crisis* (New York: Oxford University Press, 1989); J. P. Ochenkowski, "The Origins of Nullification in South Carolina," *South Carolina Historical Magazine* 83.2 (Apr. 1982): 121–153; Richard B. Latner, "The Nullification Crisis and Republican Subversion," *Journal of Southern History* 43.1 (Feb. 1977): 19–38.

8. The most significant tariff-related issue in Britain centered on the Corn Laws. For a description of the effects of these laws, with particular reference to the careers of two key Anglo-American figures who were integral to the Anti-Corn Law League (ACLL), Richard Cobden and John Bright, see Donald Read, *Cobden and Bright: A Victorian Political Partnership* (London: Edward Arnold 1967). Information on the often difficult relationship between the ACLL and the free traders of the South is provided in Simon Morgan, "The Anti-Corn Law League and British Anti-Slavery in Transatlantic Perspective, 1838–1846," *Historical Journal* 52.1 (Mar. 2009): 87–107. The laws themselves and their repeal have been the subject of a number of works; see Paul A. Pickering and Alex Tyrrell, *The People's Bread: A History of the Anti-Corn Law League* (London: Leicester University Press, 2000); Cheryl Schonhardt-Bailey, *From the Corn Laws to Free Trade: Interests, Ideas, and Institutions in Historical Perspective* (Cambridge, MA: MIT Press, 2006); Henry Miller, "Popular Petitioning and the Corn Laws, 1833–46," *English Historical Review* 127.527 (Aug. 2012): 882–919. *Cobbett's Weekly Political Register*, 19 Jan. 1833; *Aberdeen Journal*, 9 Jan. 1833; *Newcastle Courant*, 7 Sept. 1833.

9. *Morning Post*, 7 Sept. 1832; *Standard*, 4 Jan. 1833; *Standard*, 24 Jan. 1833; *Hull Packet*, 18 Jan. 1833; *Jackson's Oxford Journal*, 26 Jan. 1833; *Aberdeen Journal*, 9 and 23 Jan. 1833; *Essex Chronicle and Colchester and Country Advertiser*, 5 Jan. 1833; *Essex Standard and Colchester and Country Advertiser*, 26 Jan. 1833; *Ipswich Journal*, 19 Jan. 1833; *Leicester Chronicle or Commercial and Agricultural Advertiser*, 13 Jan. 1833; *Sheffield Independent and Yorkshire and Derbyshire Advertiser*, 19 Jan. 1833.

10. *Cobbett's Weekly Political Register*, 19 Jan. 1833; Brian Schoen, *The Fragile Fabric of Union: Cotton, Federal Politics and the Global Origins of the Civil War* (Baltimore: Johns Hopkins University Press, 2009), 131.

11. *John Bull*, 23 May 1836.

12. Campbell, *Unlikely Allies*, *115*, 126–129.

13. Ibid., 117–118, 126, 129–130; Kenneth R. Stevens, *Border Diplomacy: The Caroline and McLeod Affairs in Anglo-American-Canadian Relations, 1837–1842* (Tuscaloosa: University of Alabama Press, 1989); Francis M. Carroll, *A Good and Wise Measure: The Search For the Canadian-American Boundary, 1783–1842* (Toronto: University of Toronto Press, 2001).

14. Campbell, *Unlikely Allies,* 126; *Age,* 29 Nov. 1835; *Bell's Life in London and Sporting Chronicle,* 23 Dec. 1838, 17 Mar. 1839, 14 Apr. 1839.

15. Martineau, *Society in America,* 2:75–76, 79–80; Godley, *Letters from America,* 1:22; Lyell, *A Second Visit,* 182, 255; Stirling, *Letters from the Slave States,* 72, 128.

16. For a discussion of Martineau's connection with one of the key liberal political figures of the era, Richard Cobden, see Nicholas C. Edsall, *Richard Cobden: Independent* Radical (Cambridge, MA: Harvard University Press, 1986), 162–163. Anthony Howe, *The Cotton Masters, 1830–1860* (Oxford: Oxford University Press, 1984); Martineau, *Society in America,* 1:44–46, 182–183.

17. Martineau, *Society in America,* 1:103, 99–100.

18. Ibid., 1:185. Interestingly, Martineau noted the existence of a small and "not influential" group of New Englanders who favored the revival of the monarchy. See Martineau, *Society in America,* 3:32–32. *Bristol Mercury,* 5 Jan. 1833; *Preston Chronicle,* 5 Jan. 1833; *Leeds Mercury,* 19 Jan. 1833.

19. Martineau, *Society in America,* 1:105–106.

20. *John Bull,* 14 Jan. and 23 Sept. 1833. For the acceptance of the idea of the tyranny of the majority and the influence of Alexis de Tocqueville on the development of the concept in Britain, see Roper, *Democracy and Its Critics,* 145–156.

21. Marryat, *Diary in America,* 11; Marryat, *Diary in America Part Second,* 132–137, 190, 203.

22. The relationship between democracy and the decline into mob rule was most influentially expounded by Edmund Burke, *Reflections on the Revolution in France: and on the Proceedings in Certain Societies in London relative to that Event* (1790; repr., Harmondsworth: Penguin, 1982); *John Bull,* 4 July 1836; Marryat, *Diary in America Part Second,* 132–137. For British views on President Jackson and the mob, see Crook, *American Democracy in English Politics,* 111–113.

23. Marryat, *Diary in America Part Second,* 64.

24. Marryat, *Diary in America,* 2, 32, 254; Marryat, *Diary in America Part Second,* 60.

25. Marryat, *Diary in America,* 253; Marryat, *Diary in America Part Second,* 180.

26. Campbell, *Unlikely Allies,* 100; Brothers, *The United States of North America as they are,* 187.

27. Brothers, *The United States of North America as they are,* 62.

28. Buckingham, *America,* 1:67–69, 3:338–339. For further accounts of elections in both New York and Boston, see Buckingham, *America,* 1:71–73, 3:411–415. For the period as a whole see John Ashworth, *The Republic in Crisis, 1848–1861* (New York: Cambridge University Press, 2012).

29. Buckingham, *The Slave States,* 1:290–291; Buckingham, *America,* 3:55–56.

30. Buckingham, *America,* 1:331; Buckingham, *The Slave States,* 1:35.

31. Buckingham, *America,* 3:462.

32. Henry Miller, "Radicals, Tories, or Monomaniacs? The Birmingham Currency Reformers in the House of Commons, 1832–1867," *Parliamentary History* 31.3 (Oct. 2012): 354–377, 368; Read, *Cobden and Bright,* 29–30. Sturge was one of the most active members of the

abolitionist community in Britain to publish a travelogue during this period; for his political life, see Howard Temperley, *British Antislavery, 1833–1870* (Columbia: University of South Carolina Press, 1972); Huzzey, *Freedom Burning*; Alex Tyrrell, *Joseph Sturge and the Moral Radical Party in Early Victorian Britain* (London: Christopher Helm, 1987).

33. Joseph Sturge, *A Visit to the United States in 1841* (London: Hamilton, Adams, 1842), 180, 176, 177.

34. Combe, *Notes on the United States,* 1:255; Jenkins, *Lord Lyons,* 105.

35. William Rathbone VI to Elizabeth Rathbone, 5 June 1842, RPVIX.3.68, Rathbone Papers; Combe, *Notes on the United States,* 1:88–89, 161, 223, 290.

36. Slater, *Charles Dickens,* 175, 196; Hugh Cunningham, "Dickens as a Reformer," in David Paroissien, ed., *A Companion to Charles Dickens* (Malden, MA: Blackwell, 2008), 173. Cunningham raises questions about Dickens's reputation as a reformer. For Dickens's politics see Ackroyd, *Dickens,* 137–139, 154–155, 301–302, 325–328, 369–371, 736–742; and Andrew Sanders, *Charles Dickens* (Oxford: Oxford University Press, 2003), 46–47, 50–61. For discussions of Dickens's politics more generally, see Gold, *Charles Dickens: Radical Moralist*; and Dickens, *American Notes,* 27, 245, 119–121, 247–248.

37. Campbell, *Unlikely Allies,* 131; Jones, *The American Problem,* 7, 28–29; Benjamin Disraeli to Sarah Disraeli, 19 Feb. 1841, in M. G. Wiebe et al., eds., *Benjamin Disraeli Letters,* 10 vols. (Toronto: University of Toronto Press, 1987), vol. 3; Paul Smith, *Disraeli: A Brief Life* (Cambridge: Cambridge University Press, 1996); Lytton Strachey and Roger Fulford, eds., *The Greville Memoirs, 1814–1860,* 7 vols. (London: Macmillan, 1938), vol. 4.

38. Daubeny, *Journal of a Tour Through the United States and Canada,* 111, 122–123.

39. Morgan, "The Anti-Corn Law League," 100–103; Martineau, *Society in America,* 2:129. For McDuffie as a proslavery figure, see Charles S. Sydnor, *The Development of Southern Sectionalism, 1819–1848* (Baton Rouge: Louisiana State University Press, 1948), 336. Report of Lindsay speaking on Free Trade in North Shields, 3 July 1859, WSLC, LND.1; Schoen, *Fragile Fabric,* 190–191.

40. Stone, "Dickens' Use of His American Experiences in *Martin Chuzzlewit*"; Dickens, *Martin Chuzzlewit,* 250–251. Although the newspapers that Dickens created were all New York based, two of the stories that the newsboys highlight focus on violence in the Southwest (specifically Arkansas and Alabama). Ackroyd, *Dickens,* 379; *Morning Post,* 21 Oct. 1843; *Freeman's Journal and Daily Commercial Advertiser,* 21 Sept. 1843; Gulddal, "The Most Hateful Land," 432–435. It is worth noting that Dickens had personal reasons for targeting the American press, given the treatment *American Notes* received from reviewers following its US publication. For an illustration of Dickens's other experiences with American newspapers, including the controversy surrounding a forged letter that appeared in the New York press, see Monod, *Martin Chuzzlewit,* 50.

41. Dickens, *Martin Chuzzlewit,* 332–363, 503–504; *Ainsworth's Magazine of Romance, General Literature and Art* 2 (1842): 15–16.

42. Jones, *The American Problem,* 31–54; Bourne, *The Balance of Power,* chapters 4 and 5; Woodworth, *Manifest Destinies,* 107–108; Haynes, *Unfinished Revolution,* 236–237, 259–260, 270.

43. Haynes, *Unfinished Revolution*, 247.

44. *Blackwood's Edinburgh Magazine* 59.366 (Apr. 1846): 440; White, "The United States in the 1850s," 526; Carl N. Degler, "The Locofocos: Urban 'Agrarians,'" *Journal of Economic History* 16.3 (Sept. 1956): 322–333.

45. Lyell, *Travels in North America*, 1:242; Disraeli to Baron Lionel de Rothschild, 3 Dec. 1845, in Wiebe et al., *Benjamin Disraeli Letters*, vol. 4.

46. Godley, *Letters from America*, 2:197, 55–57.

47. Ibid., 2:195; Featherstonhaugh, *Excursion Through the Slave States*, 2:334–335, 341–342. Cooper was a keen observer of British politics, in particular the ideas of political economy that were becoming increasingly fashionable in both Britain and the South; see Schoen, *The Fragile Fabric*, 120.

48. Lyell, *A Second Visit*, 1:160–161; Prentice, *A Tour of the United States*, 46.

49. Lyell, *A Second Visit*, 1:325; Saunders, "Let America Be the Test," 85.

50. Benjamin Disraeli to Lord Malmesbury, 13 Aug. 1852, in Wiebe et al., *Benjamin Disraeli Letters*, vol. 6; Stuart-Wortley, *Travels in the United States*, 21.

51. *Leeds Mercury*, 24 July 1852.

52. Hugh Seymour Tremenheere, *Notes on Public Subjects, Made During a Tour in the United States and in Canada* (London: John Murray, 1852), 133–134; Hugh Seymour Tremenheere, *The Constitution of the United States Compared With Our Own* (London: John Murray, 1854), 221–225. For reviews, etc., see *Examiner*, 6 Mar., 20 Nov., and 24 Mar. 1852; 3 Dec. 1853; 25 Mar. 1854; *Nottinghamshire Guardian*, 29 Apr. 1852; *Morning Chronicle*, 13 May 1852; *Morning Post*, 13 May and 1 July 1852; *Bradford Observer*, 3 June 1852; *Freeman's Journal and Daily Commercial Advertiser*, 11 Aug. 1852; *Belfast News-Letter*, 4 May 1857; *Standard*, 24 Nov. 1853; Stuart-Wortley, *Travels in the United States*, 25; Houstoun, *Hesperos*, 2:237.

53. Tremenheere, *The Constitution of the United States*, 150–151, 291. For an analysis of coverage in the *London Times* see Crawford, *The Anglo-American Crisis*, 42–45.

54. Bird, *The Englishwoman in America*, 339, 415.

55. Henry Bulwer to Lord Palmerston, 27 Jan. 1851; John F. T. Crampton to Lord Malmesbury, 12 Sept. 1852; Crampton to Lord Clarendon, 7 Feb. 1853, all in Barnes and Barnes, *Private and Confidential*; Lord Clarendon to the Earl of Aberdeen, 14 May 1854, quoted in Jones, *The American Problem*, 132.

56. *Daily News*, 8 June 1855.

57. Campbell, *Unlikely Allies*, 135–137; Jones, *The American Problem*, 77–98, 134.

58. Bourne, *Britain and the Balance of Power*, 185–186; Jones, *The American Problem*, 145–146.

59. Haynes, *Unfinished Revolution*, 289; Schoen, 218–219; *Punch*, 21 June 1856.

60. Stirling, *Letters from the Slave States*, 100–101; Strachey and Fulford, *The Greville Memoirs*, vol. 7.

61. Stirling, *Letters from the Slave States*, 72, 77, 84, 340. For the rural-versus-urban dichotomy that existed in southern thought, see Frank Towers, *The Urban South and the Coming of the Civil War* (Charlottesville: University of Virginia Press, 2004); Blaine A. Brownell and David R. Goldfield, eds., *The City in Southern History: The Growth of Urban Civilization in the South* (Port Washington, NY: Kennikat, 1977); Lyle W. Dorsett and Arthur H. Shaffer, "Was the Antebellum South Antiurban? A Suggestion," *Journal of Southern History* 38.1 (Feb. 1972):

93–100; David R. Goldfield, "The Urban South: A Regional Framework," *American Historical Review* 86.5 (Dec. 1981): 1009–1034; Frank Towers, "The Southern Path to Modern Cities: Urbanization in the Slave States," in Barnes, Schoen, and Towers, *The Old South's Modern Worlds.*

62. Stirling, *Letters from the Slave States,* 60–63.

63. Ibid., 38, 70; see also 195–197.

64. Quigley, *Shifting Grounds,* 6–7, 51–52.

65. *Leeds Mercury,* 24 July 1852; *Freeman's Journal and Daily Commercial Advertiser,* 15 Oct. 1856; *Era,* 8 June 1856.

66. Gregory quoted in Brian Jenkins, *Sir William Gregory of Coole: The Biography of an Anglo-Irishman* (Gerrards Cross, UK: Colin Smythe, 1986), 143; Lord Napier to Malmesbury, 8 June 1858, in Barnes and Barnes, *Private and Confidential.*

67. Foreman, *World on Fire,* 61.

CHAPTER FOUR

1. Title quotation taken from Hugo Reid, *Sketches in North America, with some Account of Congress and of the Slavery Question* (London: Longman, Green, Longman and Roberts, 1861), 204–205.

2. For key literature on this subject, see the introduction.

3. Bellows, "A Study of British Conservative Reaction," 507. For verbatim reports of Davis's Address, see *Daily News,* 4 Mar. 1861, and *Liverpool Mercury Etc,* 4 Mar. 1861. Jones, *Blue and Gray Diplomacy,* 18. For reactions to the Morrill Tariff, see *Dundee Courier,* 15 Mar. 1861; *Essex Standard, and General Advertiser for the Eastern Counties,* 15 Mar. 1861; *Royal Cornwall Gazette, Falmouth Packet, and General Advertiser,* 15 Mar. 1861; *Preston Guardian etc,* 16 Mar. 1861. For a recent work that emphasizes the significance of the tariff debate in Anglo-American Civil War relations and demonstrates the paucity of analysis it has received, see Marc-William Palen, "The Civil War's Forgotten Transatlantic Tariff Debate and the Confederacy's Free Trade Diplomacy," *Journal of the Civil War Era* 3.1 (Mar. 2013): 35–61.

4. Jones, *Blue and Gray Diplomacy,* 23; Jenkins, *Lord Lyons,* 151; Lyons to Lindsay, 8 Apr. 1861, WSLC, LND.7.461; Lyons to Russell, 1 Apr. 1861, in James J. Barnes and Patience P. Barnes, eds., *The Civil War Through British Eyes: Dispatches from British Diplomats,* vol. 1, *November 1860–April 1862* (London: Caliban, 2003); Brian Jenkins, "William Gregory: Champion of the Confederacy," *History Today* 28.5 (May 1978): 322–330, 325. It was Gregory who introduced Yancey to William Schaw Lindsay and John Laird, both significant figures in the British Confederate lobby; see Foreman, *World on Fire,* 95.

5. *Daily News,* 18 Mar. 1861; *Glasgow Herald,* 8 Mar. 1861. Before the war Lindsay had corresponded on free trade and reform with a number of key Civil War actors in Britain, such as Bright, Cobden, and Roebuck; see WSLC LND.4, LND.5.2. Roebuck worked with Lindsay as an advocate of the Confederate cause during the conflict, while Bright and Cobden became key members of the pro-Union lobby. Adrian, "Dickens on American Slavery," 324.

6. Jones, *Blue and Gray Diplomacy,* 5–6; 16–17; Doyle, *The Cause of All Nations,* 30–31.

7. Robert Toombs to Pierre Rost, Dudley A. Mann, and William L. Yancey, 16 Mar. 1861, in Richardson, *Messages and Papers of Jefferson Davis.*

8. Toombs to Rost, Mann, and Yancey, 16 Mar. 1861; Quigley, *Shifting Grounds*, 129–134. The major exception to this pattern of British support for national liberation movements came in the form of Ireland. McDaniel, *The Problem of Slavery*, 226.

9. Crawford, *The Anglo-American Crisis*, 93–94; Brantlinger, *Spirit of Reform*, 115; Blackett, *Divided Hearts*, 21, 152. Cobden described the British as "unanimous and fanatical" in their commitment to free trade; see Palen, "The Civil War's Forgotten Transatlantic Tariff Debate," 35. Cash, *John Bright*, 151–152.

10. For British coverage of Lincoln's inauguration, see *Birmingham Daily Post*, 19 Mar. 1861; *Daily News*, 19 Mar. 1861; *Morning Post*, 19 Mar. 1861; *Caledonian Mercury*, 20 Mar. 1861; *Reynolds's Newspaper*, 24 Mar. 1861. Campbell, *English Public Opinion*, 19; Phillips, *The Cousins War*, 491; Owsley, *King Cotton Diplomacy*, 206–208; Harrison, "British Labour and the Confederacy," 304; Doyle, *The Cause of All Nations*, 55–56; Walter Stahr, *Seward: Lincoln's Indispensable Man* (New York: Simon and Schuster, 2012).

11. William Arthur, *The American Question* (London: Sampson, Low and Son, 1861), 3, 5; *Punch*, 9 Mar. 1861; *Punch*, 20 Apr. 1861.

12. Arthur, *The American Question*, 10.

13. William Tallack, *Friendly Sketches in America* (London: A. W. Bennett, 1861), 229–230.

14. Yancey and Mann to Toombs, 21 May 1861; Yancey, Mann, and Rost to Toombs, 14 Aug. 1861, sent as an enclosure in Walker Fearn to Robert Toombs, 14 Aug. 1861, in Richardson, *Messages and Papers of Jefferson Davis*; De Leon quoted in Palen, "The Civil War's Forgotten Transatlantic Tariff Debate," 45.

15. *Punch*, 25 May 1861.

16. *Punch*, 17 Aug. 1861.

17. Entry for 7 Jan. 1861, *Journal of Benjamin Moran*, vol. 1; entries for 30 Aug. and 19 Nov., *Journal of Benjamin Moran*, vol. 2; *All the Year Round*, 21 Dec. 1861; Bagehot quoted in Sexton, *Debtor Diplomacy*, 154; Lorimer, "The Role of Anti-Slavery," 409.

18. Entries for 30 Aug., 19 and 11 Nov. 1861, *Journal of Benjamin Moran*, vol. 2.

19. Butler, *Critical Americans*, 75; Charles Francis Adams to Charles Francis Adams Jr., 18 July 1861; Adams to Adams Jr., 14 June 1861, in Ford, *Cycle of Adams Letters*, vol. 1.

20. Francis W. Newman to Dr. Nicholson, 14 June 1861, in Giberne Sieveking, ed., *Memoir and Letters of Francis W. Newman* (London: Kegan Paul, Trench Trubner, 1909), 181; "Extract from a Speech delivered at a meeting at Rochdale, to promote the Election of John Cheetham, Esq. for the Southern Division of the County of Lancaster, August 1, 1861," in *Speeches of John Bright, M.P on the American Question* (Boston: Little, Brown, 1865), 6; Cash, *John Bright*, 93–94, 145–169. For dissatisfaction over Lincoln's lack of action against slavery among prominent Americans, see Butler, *Critical Americans*, 58–59.

21. Arthur, *The American Question*, 7–8; Tallack, *Friendly Sketches*, 228.

22. Lyons to Earl Russell, 8 June 1861, in Barnes and Barnes, *The Civil War Through British Eyes*. For an analysis of the military threat posed to Canada and the British response to it, see Bourne, "British Preparations."

23. William Howard Russell, *Pictures of Southern Life, Social, Political and Military* (New York: James G. Gregory, 1861), 3–4, 49. Russell subsequently published extracts from his 1861 diary in 1863; see William Howard Russell, *My Diary North and South* (1863; repr., New York:

Harper Colophon, 1965), 59. For more on Russell, see Illana D. Miller, *Reports from America: William Howard Russell and the Civil War* (Stroud: Sutton, 2001); Rupert Furneaux, *The First War Correspondent: William Howard Russell of the Times* (London: Cassell, 1944).

24. Russell, *My Diary,* 191; Russell, *Pictures of Southern Life,* 117–118; Doyle, *The Cause of All Nations,* 159.

25. Russell, *My Diary,* 78; Schoen, *The Fragile Fabric,* 199.

26. Russell, *My Diary,* 101–102.

27. Knobel, *Paddy and the Republic,* 39–40; Murphy, *American Slavery, American Freedom,* 19; Horsman, *The Origins of Racial Anglo-Saxonism,* 163–164, 160, 301; Faust, *The Creation of Confederate Nationalism,* 5–22; Michael J. Bernath, *Confederate Minds: The Struggle for Intellectual Independence in the Civil War South* (Chapel Hill: University of North Carolina Press, 2010).

28. Crawford, "William Howard Russell," 197; Russell, *My Diary,* 141; Russell, *Pictures of Southern Life,* 95; see also 70, 27, 111.

29. Russell, *My Diary,* 29–30, 174, 75; see also 77, 52, 141, 149.

30. Russell, *Pictures of Southern Life,* 3–5; Russell to J. T. Delane, 26 Mar. 1861, in Martin Crawford, ed., *William Howard Russell's Civil War Private Diary and Letters, 1861–1862* (Athens: University of Georgia Press, 1992); Richard D. Fulton, "'Now Only *The Times* is on our Side': The London *Times* and America before the Civil War," *Victorian Review* 16.1 (Summer 1990): 48–58, 48; Crawford, *The Anglo-American Crisis;* Russell, *Civil War Diary and Letters, 1861–1862,* 45; Doyle, *The Cause of All Nations,* 100–102.

31. Henry Adams to C. F. Adams, 8 May 1862, in Ford, ed., *Cycle of Adams Letters,* vol. 1. For the British reaction to the Battle of Bull Run, see Crawford, *The Anglo-American Crisis,* 117–122, 111; Foreman, *World on Fire,* 122–130; Jones, *Blue and Gray Diplomacy,* 61–64.

32. James M. Mason to Judah P. Benjamin, 2 May 1862, in Richardson, *Messages and Papers of Jefferson Davis;* Blackett, *Divided Hearts,* 139. Spence was one of the most active pro-Confederate propagandists of the war, and in addition to pamphlets he produced forty-five articles for the *London Times* between February 1862 and January 1865. For examples of reviews of *The American Union,* see *London Times,* 6 Jan. 1862; *Morning Post,* 7 Jan. 1862; and *Examiner,* 12 Apr. 1862. For an unfavorable review, see *Daily News,* 2 Dec. 1861, Robert Trimble, *A Review of the American Struggle in its Military and Political Aspects from the Inauguration of President Lincoln, 4 Mar. 1861 till his Re-election, 8 November 1864* (London: Whittaker, 1864), 46–48. Palen, "The Civil War's Forgotten Transatlantic Tariff Debate," 46; W. E. Adams, *Memoirs of a Social Atom,* vol. 2 (London: Hutchinson, 1903), 420; James Spence, *The American Union; its Effect on National Character and Policy, with an Inquiry into Secession as a Constitutional Right, and the Causes of the Disruption* (1861; repr., London: Richard Bentley, 1862), 30, 193, 196. Quigley, *Shifting Grounds,* 79.

33. Quigley, *Shifting Grounds,* 201, 209, 225–226.

34. Spence, *The American Union,* 239–240. Forsyth quoted in Bellows, "British Conservative Reaction," 516.

35. Spence, *The American Union,* 60, 70.

36. Russell, *Pictures of Southern Life,* 6, 132; Mulvey, *Transatlantic Manners,* 31; Bellows, "British Conservative Reaction," 512–513; Blackett, *Divided Hearts,* 225–227.

37. Doyle, *The Cause of All Nations,* 95–98; Cruikshank, "J. A. Roebuck M.P," 202.

38. Spence, *The American Union,* 85–86, 57.

39. *Blackwood's* quoted in Blackett, "British Views of the Confederacy," 143–144; Phillips, *The Cousins War,* 495; Bonner, "Roundheaded Cavaliers."

40. Spence, *The American Union,* 130; see also 121, 125, 136.

41. Spence, *The American Union,* 122; see also 150.

42. Betty Fladeland, "'Our Cause Being One and the Same': Abolitionists and Chartism," in Walvin, *Slavery and British Society, 1776–1846.* For O'Brien and Owen, see Harrison, "British Labour and the Confederacy," 310–311. For more on British radical opinion on the Civil War, see Kevin J. Logan, "The *Bee-Hive* Newspaper and the British Working Class Attitudes Toward the American Civil War," *Civil War History* 22.4 (Dec. 1976): 337–348; Michael J. Turner, "Perceptions of America and British Reform during the 1860s," *Civil War History* 59.3 (Sept. 2013): 320–357. Kelly J. Mays, "Slaves in Heaven, Laborers in Hell: Chartist Poets' Ambivalent Identification with the (Black) Slave," *Victorian Poetry* 39.2 (Summer 2001): 137–163, 157.

43. Schoen, *Fragile Fabric,* 235.

44. Spence, *The American Union,* 93–94, 141, 149; Lorimer Crawford, *The Anglo-American Crisis,* 82; "The Role of Anti-Slavery Sentiment," 406, 420.

45. Campbell, *Unlikely Allies,* 146–147; Spence, *The American Union,* 99–100, 109, 152–153; Lawrence Goldman, "'A Total Misconception': Lincoln, the Civil War, and the British, 1860–1865," in Jay Sexton and Richard Carwadine, eds., *The Global Lincoln* (New York: Oxford University Press, 2011), 113.

46. Reid, *Sketches in North America,* 97–98, 202–203, 176–177. Reid made specific mention of Archibald Prentice's travelogue.

47. Ibid., 193, 202–205.

48. Ibid., 162–164, 106–107. Reid was critical of the conditions of escaped slaves in Canada as well as the northern states of the Union. This being said, he implied that the conditions in the northern United States were worse than those in British North America.

49. Ibid., 39–40, 51.

CHAPTER FIVE

1. Title quotation taken from an anonymous letter sent to the American legation in London on 28 October 1863; see Foreman, *World on Fire,* 524. Campbell, *Unlikely* Allies, 149; Bourne, *The Balance of Power,* 218–247; Foreman, *World on Fire,* 170; Jones, *Blue and Gray Diplomacy,* 83–111; entries for 27 and 28 Nov. 1861, *Journal of Benjamin Moran,* vol. 2; Jordan and Pratt, *Europe and the American Civil War,* 28–47. For more on the *Trent* and possible conflict between Britain and the Union, see Sexton, *Debtor Diplomacy,* 95–104; Jones, *Blue and Gray Diplomacy,* 83–92; Campbell, *Unlikely Allies,* 150–152, 168–170; Bourne, *The Balance of Power,* 218–247; Foreman, *World on Fire,* 173–195; Stephen C. Neff, *Justice in Blue and Gray: A Legal History of the Civil War* (Cambridge, MA: Harvard University Press, 2010); Adams, *Great Britain and the American Civil War,* 1:218–237; Mahin, *One War at a Time,* 66–73; Charles Francis Adams, "The Trent Affair," *American Historical Review* 17.3 (Apr. 1912): 540–562; Victor H. Cohen, "Charles Sumner and the Trent Affair," *Journal of Southern History* 22.2 (May 1956): 205–219.

2. Blackett, *Divided Hearts,* 61; *Birmingham Daily Post,* 29 Nov. 1861; *Morning Post,* 28 Nov. 1861; *Liverpool Mercury etc.,* 28 Nov. 1861. For further examples, see *Bradford Observer,* 28 Nov. 1861; *Freeman's Journal and Daily Commercial Advertiser,* 28 Nov. 1861; *Dundee Courier and Daily Argus,* 28 Nov. 1861; *Sheffield and Rotherham Independent,* 28 Nov. 1861; *Standard,* 28 Nov. 1861. See also Jordan and Pratt, *Europe and the American Civil War,* 29–31. This must be seen as quite a shift for the Adelphi theater, given that, according to Sarah Meer, the management team had antislavery sympathies during the 1850s; see Meer, *Uncle Tom Mania,* 156–158.

3. *London Times,* 3 Dec. 1861; Adams, "The Trent Affair," 544, 547; Crawford, "William Howard Russell," 203; entry for 12 Dec. 1861, *Journal of Benjamin Moran,* vol. 2; Crawford, *The Anglo-American Crisis,* 96–97; Campbell, *Unlikely Allies,* 150; Palmerston quoted in Foreman, *World on Fire,* 174.

4. John Bright, "Speech at a Dinner at Rochdale," in *The Speeches of John Bright*; *Huddersfield Chronicle and West Yorkshire Advertiser,* 7 Dec. 1861; Henry Adams to C. F. Adams Jr., 20 Nov. 1861, in Ford, *Cycle of Adams Letters,* vol. 1.

5. Bright, "Speech at a Dinner at Rochdale," in Bright, *The Speeches of John Bright*; Cohen, "Charles Sumner and the Trent Affair," 236; Blackett, *Divided Hearts,* 152; C. F. Adams to C. F. Adams Jr., 10 Jan. 1862, in Ford, *Cycle of Adams Letters,* vol. 1; E. D. Adams, *Great Britain and the American Civil War,* 1:236; Campbell, *Unlikely Allies,* 152–152; Crawford, *The Anglo-American Crisis,* 107–111.

6. *London Times,* reprinted in the *Glasgow Herald,* 9 Dec. 1861.

7. *Blackburn Standard,* 11 Dec. 1861; *Punch,* quoted in *Glasgow Herald,* 13 Dec. 1861.

8. A. J. B. Beresford-Hope, *England, the North, and the South: being a Popular View of the American Civil War* (London: James Ridgway, 1862), 58–59; Bruce Coleman, *Conservatism and the Conservative Party in Nineteenth Century Britain* (London: Edward Arnold, 1988), 127; Blackett, *Divided Hearts,* 61. The SIA publically called on the Confederacy to eventually abolish slavery; see Adams, *Great Britain and the American Civil War,* 2:220. See also Wharncliffe Muniments, Sheffield Archives, in particular Wh.M 460 and Wh.M 461.

9. Schoen, *Fragile Fabric,* 104; McDaniel, *The Problem of Democracy,* 6; Jenkins, *Lord Lyons,* 120.

10. For Fremont's order, see Gary W. Gallagher, *The Union War* (Cambridge, MA: Harvard University Press, 2011), 94; and James Oakes, "Reluctant to Emancipate?: Another Look at the First Confiscation Act," *Journal of the Civil War Era* 3.4 (Dec. 2013): 458–466. Beresford-Hope, *England, the North, and the South,* 36–37, 67, 10–12, 59; Lyons to Russell, 16 Sept. 1861, in Barnes and Barnes, *The American Civil War Through British Eyes*; Goldman, "A Total Misconception," 113; *Index,* 8 May 1862.

11. Jenkins, *Lord Lyons,* 130; Schoen, *Fragile Fabric,* 208–209.

12. W. L. Yancey specifically focused on the possibility that the Confederacy might reopen the international slave trade; see *Daily News,* 3 Feb. 1862; *Index,* 2 Oct. 1862; Owsley, *King Cotton Diplomacy,* 169; Foreman, *World on Fire,* 214–215, 273. The format of the *Index* was a sixteen-page weekly newspaper; see Mahin, *One War at a Time,* 21; Blackett, *Divided Hearts,* 145; Oates, "Henry Hotze," 140; Henry Hotze to George Witt, 11 Aug. 1864, in Burnett, *Henry Hotze.* For more on Hotze and the *Index,* see the introduction to Burnett, *Henry Hotze*; Robert E.

Bonner, “Slavery, Confederate Diplomacy, and the Racialist Mission of Henry Hotze,” *Civil War History* 51.3 (Sept. 2005): 288–316; Barnhart, *Albert Taylor Bledsoe*; Cunliffe, *Chattel Slavery and Wage Slavery*; Bonner “Proslavery Extremism Goes to War.”

13. Beresford-Hope, *England, the North, and the South,* 6–8.

14. Ibid., 13–14, 61.

15. Ibid., 33–34; Saunders, “Let America Be the Test,” 86–87; *Morning Post,* 22 Feb. 1862.

16. G. Taylor to Lindsay, 20 Oct. 1862, WSLC, LND.7.

17. Beresford-Hope, *England, the North and the South,* 12–13, 26, 21; William Howard Russell to John T. Delane, 16 July 1861, in Crawford, *William Howard Russell's Private Diary*; Oscar Maurer, “‘Punch’ On Slavery and Civil War in America, 1841–1865,” *Victorian Studies* 1.1 (Sept. 1957): 4–28, 17; C. F. Adams to C. F. Adams Jr., 1 Aug. 1862; Henry Adams to C. F. Adams Jr., 7 Nov. 1861; Henry Adams to C. F. Adams Jr., 25 Oct. 1861, Ford, *Cycle of Adams Letters,* vol. 1.

18. Blackett, *Divided Hearts,* 84–86, 104–121; Mark Bennett, “Confederate Supporters in the West Riding, 1861–1865: ‘Cranks of the Worst English Species,’” *Northern History* 51.2 (Sept. 2014): 311-329, 135–136.

19. A. J. B. Beresford-Hope, *The Results of the American Disruption: The Substance of a Lecture Delivered by Request Before the Maidstone Literary and Mechanics Institution, in Continuation of a Popular View of the American Civil War, and England, the North and the* South (London: James Ridgway, 1862), 28; Beresford-Hope, *England, The North and the South,* 56, 74.

20. Beresford-Hope, *England, the North and the South,* 13–14; *Morning Post,* 20 Mar. 1862.

21. Jenkins, “William Gregory,” 323–325; Charles M. Hubbard, “James Mason, the ‘Confederate Lobby,’ and the Blockade Debate of March 1862,” *Civil War History* 45.3 (Sept. 1999): 223–237; Hubbard, *The Burden of Confederate Diplomacy,* 78; *Leeds Mercury,* 10 Mar. 1862. For coverage of Gregory's motion, see *Belfast News-Letter,* 8 Mar. 1862; *Dundee Courier and Daily Angus,* 8 Mar. 1862. For blockades and blockade running, see Sexton, *Debtor Diplomacy,* 165–166, 179–183.

22. Jenkins, “William Gregory,” 323–325; Hubbard, “James Mason,” *Leeds Mercury,* 10 Mar. 1862.

23. James Pope-Hennessy, *Anthony Trollope* (Boston: Little, Brown, 1971); Kinser, *The American Civil War,* 55–90.

24. Anthony Trollope, *North America,* vol. 1 (Leipzig: Bernard Tauchnitz, 1862), 174, 12, 159–165; Anthony Trollope, *North America,* 2 vols. (1862; repr., Gloucester: Alan Sutton, 1987), 2:86–87.

25. Hall, *Civilising Subjects,* 210–216, 222–223.

26. Anthony Trollope, *North America,* 1:158, 175.

27. *Index,* 1 May 1862 (this letter may actually have been written by James Spence or a member of Fraser, Trenholm, and Son, a key Confederate merchant company with offices in New York, Liverpool, and Charleston); Owsley, *King Cotton Diplomacy,* 21; Dickens quoted in Adrian, “Dickens on American Slavery,” 324–325; Dickens quoted in Slater, *Charles Dickens,* 505–506.

28. Anthony Trollope, *North America,* 2:80; Charles P. Cullop, *Confederate Propaganda in Europe, 1861-1865* (Coral Gables, FL: University of Miami Press, 1969), 57.

29. Foreman, *World on Fire,* 58–59; C. F. Adams to C. F. Adams Jr., 20 Dec. and 21 June 1861, Ford, *Cycle of Adams Letters,* vol. 1; Campbell, *English Public Opinion,* 36–38; Crook "Portents of War," 168; Campbell, *Unlikely Allies,* 156–157; Phillips, *The Cousins War,* 491; Doyle, *The Cause of All Nations,* 62; Jenkins, *Lord Lyons,* 148; Jones, *The American Problem,* 201.

30. Adams, *Great Britain and the American Civil War,* 1:113; Bourne, *Britain and the Balance,* 211; Anthony Trollope, *North America,* 1:369–370, 2:237, 304, 281–282; C. F. Adams to C. F. Adams Jr., 20 Dec. 1861; Bourne, "British Preparations for War," 601; Jay Sexton, "William H. Seward in the World," *Journal of the Civil War Era* 4.3 (Sept. 2014): 398–430.

31. James M. McPherson, *Battle Cry of Freedom: The Civil War Era* (New York: Oxford University Press, 1988), 420; Judah P. Benjamin to John Slidell and James M. Mason, 19 July 1862, in Richardson, *Messages and Papers of Jefferson Davis*; Campbell, *English Public Opinion,* 106–107; Crook, *The North, the South and the Powers,* 206; Blackett, *Divided Hearts,* 223–224.

32. *Index,* 4 Sept., 12 June, 5 June, 16 June, and 10 Nov. 1862; Blackett, *Divided Hearts,* 10; Dudley Mann to Jefferson Davis, 1 Feb. 1862, in Richardson, *Messages and Papers of Jefferson Davis.*

33. For an account of the meeting, see *Bradford Observer,* 14 Aug. 1862; see also *Reynolds's Newspaper,* 17 Aug. 1862; *Sheffield and Rotherham Independent,* 14 Aug. 1862; *Newcastle Courant Etc.,* 15 Aug. 1862; *York Herald,* 16 Aug. 1862. For the Cotton Famine in Britain, see Owsley, *King Cotton Diplomacy*; Blackett, *Divided Hearts*; Ellison, *Support of Secession*; Campbell, *English Public Opinion*; Crawford, *Anglo-American Crisis*; Foner, *British Labor and the Confederacy*; Jones, *Blue and Gray Diplomacy*; Kinser, *The American Civil War*; Myers, *Caution and Cooperation*; Brauer, "British Mediation and the American Civil War"; Michael Brook, "Confederate Sympathies in North-East Lancashire, 1862–1864," *Lancashire and Cheshire Antiquarian Society* 75–76 (1977): 211–217; N. Hall, "The Liverpool Cotton Market and the American Civil War," *Northern History* 34.1 (1998): 149–169; Lebergott, "Through the Blockade"; Frenise A. Logan, "India-Britain's Substitute for American Cotton, 1861–1865," *Journal of Southern History* 24.4 (Nov. 1958): 472–480; Douglas Maynard, "Civil War 'Care': The Mission of the George Griswold," *New England Quarterly* 34.3 (Sept. 1961): 291–310; Foreman, *World on Fire,* 281–282; Richard Cobden to Henry Ashworth, 10 Apr. 1862, in F. W. Chesson, *The Political Writings of Richard Cobden,* 2 vols. (London: T. Fisher Unwin, 1902), vol. 1. Although Palmerston and Roebuck both highlighted cotton in speeches given in Sheffield, the city had little involvement in the trade. As Palmerston indicates, the most significant impact of the cotton famine was on Lancashire.

34. Adams, *Memoirs of a Social Atom,* vol. 2; *Bradford Observer,* 14 Aug. 1862; see also *Sheffield and Rotherham Independent,* 14 Aug. 1862; *Newcastle Courant Etc.,* 15 Aug. 1862; *York Herald,* 16 Aug. 1862.

35. Charles Edward Rawlins Jr., *American Disunion: Constitutional or Unconstitutional? A Reply to Mr. James Spence upon the Question "Is Secession a Constitutional Right?" Discussed in his Recent Work, "The American Union"* (London: Robert Hardwicke, 1862), 8–9, 22.

36. Jack Stillinger, ed., *John Stuart Mill Autobiography* (Boston: Houghton Mifflin, 1969), 158; Jordan and Pratt, *Europe and the American Civil War,* 74; Campbell, *English Public Opinion,* 200; Harrison, "British Labour," 91; Jenkins, *Britain and the War for the Union,*

2:39; J. E. Cairnes, *The Slave Power: Its Character and Probable Designs: Being an Attempt to Explain the Real Issues involved in the American Contest* (New York: Carleton, 1862), xi, 17, 22, 24, 18; Jenkins, *Lord Lyons,* 199. For a biography of Cairnes, see Adelaide Weinberg, *John Elliot Cairnes and the American Civil War: A Study in Anglo-American Relations* (London: Kingswood, 1970). For the 1842 tariff, see Daniel Walker Howe, *What Hath God Wrought,* 593–594, 765.

37. Cairnes, *The Slave Power,* 18.

38. Ibid., 19, 103; McPherson, *Battle Cry of Freedom,* 352–358.

39. Cairnes, *The Slave Power,* 34.

40. Ibid., 17, 27.

41. Ibid., 21.

42. Ibid., 26, 29–31.

43. Ibid., 89–90, 210; Campbell, *English Public Opinion.*

44. Adams, *Great Britain and the American Civil War,* 2:18; Brauer, "British Mediation and the American Civil War," 49; "Speech of W. S. Lindsay to the House of Commons, 18 July 1862," included as an appendix in Nemo, *Remarks on the Policy of Recognizing the Independence of the Southern States of North America, and on the Struggle in that Continent* (London: Effingham Wilson, 1863); Stillinger, *John Stuart Mill,* 159–160; entry for 21 June 1862, *Journal of Benjamin Moran,* vol. 2.

45. Mason to Benjamin, 23 June 1862; Slidell to Benjamin, 29 Sept. 1862; Richardson, *Messages and Papers of Jefferson Davis,* vol. 2.

46. For the decision to pass the proclamation in the context of American politics and the reaction to it across the United States, see Louis P. Masur, *Lincoln's Hundred Days: The Emancipation Proclamation and the War for the Union* (Cambridge, MA: Belknap, 2012).

47. *Morning Post,* 9 Oct. 1862.

48. Ibid., Adams, *Great Britain and the American Civil War,* 2:47; Owsley, *King Cotton Diplomacy,* 19; Blackett, *Divided Hearts,* 30. For the arguments for and against the "King Cotton theory," see Owsley, *King Cotton Diplomacy*; Blackett, *Divided Hearts*; Ellison, *Support of Secession*; Campbell, *English Public Opinion*; Crawford, *Anglo-American Crisis*; Foner, *British Labor and the Confederacy*; Jones, *Blue and Gray Diplomacy*; Kinser, *The American Civil War*; Myers, *Caution and Cooperation*; Brauer, "British Mediation and the American Civil War"; Brook, "Confederate Sympathies in North-East Lancashire"; Claussen, "Peace Factors"; Gentry, "Confederate Success in Europe"; Hall, "The Liverpool Cotton Market"; Harrison, "British Labour and the Confederacy"; Hernon, "British Sympathies"; Lebergott, "Through the Blockade"; Logan, "India: Britain's Substitute for American Cotton"; Maynard, "Civil War Care"; Park, "The English Workingmen"; Sadie Daniel St Clair, "Slavery as a Diplomatic Factor in Anglo-American Relations During the Civil War," *Journal of Negro History* 30.3 (July 1945): 260–275; *Morning Post,* 9 Oct. 1862; Jenkins, *Lord Lyons,* 206.

49. Entries for 9, 6, and 8 Oct. and 8 Nov. 1862, *Journal of Benjamin Moran,* vol. 2.

50. E. D. Steele, *Palmerston and Liberalism, 1855–1865* (Cambridge: Cambridge University Press, 1991); Robert L. Reid, ed., "William E. Gladstone's 'Insincere Neutrality' during the Civil War," *Civil War History* 15 (Dec. 1969): 293–307, 294; *Liverpool Mercury,* 11 Jan. 1869.

51. *London Times,* 7 Oct. 1862; St. Clair, "Slavery as a Diplomatic Factor," 268; Blackett, *Divided Hearts,* 108. For Wilson Armistead, see Temperley, *British Antislavery, 1833–1870,* 237–238, 245–247.

52. *Index,* 16 Oct. 1862; Campbell, *English Public Opinion,* 131; Christopher Ewan, "The Emancipation Proclamation and British Public Opinion," *Historian* 67.1 (Mar. 2005): 1–19, 15–16; Mason to Benjamin, 7 Nov. 1862, in Virginia Mason, ed., *The Public Life and Diplomatic Correspondence of James M. Mason with Some Personal History* (New York: Neale, 1906); Doyle, *The Cause of All Nations,* 171.

53. *Index,* 22 Jan. 1863.

54. *Index,* 22 Jan. 1863; G. Julian Harney to Charles Sumner, 10 Dec. 1862, in Frank Gees Black and Renee Metivier Black, eds., *The Harney Papers* (Assen: Van Gorcum, 1969).

55. Mason to Benjamin, 4 Nov. 1862; Mason to Benjamin, 7 Nov. 1862, both in Mason, *The Public Life and Diplomatic Correspondence.*

56. Foreman, *World on Fire,* 731–732, 748–749; Jones, *Blue and Gray,* 318–319; Sexton, *Debtor Diplomacy,* 184–186; Crook, *The North, the South,* 356–359.

57. "Memorandum (Secret) by Mr. Gladstone on the War in America—Printed for the Use of the Cabinet on 25 Oct. 1862," in Philip Guedalla, ed., *Gladstone and Palmerston, being the Correspondence of Lord Palmerston with Mr. Gladstone, 1851–1865* (London: Victor Gollancz, 1928); Logan, "The *Bee-Hive* Newspaper," 344–345.

58. Myers, *Caution and Cooperation,* 6; Campbell, *Unlikely Allies,* 158, 160; Blackett, *Divided Hearts,* 32; Lorimer, "The Role of Anti-Slavery," 420; Logan, "The *Bee-Hive* Newspaper," 347; Gideon Welles, 7 Apr. 1863, in Howard K. Beale, ed., *Diary of Gideon Welles: Secretary of the Navy Under Lincoln and Johnson,* vol. 1 (New York: John W. W. Norton, 1960); Henry Adams to C. F. Adams Jr., 30 Jan. 1863; Henry Adams to C. F. Adams Jr., 23 Jan. 1863; C. F. Adams to C. F. Adams Jr., 23 Jan. 1863, in Ford, *Cycle of Adams Letters,* vol. 1; Jenkins, *Lord Lyons,* 218–219; entry for 22 Jan. 1863, *Journal of Benjamin Moran,* vol. 2.

59. Oates, "Henry Hotze," 151–152; Burnett, *Henry Hotze,* 22–26.

60. Jones, *Blue and Gray Diplomacy,* 255–264, 276, 287–288, 295–302, 307. A number of diplomatic developments, including a Polish uprising against Russia and the Second Schleswig War between Denmark and the German Confederation, also distracted the British public and politicians from the American conflict in this period, thereby reducing the likelihood of intervention; see Jones, *Blue and Gray Diplomacy,* 293; Laurence Fenton, *Palmerston and the Times: Foreign Policy, the Press, and Public Opinion in Mid-Victorian Britain* (London: I. B. Tauris, 2012), 216–220. In some sense, US affairs remained of limited interest from the later months of 1863 through to the end of the war. While the assassination of Lincoln in April 1865 saw Britons turn their attention to the United States temporarily, the scandal over Gov. Edward Eyre and his treatment of the Morant Bay Rebels in Jamaica in October 1865 refocused British eyes on imperial and domestic politics. For a concise and compelling overview of the British response to the assassination of Lincoln, see Blackett, *Divided Hearts,* 213–243. For Governor Eyre and Morant Bay, see Rugemer, *The Problem of Emancipation,* 291–301; B. A. Knox, "The British Government and the Governor Eyre Controversy, 1865–1875," *Historical Journal* 19.4 (Dec. 1976): 877–900.

61. Oates, "Henry Hotze," 145–146.

EPILOGUE

1. Michael F. Fitzgerald, *Splendid Failure: Postwar Reconstruction in the American South* (Chicago: Ivan R. Dee, 2007); Eric Foner, *Reconstruction: America's Unfinished Revolution, 1863–1877* (1988; repr., New York: Perennial Classics, 2002). Some US critics of Reconstruction made specific reference to the Governor Eyre controversy; see Rugemer, *The Problem of Emancipation,* 291–301. *Morning Post,* 13 Aug. 1867; *Dundee Argus,* 21 Aug. 1865; *London Times,* 16 Apr. 1866; *Morning Post,* 14 Dec. 1867, 3 Apr. 1868.

2. Jay Sexton, "The Funded Loan and the Alabama Claims," *Diplomatic History* 27.4 (Sept. 2003): 449–478; Adrian Cook, *The Alabama Claims: American Politics and Anglo-American Relations, 1865–1872* (Ithaca: Cornell University Press, 1975); Campbell, *Unlikely Allies,* 182–187; Jones, *Blue and Gray Diplomacy,* 196–201; Thomas E. Sebrell III, *Persuading John Bull: Union and Confederate Propaganda in Britain, 1860–1865* (Lanham, MD: Lexington Books, 2014). For contemporary reports of the general progress of the claims, see *London Times,* 29 Dec. and 20 Jan. 1868; *Sporting Gazette,* 31 Oct. 1868; Anonymous, *The Alabama Claims* (London: Central Press, 1872).

3. *Glasgow Herald,* 10 Apr. 1867; Campbell, *Unlikely Allies,* 176–177, 183–184; Walter LeFeber, *The New Empire: An Interpretation of American Expansion, 1860–1898* (Ithaca: Cornell University Press, 1963), 28, 22–34; Cook, *The Alabama Claims,* 38; *London Times,* 29 Mar. 1867, 1, 5, 7, and 27 May 1869.

4. León Ó'Broin, *Fenian Fever: An Anglo-American Dilemma* (New York: New York University Press, 1971); R. V. Comerford, *The Fenians in Context: Irish Politics and Society, 1848–82* (Dublin: Wolfhound, 1985); *Glasgow Herald,* 17 Jan. 1866; *Morning Post,* 27 June 1867.

5. David Sim, *A Union Forever: The Irish Question and US Foreign Relations in the Victorian Age* (Ithaca: Cornell University Press, 2014), 85, 87; Campbell, *Unlikely Allies,* 176; O'Broin, *Fenian Fever,* 9–10, 52, 60–61.

6. O'Broin, *Fenian Fever,* 52, 67, 71; *Morning Post,* 5, 20, 23, 25, and 30 Apr. 1866; *London Times,* 19 and 26 Mar., 8 Apr., 16 Sept., 10. Dec. 1867; *John Bull,* 15 Dec. 1866; *Morning Post,* 22 Sept. 1866.

7. Ó'Broin, *Fenian Fever,* 60–72, 250; *Glasgow Herald,* 28 July 1870; Cook, *The Alabama Claims,* 35, 243–244; Campbell, *Unlikely Allies,* 175.

8. George C. Herring, *From Colony to Superpower: US Foreign Relations Since 1776* (New York: Oxford University Press, 2008), 254; Jay Sexton, *The Monroe Doctrine: Empire and Nation in Nineteenth Century America* (New York: Hill and Wang, 2011), 165–167; Campbell, *Unlikely Allies,* 185–187; Sexton, "The Funded Loan and the Alabama Claims," 478–479; LaFeber, *The New Empire,* 34.

9. Sexton, *The Monroe Doctrine,* 176–177; LaFeber, *The New Empire,* 99–100; Campbell, *Unlikely Allies,* 178–179, 201, 211; Sexton, "William H. Seward in the World," 407–409.

10. Campbell, *Unlikely Allies,* 201–203; *Liverpool Mercury,* 11 Jan. 1869.

11. Campbell, *Unlikely Allies,* 203–207; *North American Review* 127.264 (Sept.–Oct. 1878): 179–212.

BIBLIOGRAPHY

MANUSCRIPT AND ARCHIVAL SOURCES

Confederate State Papers. Microfilm—MSS16550, Reels 1–11. Library of Congress, Washington, DC.

Fraser, Trenholm and Co., Business Records. Merseyside Maritime Museum, Liverpool.

Gregory Family, Papers. Emory University, Robert W. Woodruff Library, Atlanta, Georgia.

Lindsay, William Schaw, Papers. National Maritime Museum, London.

Maury, Matthew Fontaine, Papers. Virginia Military Institute, Preston Library, Lexington, Virginia.

Rathbone Family, Papers. University of Liverpool Library, Liverpool.

Wharncliffe, Lord, Papers. Sheffield Archives, Sheffield.

PUBLISHED PRIMARY SOURCES

Adams, W. E. *Memoirs of a Social Atom.* Vol. 2. London: Hutchinson, 1903.

Anonymous. *The Alabama Claims.* London: Central Press, 1872.

Arthur, William. *The American Question.* London: Sampson, Low and Son, 1861.

Ashworth, Henry. *A Tour of the United States, Cuba, and Canada: A Course of Lectures Delivered Before the Members of the Bolton Mechanics' Institution.* London: A. W. Bennett, 1861.

August, Eugene R., ed. *The Nigger Question: The Negro Question.* New York: Appleton, 1971.

Ballentine, George. *Autobiography of an English Soldier in the United States Army, Comprising Observations and Adventures in the States and Mexico.* New York: Stringer and Townsend, 1853.

Barnes, James J., and Patience P. Barnes, eds. *The American Civil War Through British Eyes: Dispatches from British Diplomats.* Vol. 1, *November 1860–April 1862.* London: Caliban, 2003.

——, eds. *Private and Confidential: Letters from British Ministers in Washington to the Foreign Secretaries in London, 1844–67.* London: Associated University Presses, 1993.

Barnes, L. Diane, Brian Schoen, and Frank Towers, eds. *The Old South's Modern Worlds: Slavery, Region and the Nation in the Age of Progress.* Oxford: Oxford University Press, 2011.

Beale, Howard K., ed. *Diary of Gideon Welles: Secretary of the Navy Under Lincoln and Johnson.* Vol. 1. New York: John W. W. Norton, 1960.

Benson, Arthur Christopher, and Viscount Esher, eds. *The Letters of Queen Victoria: A Selection from Her Majesty's Correspondence Between the Years 1837 and 1861.* 3 vols. London: John Murray, 1908.

Beresford-Hope, A. J. B. *England, the North, and the South: being a Popular View of the American Civil War.* London: James Ridgway, 1862.

——. *The Results of the American Disruption: The Substance of a Lecture Delivered by Request Before the Maidstone Literary and Mechanics Institution, in Continuation of a Popular View of the American Civil War, and England, the North and the South.* London: James Ridgway, 1862.

——. *The Social and Political Bearings of the American Disruption.* London: William Ridgway, 1863.

Bird, Isabella Lucy. *The Englishwoman in America.* 1856. Reprint, Madison: University of Wisconsin Press, 1966.

Black, Frank Gees, and Renee Metivier Black, eds. *The Harney Papers.* Assen: Van Gorcum, 1969.

Bright, John. *Speeches of John Bright, M.P. on the American Question.* Boston: Little, Brown, 1865.

Brothers, Thomas. *The United States of North America as they are; Not as they are generally Described: Being a Cure for Radicalism.* London: Longman, Orme, Brown, Green, and Longmans, 1840.

Buckingham, James Silk. *America, Historical, Statistic and Descriptive.* 3 vols. London: Fisher and Son, 1841.

——. *The Slave States of America.* 2 vols. London: Fisher, Son, 1842.

Buckle, George Earl, ed. *The Letters of Queen Victoria: A Selection from Her Majesty's Correspondence and Journal Between Years 1862 and 1878.* Vol. 1, *1862–1869.* London: John Murray, 1926.

Burke, Edmund. *Reflections on the Revolution in France: and on the Proceedings of Certain Societies in London relative to that Event.* 1790. Reprint, Harmondsworth: Penguin, 1982.

Burnett, Lonnie A. *Henry Hotze: Confederate Propagandist, Selected Writings on Revolution, Recognition, and Race.* Tuscaloosa: University of Alabama Press, 2008.

Cairnes, J. E. *The Slave Power: Its Character and Probable Designs: Being an Attempt to Explain the Real Issues involved in the American Contest.* New York: Carleton, 1862.

Chambers, William. *American Slavery and Colour.* London: W. and R. Chambers, 1857.

Chesson, F. W., ed. *The Political Writings of Richard Cobden.* 2 vols. London: T. Fisher Unwin, 1902.

Cobden, Richard. *Speech of Mr Cobden on the Foreign Enlistment Act in the House of Commons, Friday 24th April, 1863.* London: William Ridgway, 1863.

Combe, George. *Notes on the United States of North America During a Phrenological Visit in 1838–9–40.* 3 vols. Edinburgh: Maclachlan, Stewart, 1841.

Crawford, Martin, ed. *William Howard Russell's Civil War Diary, 1861–1862.* Athens: University of Georgia Press, 1992.

Daubeny, Charles. *Journal of a Tour Through the United States and Canada, made During the Years 1837–1838.* Oxford: T. Combe, 1843.

De Tocqueville, Alexis. *Democracy in America.* 2 vols. 1835. Reprint, New York: Mentor, 1955.

Dicey, Edward. *Six Months in the Federal States.* 2 vols. London: Macmillan, 1863.

Dickens, Charles. *American Notes for General Circulation.* 1842. Reprint, London: Oxford University Press, 1966.

———. *Bleak House.* London: Bradbury and Evans, 1853.

———. *The Life and Adventures of Martin Chuzzlewit.* 1844. Reprint, London: Wordsworth Classics, 1997.

Englehart, John Gardner D. *Journal of the Progress of H.R.H. Prince of Wales through British North America; and his Visit to the United States, 10th July to 15th November 1860.* London: Privately Printed, 1860.

Featherstonhaugh, G. W. *Excursion Through the Slaves States, from Washington on the Potomac to the Frontier of Mexico; With Sketches of Popular Manners and Geological Notices.* 2 vols. London: John Murray, 1844.

Foot, M. R. D., ed. *The Gladstone Diaries.* Oxford: Clarendon, 1974.

Ford, Worthington Chauncey, ed. *A Cycle of Adams Letters.* 2 vols. London: Constable, 1921.

Fremantle, Arthur James Lyon. *Three Months in the Southern States April–June 1863.* Edinburgh: William Blackwood and Sons, 1863.

Godley, John Robert. *Letters from America.* 2 vols. London: John Murray, 1844.

Gosse, Philip Henry. *Letters from Alabama (U.S.) Chiefly Relating to Natural History.* London: Morgan and Chase, 1859.

Guedalla, Philip, ed. *Gladstone and Palmerston, being the Correspondence of Lord Palmerston with Mr. Gladstone, 1851–1865.* London: Victor Gollancz, 1928.

Hall, Marshall. *The Two-Fold Slavery of the United States; With a Project for Self-Emancipation.* London: Adam Scott, 1854.

Hall, Newman. *The American War: A Lecture Delivered in London 20th October 1862.* New York: Anson, D. F. Randolph, 1862.

Hopley, Catherine C. *Life in the South from the Commencement of the War: Being a Social History of those who took part in the Battles, from a Personal Acquaintance with them in their own Homes, from the Spring of 1860 to August 1862.* 2 vols. 1863. Reprint, London: Chapman and Hall, 1974.

Houstoun, Charlotte Matilda. *Hesperos: Or, Travels in the West.* 2 vols. London: John W. Parker, 1850.

——. *Texas and the Gulf of Mexico; or, Yachting in the New World.* London: John Murray, 1844.

Johnston, James F. W. *Notes on North America: Agricultural, Economical and Social.* Vol. 2. Edinburgh: William Blackwood and Sons, 1851.

Kershaw, T. Bentley. *The Truth of the American Question: A Reply to the Prize Essay of Mr Rowan.* SIA: Bradford, 1864.

Lawrence, George Alfred. *Border and Bastille.* Leipzig: Bernhard Tauchnitz, 1863.

Leader, Robert Eadon, ed. *Life and Letters of John Arthur Roebuck with Chapters of Autobiography.* London: Edward Arnold, 1897.

Lothian, William, Marquess of. *The Confederate Secession.* Edinburgh: William Blackwood and Sons, 1864.

Lyell, Sir Charles. *A Second Visit to the United States of North America.* 2 vols. London: John Murray, 1849, 1850.

——. *Travels in North America; with Geological Observations on the United States, Canada and Nova Scotia.* 2 vols. London: John Murray, 1845.

Mackenzie, William L. *Sketches of Canada and the United States.* London: Effingham Wilson, 1833.

Marryat, Frederick. *Diary in America with Remarks on its Institutions.* Paris: Baudry's European Library, 1839.

——. *Diary in America with Remarks on its Institutions Part Second.* Paris, Baudry's European Library, 1840.

Martineau, Harriet. *Society in America.* 3 vols. London: Saunders and Otley, 1837.

Mason, Virginia, ed. *The Public Life and Diplomatic Correspondence of James M. Mason with Some Personal History.* New York: Neale, 1906.

Mitchell, D. W. *Ten Years Residence in the United States.* London: Smith, Elder, 1862.

Murray, Amelia M. *Letters from the United States, Cuba and Canada.* New York: G. P. Putnam, 1856.

Murray, Charles Augustus. *Travels in North America During the Years 1834, 1835, and 1836 Including a Summer Residence with the Pawnee tribe of Indians, in the Remote Prairies of the Missouri and a Visit to Cuba and the Azore Islands.* 2 vols. New York: Harper and Brothers, 1839.

Murray, Henry A. *Lands of the Slave and the Free: or, Cuba, The United States, and Canada.* Vol. 1. London: John Parker and Son, 1855.

Nemo. *Remarks on the Politics of Recognizing the Independence of the Southern States of North America, and on the Struggle in that Continent.* London: Effingham Wilson, 1863.

Partridge, Arthur J. *The False Nation and its Bases, or, Why the South Can't Stand.* London: Edward Stanford, 1864.

Prentice, Archibald. *A Tour of the United States with Two Lectures on Emigration, Delivered in the Mechanics' Institution Manchester.* London: John Johnson, 1849.

Rawlins, Charles Edward, Jr. *American Disunion: Constitutional or Unconstitutional? A Reply to Mr. James Spence upon the Question "Is Secession a Constitutional Right?" Discussed in his Recent Work, "The American Union."* London: Robert Hardwicke, 1862.

Ray, Gordon N., ed. *The Letters and Private Papers of William Makepeace Thackeray in Four Volumes.* Vol. 3. London: Oxford University Press, 1945.

Reid, Hugo. *The American Question in a Nut-Shell: or, Why We Should Recognize the Confederates.* London: Robert Hardwicke, 1862.

———. *Sketches in North America, with some Account of Congress and of the Slavery Question.* London: Longman, Green, Longman and Roberts, 1861.

Richardson, James D., ed. *The Messages and Papers of Jefferson Davis and the Confederacy Including Diplomatic Correspondence, 1861–1865.* 2 vols. New York: Robert Hector, 1966.

Roebuck, John Arthur. *The Colonies of England: A Plan for the Government of Some Portion of our Colonial Possessions.* London: John W. Parker, 1849.

Russell, William Howard. *My Diary North and South.* 1863. Reprint, New York: Harper Colophon, 1965.

———. *Pictures of Southern Life, Social, Political and Military.* New York: James G. Gregory, 1861.

Sala, George Augustus. *My Diary in America in the Midst of War.* 2 vols. London: Tinsley Brothers, 1865.

Senior, Nassau William. *American Slavery: A Reprint of an Article on "Uncle Tom's Cabin," of which a Portion was inserted in the 206th Number of the "Edinburgh Review"; and of Mr. Sumner's Speech on the 19th and 20th of May 1856, with a Notice of Events Which Followed that Speech.* London: Longman, Brown, Green, Longmans, and Roberts, 1856.

Shelley, Mary. *Lodore.* 1835. Reprint, Toronto: Broadview Literary Texts, 1997.

Sieveking, Giberne, ed. *Memoir and Letters of Francis W Newman.* London: Kegan Paul, Trench Trubner, 1909.

Smith, Goldwin. *A Letter to a Whig Member of the Southern Independence Association.* Boston: Ticknor and Fields, 1864.

Spence, James. *The American Union; its Effect on National Character and Policy, with an Enquiry into Secession as a Constitutional Right, and the Causes of the Disruption.* 1881. Reprint, London: Richard Bentley, 1862.

———. *On the Recognition of the Southern Confederacy.* London: Richard Bentley, 1862.

Stillinger, Jack, ed. *John Stuart Mill Autobiography.* Boston: Houghton Mifflin, 1969.

Stirling, James. *Letters from the Slave States.* London: John W. Parker and Son, 1857.

Stowe, Harriet Beecher. *Uncle Tom's Cabin.* 1852. Reprint, New York: W. W. Norton, 1994.

Strachey, Lytton, and Roger Fulford, eds. *The Greville Memoirs, 1814–1860.* 7 vols. London: Macmillan, 1938.

Stuart-Wortley, Lady Emmeline. *Travels in the United States Etc, during 1849 and 1850.* Paris: Baudry's European Library, 1851.

Sturge, Joseph. *A Visit to the United States in 1841.* London: Hamilton, Adams, 1842.

Sullivan, Edward. *Rambles and Scrambles in North and South America.* London: Richard Bentley, 1852.

Tallack, William. *Friendly Sketches in America.* London: A. W. Bennett, 1861.

Thackeray, William Makepeace. *The Virginians.* 1859. Reprint, London: Smith, Elder.

Tremenheere, Hugh Seymour. *The Constitution of the United States Compared with Our Own.* London: John Murray, 1854.

———. *Notes on Public Subjects, Made During A Tour in the United States and in Canada.* London: John Murray, 1852.

Trimble, Robert. *A Review of the American Struggle in its Military and Political Aspects from the Inauguration of President Lincoln, 4th March 1861 till his Re-election, 8th November 1864.* London: Whittaker, 1864.

Trollope, Anthony. *North America.* Vol. 1. Leipzig: Bernard Tauschitz, 1862.

———. *North America. 2 vols.* 1862. Reprint, Gloucester: Alan Sutton, 1987.

Trollope, Frances. *The Barnabys in America, or Adventures of the Widow Wedded.* Paris: Baudry's European Library, 1843.

———. *Domestic Manners of the Americans.* 1830. Reprint, London: Century, 1984.

———. *The Life and Adventures of Jonathan Jefferson Whitlaw, or Scenes on the Mississippi.* Paris: Baudry's European Library, 1836.

———. *The Refugee in America.* 3 vols. London: Whittaker, Treacher, 1832.

Tudor, Henry. *Narrative of a Tour in North America; Comprising Mexico, and the Mines of Real Del Monte, the United States, and the British Colonies: With an Excursion to the Island of Cuba, in a Series of Letters Written 1831–1832.* London: James Duncan, 1834.

Wallace, S. A., and F. E. Gillespie, eds. *The Journal of Benjamin Moran, 1857–1865.* 2 vols. Chicago: University of Chicago Press, 1948.

Wheeler, Thomas. *Sunshine and Shadow.* In Ian Haywood, ed., *Chartist Fiction.* Aldershot: Ashgate, 1999.

Wiebe, M. G., et al., eds. *Benjamin Disraeli Letters.* 10 vols. Toronto: University of Toronto Press, 1987–2014.

NEWSPAPERS, MAGAZINES, AND PERIODICALS

Aberdeen Journal

All the Year Round

Ainsworth's Magazine of Romance, General Literature and Art

Belfast News-Letter

Bell's Life in London and Sporting Chronicle

Berrow's Worcester Journal

Birmingham Daily Post

Blackburn Standard

Blackwood's Edinburgh Magazine

Bradford Observer

Bradford Observer; and Halifax, Huddersfield, and Keighley Reporter

Brighton Patriot and South of England Free Press

Bristol Mercury

Bury and Norwich Post and East Anglian

Bury and Norwich Post, and East Anglian: Or Suffolk, Norfolk, Essex, Cambridge, and Ely Intelligencer

Caledonian Mercury

Champion and Weekly Herald

Charter

Cheshire Observer and General Advertiser for Cheshire and North Wales

Cobbett's Weekly Political Register

Daily News

Derby Mercury

Dundee Argus

Dundee Courier

Dundee Courier and Daily Argus

Era

Essex Standard, and Colchester and County Advertiser

Essex Standard, and Colchester, Chelmsford, Maldon, Harwich, and General County Advertiser

Essex Standard, and General Advertiser for the Eastern Counties
Examiner
Freeman's Journal and Daily Commercial Advertiser
Glasgow Herald
Hampshire Advertiser and Salisbury Guardian
Hampshire Advertiser and Salisbury Guardian Royal Yacht Club Gazette, Southampton Town and County Herald, Isle of Wight Journal, Winchester Chronicle, and General Reporter
Hampshire Telegraph and Sussex Chronicle etc.
Huddersfield Chronicle and West Yorkshire Advertiser
Hull Packet
Hull Packet and East Riding Times
Hull Packet and Humber Mercury
Ipswich Journal
Index
Jackson's Oxford Journal
John Bull
Lancaster Gazette and General Advertiser, for Lancashire, Westmorland
Leeds Mercury
Leicester Chronicle: or, Commercial and Agricultural Advertiser
Liverpool Mercury
Lloyd's Weekly Newspaper
London Dispatch and People's Political and Social Reformer
Manchester Times
Manchester Times and Gazette
Morning Chronicle
Morning Post
Newcastle Courant
New York Times
North American Review
Northern Liberator
Northern Star and Leeds General Advertiser
Northern Star and National Trades Journal
Nottinghamshire Guardian
Nottinghamshire Guardian and Midland Advertiser
Poor Man's Guardian
Preston Chronicle
Punch
Reynolds Newspaper
Royal Cornwall Gazette, Falmouth Packet, and General Advertiser

Sheffield and Rotherham Independent
Sheffield Independent and Yorkshire and Derbyshire Advertiser
Spectator
Standard
Table Talk
Times
Trewman's Exeter Flying Post or Plymouth and Cornish Advertiser
Wolverhampton and Staffordshire Herald
Wrexham and Denbighshire Advertiser, and Cheshire, Shropshire, Flintshire and North Wales Register
York Herald and General Advertiser

PUBLISHED SECONDARY WORKS

Ackroyd, Peter. *Dickens.* New York: Harper Collins, 1990.

Adams, Charles Francis. "The Trent Affair." *American Historical Review* 17, no. 3 (April 1912): 540–562.

Adams, E. D. *British Interests and Activities in Texas, 1838–1846.* Gloucester, MA: Peter Smith, 1963.

——. *Great Britain and the American Civil War.* 2 vols. New York: Longman's, Green's, 1925.

Adams, Thomas R., and Nicolas Barker. "A New Model for the Study of the Book." In *A Potencie of Life: Books in Society,* in David Finkelstein and Alistair McCleery, eds., *The Book History Reader.* New York: Routledge, 2002.

Adrian, Arthur A. "Dickens on American Slavery: A Carlylean Slant." *PMLA* 67, no. 4 (June 1952): 315–329.

Allen, H. C., and Roger Thompson, eds. *Contrast and Connection in Bicentennial Essays in Anglo-American History.* London: G. Bell and Sons, 1976.

Altick, Richard D. *The English Common Reader: A Social History of the Mass Reading Public, 1800–1900.* Chicago: University of Chicago Press, 1957.

Armstrong, Catherine, Roger Fagge, and Tim Lockley, eds. *America in the British Imagination.* Newcastle: Cambridge Scholar, 2007.

Ashworth, John. *The Republic in Crisis, 1848–1861.* New York: Cambridge University Press, 2012.

Balee, Susan. "English Critics, American Crisis, and the Sensation Novel." *Nineteenth Century Contexts* 12, no. 2 (1993): 125–143.

Barnhart, Terry A. *Albert Taylor Bledsoe: Defender of the Old South.* Baton Rouge: Louisiana State University Press, 2011.

Bartley, Numan V. "The South and Sectionalism in American Politics." *Journal of Politics* 38, no. 3 (August 1976): 239–257.

Baxter, Maurice G. *One and Inseparable, Daniel Webster and the Union*. Cambridge, MA: University of Harvard Press, 1984.

Bayor, Ronald H., and Timothy J. Meagher, eds. *The New York Irish*. Baltimore: Johns Hopkins University Press, 1996.

Beckert, Sven. *Empire of Cotton: A Global History*. New York: Alfred A. Knopf, 2014.

——. *The Monied Metropolis: New York City and the Consolidation of the American Bourgeoisie, 1850–1896*. Cambridge: Cambridge University Press, 2001.

Belchem, John. "Republican Spirit and Military Science: The Irish Brigade and Irish-American Nationalism in 1848." *Irish Historical Studies* 29 (1994): 44–65.

Bellows, Donald. "A Study of British Conservative Reaction to the American Civil War." *Journal of Southern History* 51, no. 4 (November 1985): 505–526.

Bennett, Mark. "Confederate Supporters in the West Riding, 1861–1865: Cranks of the Worst English Species." *Northern History* 51, no. 2 (September 2014): 311–329.

Berger, Max. "American Slavery as Seen by British Visitors, 1836–1860." *Journal of Negro History* 30, no. 2 (April 1945): 181–202.

——. *The British Traveler in America, 1836-1860*. New York: Columbia University Press, 1943.

Bernath, Michael J. *Confederate Minds: The Struggle for Intellectual Independence in the Civil War South*. Chapel Hill: University of North Carolina Press, 2010.

Blackett, R. J. M. *Building an Anti-Slavery Wall: Black Americans and the Atlantic Abolitionist Movement, 1830–1860*. Baton Rouge: Louisiana State University Press, 1983.

——. "Cracks in the Anti-Slavery Wall: Frederick Douglass's Second Visit to England (1859–1860) and the Coming of the Civil War." In Rice and Crawford, *Liberating Sojourn*.

——. *Divided Hearts: Britain and the American Civil War*. Baton Rouge: Louisiana State University Press, 2001.

——. *Making Freedom: The Underground Railroad and the Politics of Slavery*. Chapel Hill: University of North Carolina Press, 2013.

Boltwood, Scott. "'The Ineffaceable Curse of Cain': Race, Miscegenation, and the Victorian Staging of Irishness." *Victorian Literature and Culture* 29, no. 2 (September 2001): 383–396.

Bonner, Robert E. "Proslavery Extremism Goes to War: The Counterrevolutionary Confederacy and Reactionary Militarism." *Modern Intellectual History* 6, no. 2 (2009): 161–185.

——. "Roundheaded Cavaliers?: The Context and Limits of a Confederate Racial Project." *Civil War History* 48, no. 1 (March 2002): 34–59.

——. "Slavery, Confederate Diplomacy, and the Racialist Mission of Henry Hotze." *Civil War History* 51, no. 3 (September 2005): 288–316.

Bourne, Kenneth. *Britain and the Balance of Power in North America, 1815–1908.* London: Longman's, 1967.

——. "British Preparations for War with the North, 1861–1862." *English Historical Review* 76, no. 301 (October 1961): 600–632.

Bowley, Marian. *Nassau Senior and Classical Economics.* London: George Allen and Unwin, 1967.

Bradbury, Malcolm. *Dangerous Pilgrimages: Trans-Atlantic Mythologies and the Novel.* London: Secker and Warburg, 1995.

Brantlinger, Patrick. *The Spirit of Reform: British Literature and Politics, 1832–1867.* Cambridge, MA: Harvard University Press, 1977.

Bratton, J. S. "English Ethiopians: British Audiences and Black-Face Acts, 1835–1865." *Yearbook of English Studies* 11, special number, "Literature and Its Audience" 2 (1981): 127–142.

——, ed. *Music Hall: Performance and Style.* Milton Keynes: Open University Press, 1986.

Brauer, Kinley J. "The United States and British Imperial Expansion, 1815–1860." *Diplomatic History* 12, no. 1 (January 1988): 19–37.

Bric, Maurice. "Debating Slavery and Empire: The United States, Britain and the World's Anti-slavery Convention of 1840." In William Mulligan and Maurice Bric, eds., *A Global History of Anti-slavery Politics in the Nineteenth Century.* Houndsmill: Palgrave Macmillan, 2013.

Brock, Michael. *The Great Reform Act.* London: Hutchinson, 1973.

Brock, William. "The Image of England and American Nationalism." *Journal of American Studies* 5 (December 1971): 225–245.

Bronstein, Jamie L. *Land Reform and Working-Class Experience in Britain and the United States, 1800–1862.* Stanford, CA: Stanford University Press, 1999.

Brook, Michael. "Confederate Sympathies in North-East Lancashire, 1862–1864." *Lancashire and Cheshire Antiquarian Society* 75–76 (1977): 211–217.

Brownell, Blaine A., and David R. Goldfield, eds. *The City in Southern History: The Growth of Urban Civilization in the South.* Port Washington: Kennikat, 1977.

Burk, Kathleen. *Old World, New World: Great Britain and America from the Beginning.* New York: Atlantic University Press, 2007.

Butler, Leslie. *Critical Americans: Victorian Intellectuals and Transatlantic Liberal Reform.* Chapel Hill: University of North Carolina Press, 2007.

Campbell, Charles S. *From Revolution to Rapprochement: The United States and Great Britain, 1783-1900.* New York: John Wiley and Sons, 1974.

Campbell, Duncan Andrew. *English Public Opinion and the American Civil War.* Woodbridge: Boydell, 2003.

——. *Unlikely Allies: Britain, America, and the Victorian Origins of the Special Relationship.* London: Hambledon Continuum, 2007.

Campbell, Stanley W. *The Slave Catchers: Enforcement of the Fugitive Slave Law, 1850–1860.* Chapel Hill: University of North Carolina Press, 1968.

Carey, Brycchan, Markman Ellis, and Sara Salih, eds. *Discourses of Slavery and Abolition: Britain and Its Colonies, 1760–1838.* Houndsmill: Palgrave, 2004.

Carroll, Francis M. *A Good and Wise Measure: The Search For the Canadian-American Boundary, 1783–1842.* Toronto: University of Toronto Press, 2001.

Cash, Bill. *John Bright: Statesman, Orator, Agitator.* New York: I. B. Tauris, 2012.

Cash, W. J. *The Mind of the South.* New York: A. A. Knopf, 1941.

Chase, Malcolm. *Chartism: A New History.* Manchester: Manchester University Press, 2007.

Childers, Christopher. *The Failure of Popular Sovereignty: Slavery, Manifest Destiny, and the Radicalization of Southern Politics.* Lawrence: University of Kansas Press, 2012.

Christie, O. F. *The Transition from Aristocracy, 1832–1867: An Account of the Passing of the Reform Bill, The Cause Which Led Up to It, and Its Far Reaching Consequences on the Life and Manners of All Grades of Society.* London: Seeley, Service, 1927.

Clark, J. C. D. *English Society, 1660–1832: Religion, Ideology, and Politics During the Ancien Regime.* Cambridge: Cambridge University Press, 2000.

———. *The Language of Liberty, 1660–1832: Political Discourse and Social Dynamics in the Anglo-American World.* Cambridge: Cambridge University Press, 1994.

Claussen, Martin P. "Peace Factors in Anglo-American Relations, 1861–1865." *Mississippi Valley Historical Review* 26, no. 4 (March 1940): 511–522.

Claybaugh, Amanda. "Toward a New Transatlanticism: Dickens in the United States." *Victorian Studies* 48, no. 3 (Spring 2006): 439–460.

Cohen, Victor H. "Charles Sumner and the Trent Affair." *Journal of Southern History* 22, no. 2 (May 1956): 205–219.

Colby, Robert A. "'Rational Amusement': Fiction Vs. Useful Knowledge in the Nineteenth Century." In James R. Kincaid and Robert J. Kuhn, eds., *Victorian Literature and Society: Essays Presented to Richard D. Altick.* Columbus: Ohio State University Press, 1984.

Coleman, Bruce. *Conservatism and the Conservative Party in Nineteenth Century Britain.* London: Edward Arnold, 1988.

Colley, Linda. *Britons: Forging the Nation, 1707–1837.* New Haven: Yale University Press, 1992.

Collini, Stefan. *Public Moralists: Political Thought and Intellectual Life in Britain, 1850–1930.* Oxford: Clarendon, 1991.

Comerford, R. V. *The Fenians in Context: Irish Politics and Society, 1848–82.* Dublin: Wolfhound, 1985.

Conrad, Peter. *Imagining America.* New York: Oxford University Press, 1980.

Cook, Adrian. *The Alabama Claims: American Politics and Anglo-American Relations, 1865–1872.* Ithaca: Cornell University Press, 1975.

Cox, Karen L. *Dreaming of Dixie: How the South Was Created in American Popular Culture.* Chapel Hill: University of North Carolina Press, 2011.

Cramer, Richard S. "British Magazines and the Oregon Question." *Pacific Historical Review* 32, no. 4 (November 1963): 369–382.

Craven, Avery O. *The Growth of Southern Nationalism, 1848–1861.* Baton Rouge: Louisiana State University Press, 1953.

Crawford, Martin. *The Anglo-American Crisis of the Mid-Nineteenth Century: The Times and America, 1850–1862.* Athens: University of Georgia Press, 1987.

———. "British Travelers and the Anglo-American Relationship in the 1850s." *Journal of American Studies* 12, no. 2 (August 1978): 203–219.

Crocker, Matthew H. "The Missouri Compromise, the Monroe Doctrine, and the Southern Strategy." *Journal of the West* 43, no. 3 (Summer 2004): 45–52.

Crook, D. P. *American Democracy in English Politics, 1815–1850.* Oxford: Clarendon, 1965.

Cruikshank, A. F. "J. A. Roebuck M.P.: A Re-Appraisal of Liberalism in Sheffield, 1849–1879." *Northern History* 16 (January 1980): 196–214.

Cullop, Charles P. *Confederate Propaganda in Europe, 1861–1865.* Coral Gables, FL: University of Miami Press, 1969.

Cunliffe, Marcus. *Chattel Slavery and Wage Slavery: The Anglo American Context, 1830–1860.* Athens: University of Georgia Press, 1979.

Cunningham, Hugh. "Dickens as a Reformer." In David Paroissien, ed., *A Companion to Charles Dickens.* Malden, MA: Blackwell, 2008.

Curry, Leonard P. *The Free Black in Urban America, 1800–1850: The Shadow of a Dream.* Chicago: University of Chicago Press, 1981.

Curtin, Philip D. *The Image of Africa: British Ideas and Action, 1780–1850.* Madison: University of Wisconsin Press, 1964.

Curtis, L. Perry. *Apes and Angels: The Irishman in Victorian Caricature.* Washington: Smithsonian Institute Press, 1971.

Curtis, Michael Kent. "The 1837 Killing of Elijah Lovejoy by an Anti-Abolition Mob: Free Speech, Mobs, Republican Government, and the Privileges of American Citizens." *UCLA Law Review* 44 (April 1997): 1109–1185.

Davis, David Brion. *The Problem of Slavery in Western Culture.* Ithaca: Cornell University Press, 1966.

Davis, Richard P. *The Young Ireland Movement.* Dublin: Macmillan, 1987.

Dawson, Jan C. "The Puritan and the Cavalier: The South's Perception of Contrasting Traditions." *Journal of Southern History* 44, no. 4 (November 1978): 597–614.

Degler, Carl N. "The Locofocos: Urban 'Agrarians.'" *Journal of Economic History* 16, no. 3 (September 1956): 322–333.

Delahanty, Ian. "'A Noble Empire in the West': Young Ireland, the United States and Slavery." *Britain and the World* 6, no. 2 (2013): 171–191.

De Nie, Michael. *The Eternal Paddy: Irish Identity and the British Press, 1798–1882.* Madison: University of Wisconsin Press, 2004.

Dillon, Merton L. *Elijah P. Lovejoy: Abolitionist Editor.* Urbana: University of Illinois Press, 1961.

Diner, Hasia R. "Overview: 'The Most Irish City in the Union': The Era of Great Migration, 1844–1877." In Bayor and Meagher, *The New York Irish.*

Dorsett, Lyle W., and Arthur H. Shafer. "Was the Antebellum South Antiurban? A Suggestion." *Journal of Southern History* 38, no. 1 (February 1972): 93–100.

Doyle, Don H. *The Cause of All Nations: An International History of the American Civil War.* New York: Basic Books, 2015.

Drescher, Seymour. *Abolition: A History of Slavery and Anti-Slavery.* Cambridge: Cambridge University Press, 2009.

———. *Capitalism and Antislavery: British Mobilization in Comparative Perspective.* London: Macmillan, 1986.

———. *From Slavery to Freedom: Comparative Studies in the Rise and Fall of Atlantic Slavery.* New York: New York University Press, 1999.

———. *The Mighty Experiment: Free Labor Versus Slavery in British Emancipation.* New York: New York University Press, 2002.

Dugger, Julie M. "Black Ireland's Race: Thomas Carlyle and the Young Ireland Movement." *Victorian Studies* 48, no. 3 (Spring 2006): 461–485.

Dusinberre, William. *Slavemaster President: The Double Career of James Polk.* New York: Oxford University Press, 2003.

Dykstra, David L. *The Shifting Balance of Power: American-British Diplomacy in North America, 1842–1848.* Lanham, MD: University Press of America, 1999.

Eaton, Joseph. *The Anglo-American Paper War: Debates about the New Republic, 1800–1825.* Houndsmill: Palgrave Macmillan, 2012.

Edsall, Nicholas C. *Richard Cobden: Independent Radical.* Cambridge, MA: Harvard University Press, 1986.

Eliot, Simon. "Some Trends in British Book Production, 1800–1919." In John O. Jordan and Robert L. Patten, eds., *Literature in the Marketplace: Nineteenth-Century British Publishing and Reading Practices.* Cambridge: Cambridge University Press, 1995.

Ellis, Richard E. *The Union at Risk: Jacksonian Democracy, States' Rights, and the Nullification Crisis.* New York: Oxford University Press, 1989.

Ellison, Mary. *Support for Secession: Lancashire and the American Civil War.* Chicago: University of Chicago Press, 1972.

Epstein, James. "'America' in the Victorian Cultural Imagination." In Levanthal and Quinault, *Anglo-American Attitudes from Revolution to Partnership.*

Ewan, Christopher. "The Emancipation Proclamation and British Public Opinion." *Historian* 67, no. 1 (March 2005): 1–19.

Faust, Drew Gilpin. *The Creation of Confederate Nationalism: Ideology and Identity in the Civil War South.* Baton Rouge: Louisiana State University Press, 1988.

Feldberg, Michael. *The Turbulent Era: Riot and Disorder in Jacksonian America.* New York: Oxford University Press, 1980.

Fenton, Laurence. *Palmerston and the Times: Foreign Policy, the Press, and Public Opinion in Mid-Victorian Britain.* London: I. B. Tauris, 2012.

Ferris, Norman S. *Desperate Diplomacy: William H. Seward's Foreign Policy, 1861.* Knoxville: University of Tennessee Press, 1976.

Fielding, K. J. "Carlyle and the Americans: 'Eighteen Million Bores.'" *Carlyle Studies Annual* (1997): 55–64.

Fisch, Audrey, ed. *The African American Slave Narrative.* New York: Cambridge University Press, 2007.

——. *American Slaves in Victorian England: Abolitionist Politics and Popular Literature and Culture.* Cambridge: Cambridge University Press, 2000.

Fischer, David Hackett. *Albion's Seed: Four British Folkways in America.* New York: Oxford University Press, 1989.

Fitzgerald, Michael W. *Splendid Failure: Postwar Reconstruction in the American South.* Chicago: Ivan R. Dee, 2007.

Fladeland, Betty. *Abolitionists and Working-Class Problems in the Age of Industrialization.* Baton Rouge: Louisiana State University Press, 1984.

——. *Men and Brothers: Anglo-American Anti-Slavery Co-operation.* Urbana: University of Illinois Press, 1972.

——. "'Our Cause Being One and the Same' Abolitionists and Chartism." In Walvin, *Slavery and British Society.*

Fleming, George H. *George Alfred Lawrence and the Victorian Sensation Novel.* Tucson: University of Arizona, 1952.

Floan, H. R. *The South in Northern Eyes, 1831 to 1861.* Austin: University of Texas Press, 1958.

Foner, Eric. *Reconstruction: America's Unfinished Revolution, 1863–1877.* 1988. Reprint, New York: Perennial Classics, 2002.

Foner, Philip S. *British Labor and the American Civil War.* New York: Holmes and Meier, 1981.

Forbes, Robert Pierce. *The Missouri Compromise and Its Aftermath: Slavery and the Meaning of America.* Chapel Hill: University of North Carolina Press, 2007.

Ford, Lacy K. *Deliver Us from Evil: The Slavery Question in the Old South.* Oxford: Oxford University Press, 2009.

Foreman, Amanda. *World on Fire: An Epic History of Two Nations Divided.* London: Penguin, 2011.

Foster, R. F. *Paddy and Mr. Punch: Connections in Irish and English History*. London: Penguin, 1993.

Fox-Genovese, Elizabeth, and Eugene D. Genovese. *The Mind of the Master Class: History and Faith in the Southern Slaveholders' Worldview*. Cambridge: Cambridge University Press, 2005.

Frederickson, George M. *The Inner Civil War: Northern Intellectuals and the Crisis of the Union*. 1965. Reprint, Urbana: University of Illinois Press, 1993.

Freehling, William W. *Prelude to Civil War: The Nullification Controversy in South Carolina, 1816–1836*. 1965. Reprint, New York: Oxford University Press, 1992.

———. *The Road to Disunion*. Vol. 1, *Secessionists at Bay, 1776–1854*. New York: Oxford University Press, 1990.

———. *The South Vs. the South: How Anti-Confederate Southerners Shaped the Course of the Civil War*. Oxford: Oxford University Press, 2001.

Fulton, Richard D. "'Now Only *The Times* Is on Our Side': The London *Times* and America before the Civil War." *Victorian Review* 16, no. 1 (Summer 1990): 48–58.

Furneaux, Rupert. *The First War Correspondent: William Howard Russell of the Times*. London: Cassell, 1944.

Fyfe, Aileen. *Steam-Powered Knowledge: William Chambers and the Business of Publishing, 1820–1860*. Chicago: University of Chicago Press, 2012.

Gallagher, Gary W. *The Union War*. Cambridge, MA: Harvard University Press, 2011.

Genovese, Eugene D. *The Southern Front: History and Politics in the Cultural War*. Columbia: University of Missouri Press, 1995.

Genovese, Eugene D., and Elizabeth Fox-Genovese. *Fatal Self-Deception: Slaveholding Paternalism in the Old South*. Cambridge: Cambridge University Press, 2011.

Gentry, Judith Fenner. "A Confederate Success in Europe: The Erlanger Loan." *Journal of Southern History* 36, no. 2 (May 1970): 157–188.

Giles, Paul. *Atlantic Republic: The American Tradition in English Literature*. Oxford: Oxford University Press, 2006.

———. *Virtual Americas: Transnational Fictions and the Transatlantic Imaginary*. Durham: Duke University Press, 2002.

Gilje, Paul A. "The Development of an Irish American Community in New York before the Great Migration." In Bayor and Meagher, *The New York Irish*.

———. *The Road to Mobocracy: Popular Disorder in New York City, 1763–1834*. Chapel Hill: University of North Carolina Press, 1987.

Gill, John. *Tide Without Turning: Elijah P. Lovejoy and the Freedom of the Press*. Boston: Starr King, 1970.

Gleeson, David T. *The Irish in the South, 1815–1877*. Chapel Hill: University of North Carolina Press, 2001.

Gold, Joseph. *Charles Dickens: Radical Moralist*. Minneapolis: University of Minnesota Press, 1972.

Goldfield, David R. "The Urban South: A Regional Framework." *American Historical Review* 86, no. 5 (December 1981): 1009–1034.

Goldman, Lawrence. "'A Total Misconception': Lincoln, the Civil War, and the British, 1860–1865." In Jay Sexton and Richard Carwadine, eds., *The Global Lincoln*. New York: Oxford University Press, 2011.

Goodman, Paul. "Ethics and Enterprise: The Values of a Boston Elite, 1800–1860." *American Quarterly* 18, no. 3 (Autumn 1966): 437–451.

Grant, Susan-Mary. *North over South: Northern Nationalism and American Identity in the Antebellum Era*. Lawrence: University of Kansas Press, 2000.

Gravil, Richard. *Romantic Dialogues: Anglo-American Continuities, 1776–1862*. London, Macmillan, 2000.

Greeson, Jennifer Rae. *Our South: Geographic Fantasy and the Rise of National Literature*. Cambridge, MA: Harvard University Press, 2010.

Grimsted, David. *American Mobbing, 1828–1861: Toward Civil War*. New York: Oxford University Press, 1998.

Grubb, Gerald G. "Dickens' Western Tour and the Cairo Legend." *Studies in Philology* 48, no. 1 (January 1951): 87–97.

Gulddal, Jesper. "The Most Hateful Land: Romanticism and the Birth of Modern Anti-Americanism." *Journal of European Studies* 39 (2009): 419–454.

Hall, Catherine. *Civilising Subjects: Metropole and Colony in the English Imagination, 1830–1867*. Cambridge: Polity, 2002.

——. "Troubling Memories: Nineteenth-Century Histories of the Slave Trade and Slavery." *Transactions of the Royal Historical Society* 21 (December 2011): 147–169.

Hall, N. "The Liverpool Cotton Market and the American Civil War." *Northern History* 34, no. 1 (1998): 149–169.

Hall, N. John. "Trollope and Carlyle." *Nineteenth Century Fiction* 27, no. 2 (September 1972): 197–205.

Hamand, Wendy F. "'No Voice from England': Mrs. Stowe, Mr. Lincoln, and the British in the Civil War." *New England Quarterly* 61, no. 1 (March 1988): 3–24.

Hamer, Philip M. "British Consuls and the Negro Seamen Acts, 1850–1860." *Journal of Southern History* 1, no. 2 (May 1935): 138–168.

——. "Great Britain, the United States, and the Negro Seamen Acts, 1822–1848." *Journal of Southern History* 1, no. 2 (February 1935): 3–28.

Hamilton, Homan. *Prologue to Conflict: The Crisis and Compromise of 1850*. Lexington: University of Kentucky Press, 1964.

Hannay, David. *Life of Frederick Marryat*. London: Walter Scott, 1889.

Harrison, Royden. "British Labour and the Confederacy." *International Review of Social History* 2, no. 1 (April 1957): 78–105.

Haynes, Sam W. "Anglophobia and the Annexation of Texas: The Quest for National Security." In Sam W. Haynes and Christopher Morris, eds., *Manifest Destiny and Empire: American Antebellum Expansionism.* College Station: Texas A&M University Press, 1997.

——. *Unfinished Revolution: The Early American Republic in a British World.* Charlottesville: University of Virginia Press, 2010.

Heffer, Simon. *Moral Desperado: A Life of Thomas Carlyle.* London: Weidenfeld and Nicholson, 1995.

Hegarty, Aidan. *John Mitchel: A Cause Too Many.* Belfast: Camlane, 2005.

Hernon, Joseph M. "British Sympathies in the American Civil War: A Reconsideration." *Journal of Southern History* 33, no. 3 (August 1967): 356–367.

Herring, George C. *From Colony to Superpower: US Foreign Relations since 1776.* New York: Oxford University Press, 2008.

Hershkowitz, Leo. "Overview: The Irish and the Emerging City: Settlement to 1844." In Bayor and Meagher, *The New York Irish.*

Hess, Earl J. *Liberty, Virtue and Progress: Northerners and Their War for the Union.* New York: Fordham University Press, 1997.

Holt, Thomas C. "The Essence of the Contract: The Articulation of Race, Gender, and Political Economy in British Emancipation Policy, 1838–1866." In Frederick Cooper, Thomas C. Holt, and Rebecca J. Scott, eds., *Beyond Slavery: Exploration of Race, Labor and Citizenship in Postemancipation Societies.* Chapel Hill: University of North Carolina Press, 2000.

——. *The Problem of Freedom: Race, Labor and Politics in Jamaica and Britain, 1832–1938.* Baltimore: Johns Hopkins University Press, 1992.

Horsman, Reginald. "Origins of Racial Anglo-Saxonism in Great Britain before 1850." *Journal of the History of Ideas* 37, no. 3 (July–September 1976): 387–410.

——. *Race and Manifest Destiny: The Origins of American Racial Anglo-Saxonism.* Cambridge, MA: Harvard University Press, 1981.

Horton, James Oliver, and Lois E. Horton. "A Federal Assault: African Americans and the Impact of the Fugitive Slave Law of 1850." *Chicago-Kent Law Review* 68, no. 3 (Summer 1993): 1179–1197.

——. *In Hope of Liberty: Culture, Community, and Protest Among Northern Free Blacks, 1700–1860.* New York: Oxford University Press, 1997.

Howe, Anthony. *The Cotton Masters, 1830–1860.* Oxford: Oxford University Press, 1984.

Howe, Daniel Walker. *What Hath God Wrought: The Transformation of America, 1815–1848.* New York: Oxford University Press, 2007.

Hubbard, Charles M. "James Mason, the 'Confederate Lobby,' and the Blockade Debate of March 1862." *Civil War History* 45, no. 3 (September 1999): 223–237.

Huzzey, Richard. *Freedom Burning: Anti-Slavery and Empire in Victorian Britain.* Ithaca: Cornell University Press, 2012.

——. "The Moral Geography of British Anti-Slavery Responsibilities." *Transactions of the Royal Historical Society* 22 (December 2012): 111–139.

Jackson, Alvin. *Ireland, 1798–1998: War, Peace, and Beyond.* 1999. Reprint, Chichester: Wiley-Blackwell, 2010.

Jacobson, Matthew Frye. *Whiteness of a Different Color: European Immigrants and the Alchemy of Race.* Cambridge, MA: Harvard University Press, 1998.

James, Clayton D. *Antebellum Natchez.* Baton Rouge: Louisiana State University Press, 1968.

Jenkins, Brian. *Sir William Gregory of Coole: The Biography of an Anglo-Irishman.* Gerrards Cross, UK: Colin Smythe, 1986.

———. "William Gregory: Champion of the Confederacy." *History Today* 28, no. 5 (May 1978): 322–330.

Johnson, Linck C. "'Liberty Is Never Cheap': Emerson, 'The Fugitive Slave Law,' and the Antislavery Lecture Series at the Broadway Tabernacle." *New England Quarterly* 76, no. 4 (December 2003): 550–592.

Johnson, Walter. *Soul by Soul: Life Inside the Antebellum Slave Market.* Cambridge, MA: Harvard University Press, 1999.

Johnston, Joanna. *The Life, Manners, and Travels of Fanny Trollope: A Biography.* New York: Hawthorn, 1978.

Jones, Howard. *Blue and Gray Diplomacy: A History of Union and Confederate Foreign Relations.* Chapel Hill: University of North Carolina Press, 2010.

Jones, Iva G. "Trollope, Carlyle, and Mill on the Negro: An Episode in the History of Ideas." *Journal of Negro History* 52, no. 3 (July 1967): 185–199.

Jones, Wilbur D. *The American Problem in British Diplomacy, 1841–1861.* London: Macmillan, 1974.

Jordan, Donaldson, and Edwin J. Pratt. *Europe and the American Civil War.* Cambridge, MA: Riverside, 1931.

Kaufman, Scott. *The Pig War: The United States, Britain, and the Balance of Power in the Pacific Northwest, 1846–72.* Lanham, MD: Lexington, 2004.

Kelley, Robert. *The Transatlantic Persuasion: The Liberal Democratic Mind in the Age of Gladstone.* New York: Alfred J. Knopf, 1969.

Kelly, Patrick J. "The European Revolutions in 1848 and the Transnational Turn in Civil War History." *Journal of the Civil War Era* 4, no. 3 (September 2014): 431–443.

Kerr, Donal A. *'A Nation of Beggars?': Priests, People, and Politics in Famine Ireland, 1846–1852.* Oxford: Clarendon, 1994.

Kilbride, Daniel. *Being American in Europe, 1750–1860.* Baltimore: Johns Hopkins University Press, 2013.

Kinealy, Christine. *Daniel O'Connell and the Anti-Slavery Movement.* London: Pickering and Chatto, 2010.

Kinser, Brent E. *The American Civil War and the Shaping of British Democracy.* Farnham, UK: Ashgate, 2011.

Knobel, Dale T. *Paddy and the Republic: Ethnicity and Nationality in Antebellum America.* Middletown, CT: Wesleyan University Press, 1986.

Knox, B. A. "The British Government and the Governor Eyre Controversy, 1865–1875." *Historical Journal* 19, no. 3 (December 1975): 877–900.

Koss, Stephen. *The Rise and Fall of the Political Press.* 2 vols. London: Hamish Hamilton, 1981.

LaFeber, Walter. *The New Empire: An Interpretation of American Expansion, 1860–1898.* Ithaca: Cornell University Press, 1963.

Larkin, Hilary. *A History of Ireland, 1800–1922: Theatres of Disorder.* New York: Anthem, 2014.

Latner, Richard B. "The Nullification Crisis and Republican Subversion." *Journal of Southern History* 43, no. 1 (February 1977): 19–38.

Lebergott, Stanley. "Through the Blockade: The Profitability and Extent of Cotton Smuggling, 1861–1865." *Journal of Economic History* 41, no. 4 (December 1961): 867–888.

Levanthal, Fred M., and Roland Quinault, eds. *Anglo-American Attitudes from Revolution to Partnership.* Aldershot: Ashgate, 2000.

Levine, Bruce. *Half Slave and Half Free: The Roots of Civil War.* 1992. Reprint, New York: Hill and Wang, 1992.

Lillibridge, G. D. *Beacon of Freedom: The Impact of American Democracy upon Great Britain, 1830–1870.* Philadelphia: University of Pennsylvania Press, 1955.

Litwack, Leon F. "The Federal Government and the Free Negro, 1790–1860." *Journal of Negro History* 43, no. 4 (October 1958): 261–278.

———. *North of Slavery: The Negro in the Free States, 1790–1860.* Chicago: University of Chicago Press, 1961.

Logan, Deborah A. "The Redemption of a Heretic: Harriet Martineau and Anglo-American Abolitionism." In Kathryn Kish Sklar and James Brewer Stewart, eds., *Women's Rights and Transatlantic Antislavery in the Era of Emancipation.* New Haven: Yale University Press, 2007.

Logan, Frenise A. "India-Britain's Substitute for American Cotton, 1861–1865." *Journal of Southern History* 24, no. 4 (November 1958): 472–480.

Logan, Kevin J. "The *Bee-Hive* Newspaper and the British Working Class Attitude Toward the American Civil War." *Civil War History* 22, no. 4 (December 1976): 337–348.

Lorimer, Douglas A. "The Role of Anti-Slavery Sentiment in English Reactions to the American Civil War." *Historical Journal* 19, no. 2 (1976): 405–420.

Loveland, Anne C. "Evangelicalism and 'Immediate Emancipation' in American Antislavery Thought." *Journal of Southern History* 32, no. 2 (May 1966): 172–188.

Ludlum, Robert P. "The Antislavery 'Gag-Rule': History and Argument." *Journal of Negro History* 26, no. 2 (April 1941): 203–243.

MacDonagh, Oliver. *The Emancipist: Daniel O'Connell, 1830–47.* London: Weidenfeld and Nicholson, 1989.

MacRaild, Donald M. *Irish Migrants in Modern Britain, 1750–1922.* New York: St. Martin's, 1999.

Mahin, Dean B. *One War at a Time: The International Dimensions of the American Civil War.* Washington, DC: Brassey's, 1999.

Mason, Matthew. "The Battle of the Slaveholding Liberators: Great Britain, the United States, and Slavery in the Early Nineteenth Century." *William and Mary Quarterly,* 3rd ser., 59, no. 33 (July 2002): 665–696.

Masur, Louis P. *Lincoln's Hundred Days: The Emancipation Proclamation and the War for the Union.* Cambridge, MA: Belknap, 2012.

Maurer, Oscar. "'Punch' On Slavery and Civil War in America, 1841–1865." *Victorian Studies* 1, no. 1 (September 1957): 4–28.

Maynard, Douglas. "Civil War 'Care': The Mission of the George Griswold." *New England Quarterly* 34, no. 3 (September 1961): 291–310.

Mays, Kelly J. "Slaves in Heaven, Laborers in Hell: Chartist Poets' Ambivalent Identification with the (Black) Slave." *Victorian Poetry* 39, no. 2 (Summer 2001): 137–163.

McCardell, John. *The Idea of a Southern Nation: Southern Nationalists and Southern Nationalism, 1830–1860.* New York: W. W. Norton, 1979.

McDaniel, W. Caleb. "Repealing Unions: American Abolitionists, Irish Repeal, and the Origins of Garrisonian Disunionism." *Journal of the Early Republic* 28, no. 2 (Summer 2008): 243–269.

———. *The Problem of Democracy in the Age of Slavery: Garrisonian Abolitionists and Transatlantic Reform.* Baton Rouge: Louisiana State University Press, 2013.

McGovern, Bryan P. *John Mitchel: Irish Nationalist, Southern Secessionist.* Knoxville: University of Tennessee Press, 2009.

McMahon, Cian. "Ireland and the Birth of the Irish-American Press, 1842–1861." *American Periodicals: A Journal of History and Criticism* 19, no. 1 (2009): 5–20.

McPherson, James M. *Battle Cry of Freedom: The Civil War Era.* New York: Oxford University Press, 1988.

Meckier, Jerome. *Innocent Abroad: Charles Dickens's American Engagements.* Lexington: University Press of Kentucky, 1990.

Meer, Sarah. *Uncle Tom Mania: Slavery, Minstrelsy and Transatlantic Culture in the 1850s.* Athens: University of Georgia Press, 2005.

Meinke, Scott R. "Slavery, Partisanship, and Procedure in the U.S. House: The Gag Rule, 1836–1845." *Legislative Studies Quarterly* 32, no. 1 (February 2007): 33–57.

Melish, Joanna Pope. *Disowning Slavery: Gradual Emancipation and "Race" in New England, 1780–1860.* Ithaca: Cornell University Press, 1998.

Merk, Frederick. *Slavery and the Annexation of Texas.* New York: Knopf, 1972.

Michie, Elsie B. "Morbidity in Fairyland: Frances Trollope, Charles Dickens, and the Rhetoric of Abolition." *Partial Answers* 9, no. 2 (2011): 233–251.

Miller, Henry. "Popular Petitioning and the Corn Laws, 1833–46." *English Historical Review* 127, no. 527 (August 2012): 882–919.

———. "Radicals, Tories, or Monomaniacs? The Birmingham Currency Reformers in the House of Commons, 1832–1867." *Parliamentary History* 3, no. 3 (October 2012): 354–377.

Miller, Ilana D. *Reports from America: William Howard Russell and the Civil War.* Stroud: Sutton, 2001.

Miller, Kerby A. *Emigrants and Exiles: Ireland and the Irish Exodus to North America.* New York: Oxford University Press, 1985.

Monod, Sylvere. *Martin Chuzzlewit.* London: George Allen and Unwin, 1985.

Morgan, Simon. "The Anti-Corn Law League and British Anti-Slavery in Transatlantic Perspective, 1838–1846." *Historical Journal* 52, no. 1 (March 2009): 87–107.

Moss, D. J. "A Study in Failure: Thomas Attwood, M.P. for Birmingham, 1832–1839." *Historical Journal* 21, no. 3 (September 1978): 545–571.

Mulvey, Christopher. *Anglo-American Landscapes: A Study of 19th Century Anglo-American Travel Literature.* Cambridge: Cambridge University Press, 1983.

———. *Transatlantic Manners: Social Patterns in Nineteenth Century Anglo-American Travel Literature.* Cambridge: University of Cambridge Press, 1990.

Murphy, Angela F. *American Slavery, Irish Freedom: Abolition, Immigrant Citizenship, and the Transatlantic Movement for Irish Repeal.* Baton Rouge: Louisiana State University Press, 2010.

Murphy, James H. *Abject Loyalty: Nationalism and Monarchy in Ireland During the Reign of Queen Victoria.* Cork: Cork University Press, 2001.

Myers, Phillip E. *Caution and Cooperation: The American Civil War in British-American Relations.* Kent, OH: Kent State University Press, 2008.

Nagel, Paul C. *One Nation Indivisible: The Union in American Thought, 1776–1861.* New York: Oxford University Press, 1964.

Neem, Johann M. "Taking Modernity's Wager: Tocqueville, Social Capital and the American Civil War." *Journal of Interdisciplinary History* 41, no. 4 (Spring 2011): 591–618.

Neff, Stephen C. *Justice in Blue and Gray: A Legal History of the Civil War.* Cambridge, MA: Harvard University Press, 2010.

Oakes, James. "Reluctant to Emancipate?: Another Look at the First Confiscation Act." *Journal of the Civil War Era* 3, no. 3 (December 2013): 458–466.

———. *The Ruling Race: A History of American Slaveholders.* New York: Knopf, 1982.

Oates, Stephen B. "Henry Hotze: Confederate Agent Abroad." *Historian* 27 (1965): 131–154.

O'Brien, Michael. *Conjectures of Order: Intellectual Life and the American South, 1810–1860.* 2 vols. Chapel Hill: University of North Carolina Press, 2004.

Ó'Broin, León. *Fenian Fever: An Anglo-American Dilemma.* New York: New York University Press, 1971.

Ochenkowski, J. P. "The Origins of Nullification in South Carolina." *South Carolina Historical Magazine* 83, no. 2 (April 1982): 121–153.

O'Cinneide, Muireann. *Aristocratic Women and the Literary Nation, 1832–1867.* Basingstoke: Palgrave, 2008.

Onuf, Peter S. "Antebellum Southerners and the National Idea." In Barnes, Schoen, and Towers, *The Old South's Modern Worlds.*

Osofsky, Gilbert. "Abolitionists, Irish Immigrants and the Dilemmas of Romantic Nationalism." *American Historical Review* 80, no. 4 (October 1975): 889–912.

Osterweis, Rollin G. *Romanticism and Nationalism in the Old South.* New Haven: Yale University Press, 1949.

Owsley, Frank Lawrence. *King Cotton Diplomacy: Foreign Relations of the Confederate States of America.* Chicago: University of Chicago Press, 1931.

Palen, Marc-William. "The Civil War's Forgotten Transatlantic Tariff Debate and the Confederacy's Free Trade Diplomacy." *Journal of the Civil War Era* 3, no. 1 (March 2013): 35–61.

Park, Joseph H. "The English Workingmen and the America Civil War." *Political Science Quarterly* 39, no. 3 (September 1924): 432–457.

Perkins, Howard C. "The Defense of Slavery in the Northern Press on the Eve of the Civil War." *Journal of Southern History* 9, no. 4 (November 1943): 501–531.

Perman, Michael. *The Southern Political Tradition.* Baton Rouge: Louisiana State University Press, 2012.

Pessen, Edward. "How Different From Each Other Were the Antebellum North and South?" *American Historical Review* 85, no. 5 (December 1980): 1119–1149.

Petley, Christopher. "New Perspectives on Slavery and Emancipation in the British Caribbean." *Historical Journal* 54, no. 3 (September 2011): 855–880.

Phillips, John A., and Charles Wetherell. "The Great Reform Act of 1832 and the Political Modernization of England." *American Historical Review* 100, no. 2 (April 1995): 411–436.

Phillips, Kevin. *The Cousins War: Religion, Politics and the Triumph of Anglo-America.* New York: Basic Books, 1999.

Pickering, Paul A., and Alex Tyrrell. *The People's Bread: A History of the Anti-Corn Law League.* London: Leicester University Press, 2000.

Pletcher, David M. *The Diplomacy of Annexation: Texas, Oregon and the Mexican War.* Columbia: University of Missouri Press, 1973.

Pope-Hennessy, James. *Anthony Trollope.* Boston: Little, Brown, 1971.

Potter, David M. *The Impending Crisis, 1848–1861.* New York: Harper and Row, 1976.

Price, Richard. *British Society, 1680–1880: Dynamism, Containment, and Change.* Cambridge: Cambridge University Press, 1999.

Prochaska, Frank. *The Eagle and the Crown: Americans and the British Monarchy.* New Haven: Yale University Press, 2008.

———. *Eminent Victorians on American Democracy: The View from Albion.* Oxford: Oxford University Press, 2012.

Quigley, Paul. *Shifting Grounds: Nationalism and the American South, 1848–1865.* New York: Oxford University Press, 2012.

Quinault, Roland. "Anglo-American Attitudes to Democracy from Lincoln to Churchill." In Levanthal and Quinault, *Anglo-American Attitudes from Revolution to Partnership.*

———. "Gladstone and Slavery." *Historical Journal* 52, no. 2 (2009): 363–383.

Ratner, Lorman. *Powder Keg: Northern Opposition to the Antislavery Movement, 1831–1840.* New York: Basic Books, 1968.

Read, Donald. *Cobden and Bright: A Victorian Political Partnership.* London: Edward Arnold, 1967.

Read, James J. *Majority Rule Versus Consensus: The Political Thought of John C. Calhoun.* Lawrence: University Press of Kansas, 2009.

Rehin, George F. "Blackface Street Minstrels in Victorian London and Its Resorts: Popular Culture and Its Racial Connotations as Revealed in Polite Opinion." *Journal of Popular Culture* 15, no. 1 (Summer 1981): 19–38.

Reid, Robert L., ed. "William E. Gladstone's 'Insincere Neutrality' during the Civil War." *Civil War History* 15 (December 1969): 293–307.

Remini, Robert V. *Andrew Jackson and the Course of American Democracy, 1833–1845.* Vol. 3. New York: Harper and Row, 1984.

Rice, Alan J., and Martin Crawford, eds. *Liberating Sojourn: Frederick Douglass and Transatlantic Reform.* Athens: University of Georgia Press, 1999.

Richards, Leonard L. *"Gentlemen of Property and Standing": Anti-Abolition Mobs in Jacksonian America.* New York: Oxford University Press, 1970.

———. *The Slave Power: The Free North and Southern Domination, 1780–1860.* Baton Rouge: Louisiana State University Press, 2000.

Robbins, Keith. *John Bright.* London: Routledge and Kegan Paul, 1979.

Roberts, David. *Paternalism in Early Victorian England.* New Brunswick, NJ: Rutgers University Press, 1979.

Robertson, Andrew W. *The Language of Democracy: Political Rhetoric in the United States and Great Britain, 1790–1900.* Ithaca: Cornell University Press, 1995.

Romani, Roberto. "British Views on Irish National Character, 1800–1846: An Intellectual History." *History of European Ideas* 23, no. 5/6 (1998): 193–219.

Roper, Jon. *Democracy and Its Critics: Anglo-American Democratic Thought in the Nineteenth Century.* London: Unwin Hyman, 1989.

Rose, Jonathan. "Rereading the English Common Reader: A Preface to the History of Audiences." *Journal of the History of Ideas* 58, no. 1 (January–March 1992): 47–70.

Ross, Dorothy. "'Are We a Nation?': The Conjuncture of Nationhood and Race in the United States, 1850–1876." *Modern Intellectual History* 2, no. 3 (2005): 327–360.

Rothman, Adam. "Elizabeth Fox-Genovese, Eugene Genovese, and the Proslavery Worldview." *Reviews in American History* 41, no. 3 (September 2013): 563–569.

Rugemer, Edward Bartlett. *The Problem of Emancipation: The Caribbean Roots of the American Civil War.* Baton Rouge: Louisiana State University Press, 2008.

———. "The Southern Response to British Abolitionism: The Maturation of Proslavery Apologetics." *Journal of Southern History* 70, no. 2 (May 2004): 221–248.

Samito, Christian G. *Becoming American Under Fire: Irish Americans, African Americans, and the Politics of Citizenship During the Civil War Era.* Ithaca: Cornell University Press, 2009.

Sanders, Andrew. *Charles Dickens.* Oxford: Oxford University Press, 2003.

———. *The Victorian Historical Novel, 1840–1880.* London: Macmillan, 1978.

Saum, Lewis O. *The Popular Mood of Pre-Civil War America.* Westport, CT: Greenwood, 1980.

Saunders, Robert. "'Let America Be the Test': Democracy and Reform in Britain, 1832–1867." In Ella Dzelzainis and Ruth Livesey, eds., *The American Experiment and the Idea of Democracy in British Culture, 1776–1914.* Farnham, UK: Ashgate, 2013.

Scarborough, William Kauffman. *Masters of the Big House: Elite Slaveholders of the Mid-Nineteenth-Century South.* Baton Rouge: Louisiana State University Press, 2003.

Schoen, Brian. *The Fragile Fabric of Union: Cotton, Federal Politics, and the Global Origins of the Civil War.* Baltimore: Johns Hopkins University Press, 2009.

Schonhardt-Bailey, Cheryl. *From the Corn Laws to Free Trade: Interests, Ideas, and Institutions in Historical Perspective.* Cambridge, MA: MIT Press, 2006.

Sebrell, Thomas E., II. *Persuading John Bull: Union and Confederate Propaganda in Britain, 1860–1865.* Lanham, MD: Lexington Books, 2014.

Sexton, Jay. *Debtor Diplomacy: Finance and American Foreign Relations in the Civil War Era, 1837–1873.* Oxford: Clarendon, 2005.

———. "The Funded Loan and the *Alabama* Claims." *Diplomatic History* 27, no. 4 (September 2003): 449–478.

———. *The Monroe Doctrine: Empire and Nation in Nineteenth-Century America.* New York: Hill and Wang, 2011.

———. "William H. Seward in the World." *Journal of the Civil War Era* 4, no. 3 (September 2014): 398–430.

Shain, Charles E. "The English Novelists and the American Civil War." *American Quarterly* 14, no. 3 (October 1962): 399–421.

Sheidley, Harlow W. *Sectional Nationalism: Massachusetts Conservative Leaders and the Transformation of America, 1815–1836.* Boston: Northeastern University Press, 1998.

Shillingsburg, Peter L. *Pegasus in Harness: Victorian Publishing and W. M. Thackeray.* Charlottesville: University Press of Virginia, 1992.

Silbey, Joel H. *The Partisan Imperative: The Dynamics of American Politics Before the Civil War.* New York: Oxford University Press, 1985.

Sim, David. *A Union Forever: The Irish Question and US Foreign Relations in the Victorian Age.* Ithaca: Cornell University Press, 2014.

Simpson, Lewis P. *The Man of Letters in New England and the South: Essays on the History of the Literary Vocation in America.* Baton Rouge: Louisiana State University Press, 1973.

Slater, Michael. *Charles Dickens.* New Haven: Yale University Press, 2009.

Sloan, Robert. *William Smith O'Brien and the Young Ireland Rebellion of 1848.* Dublin: Four Courts, 2000.

Smith, Paul. *Disraeli: A Brief Life.* Cambridge: Cambridge University Press, 1996.

St. Clair, Sadie Daniel. "Slavery as a Diplomatic Factor in Anglo-American Relations During the Civil War." *Journal of Negro History* 30, no. 3 (July 1945): 260–275.

Stahr, Walter. *Seward: Lincoln's Indispensable Man.* New York: Simon and Schuster, 2012.

Steele, E. D. *Palmerston and Liberalism, 1855–1865.* Cambridge: Cambridge University Press, 1991.

Stevens, Kenneth R. *Border Diplomacy: The Caroline and McLeod Affairs in Anglo-American-Canadian Relations, 1837–1842.* Tuscaloosa: University of Alabama Press, 1989.

Stoddart, Anna M. *The Life of Isabella Bird.* London: John Murray, 1906.

Stone, Harry. "Charles Dickens and Harriet Beecher Stowe." *Nineteenth Century Fiction* 12, no. 3 (December 1957): 188–202.

——. "Dickens' Use of His American Experiences in Martin Chuzzlewit." *PMLA* 72, no. 3 (June 1957): 464–478.

Stuart, Reginald C. *United States Expansionism and British North America, 1775–1871.* Chapel Hill: University of North Carolina Press, 1988.

Sutherland, John. "Thackeray as Victorian Racialist." *Essays in Criticism* 20, no. 4 (October 1970): 441–445.

——. *Victorian Fiction: Writers, Publishers, Readers.* New York: St. Martin's, 1995.

——. *Victorian Novelists and Publishers.* London: Athlone, 1976.

Sydnor, Charles S. *The Development of Southern Sectionalism, 1819–1848.* Baton Rouge: Louisiana State University Press, 1948.

Tate, Adam L. *Conservatism and Southern Intellectuals, 1789–1861: Liberty, Tradition, and the Good Society*. Columbia: University of Missouri Press, 2005.

Taylor, Miles. "The 1848 Revolutions and the British Empire." *Past and Present* 1, no. 166 (February 2000): 146–180.

——. *The Decline of British Radicalism, 1847–1860*. Oxford: Clarendon, 1995.

Taylor, William R. *Cavalier and Yankee: The Old South and American National Character*. New York: George Braziller, 1961.

Temperley, Howard. *British Antislavery, 1833–1870*. Columbia: University of South Carolina Press, 1972.

——. "Capitalism, Slavery and Ideology." *Past and Present* 75, no 1 (May 1977): 94–118.

Thistlethwaite, Frank. *The Anglo-American Connection in the Early Nineteenth Century*. Philadelphia: University of Pennsylvania Press, 1959.

Thomas, Deborah A. *Thackeray and Slavery*. Athens: Ohio University Press, 1993.

Thomas, William. "Religion and Politics in the *Quarterly Review*, 1809–1853." In Stefan Collini, Richard Whatmore, and B. W. Young, eds., *History, Religion and Culture: British Intellectual History, 1750–1950*. Cambridge: Cambridge University Press, 2000.

Thornton, A. P. *The Habit of Authority: Paternalism in British History*. Toronto: University of Toronto Press, 1966.

Towers, Frank. "The Southern Path to Modern Cities: Urbanization in the Slave States." In Barnes, Schoen, and Towers, *The Old South's Modern Worlds*.

——. *The Urban South and the Coming of the Civil War*. Charlottesville: University of Virginia Press, 2004.

Turner, Michael J. "Chartism, Bronterre O'Brien, and the 'Luminous Political Example of America.'" *History* 97, no. 325 (January 2012): 43–69.

——. *Liberty and Liberticide: The Role of America in Nineteenth-Century British Radicalism*. Lanham, MD: Lexington Books, 2014.

——. "Perceptions of America and British Reform during the 1860s." *Civil War History* 59, no. 3 (September 2013): 320–357.

Turner, Ralph E. *James Silk Buckingham, 1786–1855: A Social Biography*. New York: McGraw-Hill, 1934.

Tyrrell, Alex. *Joseph Sturge and the Moral Radical Party in Early Victorian Britain*. London: Christopher Helm, 1987.

Vanauken, Sheldon. *The Glittering Illusion: English Sympathy for the Southern Confederacy*. Worthing: Churchman, 1988.

Varouxakis, Georgios. "'Negrophilist' Crusader: John Stuart Mill on the American Civil War and Reconstruction." *History of European Ideas* 39, no. 5 (2013): 729–754.

Vernon, James. *Politics and the People: A Study in English Political Culture, c. 1815–1867*. Cambridge: Cambridge University Press, 1993.

Vincent, David. *The Rise of Mass Literacy*. Cambridge: Polity, 2000.

Waller, John O. "Charles Kingsley and the American Civil War." *Studies in Philology* 30, no. 3 (July 1963): 554–568.

Walther, Eric H. *The Fire-Eaters*. Baton Rouge: Louisiana State University Press, 1992.

Walvin, James. *Questioning Slavery*. London: Routledge, 1996.

——, ed. *Slavery and British Society, 1776–1846*. London: Macmillan, 1982.

Webb, R. K. *Harriet Martineau: A Radical Victorian*. New York: Columbia University Press, 1960.

Webb, Robert K. "Working Class Readers in Early Victorian England." *English Historical Review* 65, no. 256 (July 1950): 333–351.

Weber, Jennifer L. *Copperheads: The Rise and Fall of Lincoln's Opponents in the North*. Oxford: Oxford University Press, 2006.

Weinberg, Adelaide. *John Elliot Cairnes and the American Civil War: A Study in Anglo-American Relations*. London: Kingswood, 1970.

Weisbuch, Robert. *Atlantic Double-Cross: American Literature and British Influence in the Age of Emerson*. Chicago: University of Chicago Press, 1986.

Wesley, Timothy L. *The Politics of Faith During the Civil War*. Baton Rouge: Louisiana State University Press, 2013.

White, Laura A. "The United States in the 1850s as Seen by British Consuls." *Mississippi Valley Historical Review* 19, no. 4 (March 1933): 509–536.

Whitridge, Arnold. "Dickens and Thackeray in America." *New York Historical Society Quarterly* 52 (1978): 219–237.

Whyte, Iain. *"Send Back the Money!": The Free Church of Scotland and American Slavery*. Cambridge: James Clarke, 2012.

Williams, Raymond. *Keywords: A Vocabulary of Science and Culture*. London: Fontana, 1976.

Wilson, A. N. *The Victorians*. London: Hutchinson, 2002.

Wood, Marcus. "The American South and English Print Satire, 1760–1865." In Franklin T. Lambert and Joseph P. Ward, eds., *Britain and the American South from Colonialism to Rock and Roll*. Jackson: University of Mississippi Press, 2003.

Woodworth, Steven E. *Manifest Destinies: America's Westward Expansion and the Road to the Civil War*. New York: Alfred A. Knopf, 2011.

Worth, Tim. "'An Extraordinary Species of Tyranny': Fanny Trollope and the Domestic Manners of the Americans." *Symbiosis* 5, no. 1 (2001): 17–32.

Wyatt-Brown, Bertram. *Southern Honor: Ethics and Behavior in the Old South*. New York: Oxford University Press, 1982.

Young, Jeffrey Robert. *Domesticating Slavery: The Master Class in Georgia and South Carolina, 1670–1837*. Chapel Hill: University of North Carolina Press, 1999.

UNPUBLISHED DISSERTATIONS AND THESES

Keiser, Thomas J. "The English Press and the American Civil War." PhD thesis, University of Reading, 1971.

Schoeppner, Michael Alan. "Navigating the Dangerous Atlantic: Racial Quarantines, Black Sailors, and United States Constitutionalism." PhD diss., University of Florida, 2010.

Smith, R. T. "The Confederate Index and the American Civil War." MA thesis, University of Washington, 1961.

INDEX